FINANCIAL MANAGEMENT OF UNIVERSITIES IN INDIA

About the Auther

Madan Mohan Sharma (Gold Medalist) is an administrator by profession and a researcher by interest. He did his M.A. (Statistics) from Panjab University, Chandigarh, in 1968 and Ph.D. (Business Management) in 1989 from Punjabi University, Patiala. Dr. Sharma is deeply involved in Indian University system for two decades in diverse capacities, as a teacher, a researcher, a university administrator and an education planner. Dr. Sharma (b. 1937) was Comptroller (equivalent to Registrar) with Himachal Pradesh Krishi Vishva Vidyalaya in 1979. Dr. Sharma has been actively associated with various professional bodies. He has contributed extensively to scholarly journals, conferences and seminars. He is Consultant with the Indian Council of Social Science Research. He has published Accounts Manual of the University. His forthcoming publications include a book on "*Comparative Financial Management of University Institution* (U.K., Canada and India)"

FINANCIAL MANAGEMENT OF UNIVERSITIES IN INDIA

MADAN MOHAN SHARMA

CONCEPT PUBLISHING COMPANY PVT. LTD.
NEW DELHI-110059

The Indian Council of Social Science Research gave the financial support towards the publication of this work. However, the responsibility for the contents of the book — facts, opinions, conclusions, etc. — is entirely that of the author and not of the ICSSR.

ICSSR Consultant : **J.L. Azad**

ISBN: 978-81-7022-278-1

Edition 2022

Published and Printed by

Concept
Since 1974

Concept Publishing Company Pvt. Ltd.
A/15-16, Commercial Block, Mohan Garden
New Delhi-110059 (India)
T : 91 11 41101460
E : publishing@conceptpub.com, *W*: www.conceptpub.com

Cataloging in Publication Data--Courtesy: D.K. Agencies (P) Ltd. <docinfo@dkagencies.com>

Sharma, Madan Mohan, 1937- **author.**
Financial management of universities in India / Madan Mohan Sharma.
pages cm
ISBN 9788170222781

1. Universities and colleges--India--Finance. I. Title.

LCC LB2342.2.I5S53 2022 | DDC 378.1060954 23

To

the loving and cherishing memory

of my father

Pandit Dhani Ram

FOREWORD

FINANCIAL ADMINISTRATION is central to the functioning of the democratic system from the view points of rationality, accountability and distributive justice since the resources are often limited while demands are manifold and competing too. The union government, state governments and other funding agencies are investing considerably in various socio-economic activities for the speedier development of the country. By spending on higher education through about 188 University Institutions in India, manpower is being produced to serve the country and the community in various capacities. They are making investment decisions no different from those of various development agencies.

During the post Independence period the University Institutions in India have developed very rapidly. Though substantial increase has been made in the number of the University Institutions and in terms of expenditure on university education yet the financial position of most of the existing University Institutions is far from satisfactory and many of them are facing rough weather and operating with heavy deficits. These Institutions are mainly dependent on the government for finances and the country, being in a developing stage, is not in a position to meet the growing requirements to the desired extent. Somewhat unplanned growth together with lack of efficient and effective management in most of he universities has led to a general feeling with the concerned governments that the universities, being autonomous institutions, do not exercise effective control in the management of their finances. The situation of budget deficit and paucity of funds does not permit the University Institutions to provide adequate funds for various programmes. Thus, the management of university finances is presently undergoing severe internal stresses and strains resulting in low academic standards and low rated performances. It is at this critical juncture that the improvement in the existing management system can go a long way in bringing the University Institutions out of the present financial crisis and in helping them to achieve the objectives/goals for which they have been established.

The present study by Dr. Madan Mohan Sharma has depicted a picture of the entire financial system of the University Institutions in India. He has projected the total conceptual framework of (i) existing sources of finances (grants-in-aid), (ii) criteria for fixation of grants-in-aid, (iii) grants-in-aid rules, (iv) allocation of available funds, (v) pattern of expenditure, (vi) financial health of the University Institutions, (vii) existing budgeting and planning systems, and (viii) existing accounting and auditing systems. Dr. Sharma has also made sincere attempts to develop a model composition of a Finance Committee, model grants-in-aid rules, criteria for fixation of grants-in-aid, optimal allocation of available funds and normative pattern of expenditure. He has given useful suggestions for improving the effectiveness and efficiency of the existing financial management of the University Institutions in India.

His suggestions merit serious consideration for improving the financial management systems of the University Institutions. His findings on policy implications deserve the attention of the policy makers. Students of educational finance would find this study novel and useful. The material so built up by Dr. Sharma will serve the purpose of training the university administrators and other junior staff.

S.K. KHANNA
Vice-Chairman
University Grants Commission

PREFACE

THE FINANCIAL management system is the backbone for efficient development and growth of a University Institution. It helps independent functioning and is a shield against external criticism as well as undue interference from the government. It is a necessity which creates a healthy atmosphere and a feeling of security in the University community. Though there is internal security, yet it has led to certain working problems such as costs rising at a rapid rate while on the other hand the growth rate of income being almost steady. The financial constraints are not only being felt in India but also in several other countries of the world. There is a need to give more attention on different aspects of financial management of universities so that education must satisfy its cost. The resource position of the governments and national priorities preclude the possibility of substantially increasing government assistance to the universities. Probing and understanding of the budgetary accounting, auditing concepts and transactions, development and maintenance plans of the universities, composition and powers of fiscal policy laying authorities, grants-in-aid rules, criterion/formulae for fixation of grants-in-aid, optimal allocation of available funds amongst the different activities of universities, and a normative pattern of expenditure are the *sine quo non* for proper planning of the University finances and their management.

This book presents an in-depth study of certain aspects of the financial management system of University Institutions. It gives information on the extent to which inefficiencies in the financial management of University Institutions have been responsible for their unsatisfactory performance. The study offers suggestions regarding (i) powers and functions of fiscal policy making authorities, (ii) model composition of a Finance Committee, (iii) model grants-in-aid rules, (iv) model criterion/formulae for fixation of grants-in-aid, (v) optimal allocation of available funds, (vi) normative pattern of expenditure, (vii) budgeting and planning systems and (viii) accounting and auditing systems. The suggestions so made will go a long way for the improvement of the existing financial management systems and will also ease the overall position of University Institutions in achievement of the objectives for which they have been established.

My deep sense of gratitude to Dr. B.S. Bhatia, Professor of Management, Department of Business Management, Punjabi University, Patiala for his judicious guidance, constructive criticism and sustenance through out the period of investigation.

I owe humble gratitude to Dr. S.P. Arora, Professor of Eminence (Retd.), Additional Director of Research, Himachal Pradesh Krishi Vishvavidyalaya, Palampur for taking interest in my work, thoroughly reading the manuscript of the book and contributing valuable suggestions. The author is highly thankful to Dr. (Mrs.) H. Prim, Associate Professor (Retd.) for perusal of the script and for making valuable suggestions.

I am extremely grateful and deeply indebted to my Vice-Chancellor, Prof. (Dr.) Kirti Singh, whose constant guidance and encouragement made the publication of the book possible.

I deeply acknowledge with pleasure the help received by me from my colleagues, Mr. R.C. Kapil, HAS, W.C. Sharma and Surinder Kumar.

The author is thankful to Dr. J.L. Azad, Consultant from the Indian Council of Social Science Research for his useful and encouraging comments and the Indian Council of Social Science Research for providing the publication grant.

The person whom I wanted to thank first is being mentioned last. I deeply appreciate the inspirations and the ideal conditions provided at home by my wife Chander Kanta whose constant help and understanding made this treatise possible. And then I owe thanks to my daughters Rajni, Poonam and son Neeraj, who always kept me alive to accomplish this work despite my 'dawn to dusk' busy schedule of work.

I am also thankful to Prof. (Dr.) S.K. Khanna, Vice-Chairman, University Grants Commission, who has so generously written the foreword for this humble effort.

Finally, I present this treatise to my worthy readers for their reactions, suggestions and guidance which I shall always value greatly.

MADAN MOHAN SHARMA

CONTENTS

LIST OF TABLES

LIST OF FIGURES

1

INTRODUCTION

THE MANAGEMENT of an organisation like a University Institution requires special administrative and budgetary techniques, collectively known as 'modern management techniques'. Modern techniques provide a sound framework for efficient management and thus they should replace traditional impractical techniques. It may be advisable, at this stage, to attempt a definition of the term 'modern management techniques'. Management is recognized as the process involving (i) judgement and decisions in determining plans and using data to control performance and progress against plans, and (ii) the guidance, integration, motivation and supervision of personnel in carrying out operations. Every method and procedure used in that process, will fall into the category of management techniques.

Financial Management is an integral part of overall management, rather the staff is specially concerned with fund arranging operations. It is one of the four functional areas of the process of management. The central feature of Financial Management is the formulation of organisational strategies to determine the most effective use of available funds at the disposal of the organisation and the exploration of the most favourable sources of additional funds which the organisation will need in the foreseeable future. The central issue of financial policy therefore, is the proper use of funds. This process involves rational matching of advantages of potential use against the cost of alternative potential sources, so as to achieve the broad financial goals which an enterprise sets before itself. The art lies in using these funds as profitably as possible; planning future operations, controlling current performances and future development through financial accounting, cost accounting, budgeting, statistics and other means. Financial Management is a sub-function of total management and its task is to assist in (i) allocation of resources, (ii) utilisation of resources, and (iii) evaluation of results.

The university system can be defined as a group of units as a part of the organisation which works for achieving the objectives of higher education. In the functioning of any system, the constituents of the system play an important role. In case of the educational system, particularly higher education, teachers, teaching materials, para-educational infrastructure, their recruitment and management are crucial to the efficient functioning of the system. The nature and the extent of availability of funds and their management therefore, become key factors in the working of educational institutions. Agencies which provide funds; procedure through which funds are made available; the time period involved; and the conditions which are imposed to their availability, significantly influence the working of the system.

Review of Related Research Work

Studies on the university finances have been carried out by researchers in respect of some individual universities which are restrictive in nature and do not give a comprehensive picture. Studies on Financial Management Practices of all types of universities in the country are scarce. The Union Government, State Governments, University Grants Commission (UGC), Indian Council of Agricultural Research (ICAR) and the Association of Indian Universities have constituted Commissions/Committees for suggesting various measures for the governance of universities and the development of higher education in the country. The recommendations of such Commissions/Committees have been published in the forms of reports. Vice-Chancellors in their conferences, annual meets, have also made recommendations on management of University finances which are published by the Association of Indian Universities and the University Grants Commission. The Association of Indian Universities and the National Institute of Educational Planning and Administration are also conducting Financial Management Programmes for Vice-Chancellors/ Directors, Finance Officers/Comptrollers of the Universities and the recommendations made in such programmes are compiled in some cases and published for the benefit of the users.

The Committee on 'Model Act' (1961)[1] for the organisational structure of the universities in India and the Committee on 'Governance of Universities and Colleges' (1971)[2] in their reports have examined besides other issues, the questions of governance of universities with special reference to the organisational set up, categories and classification of officers, composition, functions and powers of various statutory bodies. They have also suggested statutory provisions for the audit of university accounts, adequate delegation of powers to teaching departments and toning up of administrative and financial procedures. Maynard James (1971)[3] examined the long and short run cost curves in the operation of higher education. He has attempted to find out the size of enrolment when the cost of operating institutions of higher learning was minimum. The Centre of Educational Research and Innovations (1972)[4] conducted a study on Costs and Potential Economics in the Institution of Higher Education mainly related to cost effectiveness in education. Hallak (1972)[5] carried out an international comparative study on management of educational costs, for reducing the cost of education and using available resources for better education. Lakdawala and Shah (1975)[6] studied university expenditure in Gujarat on revenue account of hostels. This research study has shown that the universities provide hostel services at considerably subsidised rates. Nigam (1975)[6a] examined the income, expenditure and financial procedures of Rajasthan University. He found that the per capita availability of educational facilities, in real terms, does not fall either due to increased students enrolment or due to inflation which effects supplies of material to libraries and laboratories. Azad (1976)[7] made an analytical study of the patterns and procedures of State Grants to Colleges. Mukerjee (1976)[8] attempted to throw light on the pattern of income and expenditure of Calcutta University. Nanjundappa (1976)[9] studied the criteria for fixation of grants, the format for the presentation of the budget and inter functional allocation of funds for academic services, of Karnataka University. Planning Committees for universities at the State Government level, Planning Advisory Boards, Planning Cells at the university levels, and closer alignment between the costs and fees have been recommended. Panchamukhi (1977)[10] examined the economic aspects of the behaviour of the universities in general and Bombay University in particular as a non-profit institution and evolved some general principles for effective management. Sharma (1979)[11] and Sharma (1980)[12] pointed out that some economics can be achieved by restructuring of educational programmes presently run by the colleges of Delhi University. In his unit cost study of university education he found that the higher education system was operating at a sub-optimal level and this called for remedial action. Balbir Singh and Satya Paul (1981)[13] examined major trends in the expenditure pattern of different teaching departments of Delhi University. Garg (1981)[14] discussed the finances of Punjab University by highlighting sources and objectives, salary structure of faculty members, and per capita analysis of institutional incomes and expenditure, both at current and constant prices. Ruddar Datt (1981)[15] gave a comparative picture of income and expenditure of four institutions of correspondence from four different universities. Ghosh (1983)[16] threw light broadly on norms for fixing finance in a two-tier system of maintenance grants, development grants and merits and demerits of deficit and block grants. Balachandran (1984)[17] and Balachandran (1986)[18] examined the justification for public expenditure, development of higher education in India, financing of higher education and its different constituents, per capita and per student finances and patterns, policies of grant-in-aid adopted by the State Government and the University Grants Commission and the mixed system of financing higher education. He observed that expenditure on equipment has declined over the years in Tamil Nadu, Rajasthan and Orissa whereas there had been an increase in Bihar, Maharashtra and Kerala. He pointed out the vagueness in admissibility of several legitimate items of expenditure for grants and non-existence of provision for adequate relief to neutralise the effects of inflation. He also suggested that a mixed system of financing higher education and blending of public and private funds should be adopted to avoid over dependence on Government funds. Bhardwaj and Balachandran (1985)[19] studied the extent of the shift in the expenditure patterns and its possible implications on quality in the context of unfolding socio-technological setting. They observed the basis of item-wise analysis of distribution of direct expenditure on higher education. In the Group discussion-cum-Orientation Programme on financial administration in Universities (1988)[20] organised by the Association of Indian Universities, it was recommended that the University Grants Commission should pay cent per cent developmental grant on all approved items of assistance, payment of grants by cheque/draft, non-deduction of unspent balance from the subsequent grant at the close of the period of grant on genuine grounds. Further, it was stressed that the recommendation of recoupment of existing deficits of the universities, re-designation of the posts of Finance Officer to that of Controller of Finances with the same status as that of Registrar, his membership to the statutory authority of the University be implemented. Provision for depreciation of funds and non-deduction of domestic income from grants and strong internal audit are also a requirement.

Need for the Study

Very little attention has been given to different aspects of financial management of universities in the country and abroad, yet the public all over the world demands that education must satisfy its cost. Even in the more developed counties, higher education faces recessionary economics, a shrinking pool of students, a diminishing budget and escalating costs. The financial position of most of existing Indian universities is far from satisfactory, as is evidenced from the huge deficit budget presented by various universities and the statements made out by the Vice-Chancellors. The financial crisis of universities is partly due to the fact that on the one hand costs are rising at a faster rate and, on the other hand the rate and growth of income is almost steady and this gap is widening year after year. In fact, providing full resources for university education is a problem all over the world. The resource position of the Government and national priorities preclude the possibility of substantially increasing Government assistance to the universities. Unplanned growth together with lack of efficient and effective management in most of the universities has given a general feeling to the concerned Governments that universities being autonomous institutions do not exercise effective control in the management of their finances.

The management of university finances is presently undergoing severe internal stresses and strains resulting in low academic standards. This necessitates a detailed systematic study, both at the aggregate and individual levels. Accordingly the present study entitled, "Financial Management of Universities in India" was undertaken with the following specific objectives:

Objectives

1. To make an appraisal of the University Institutions in India and their linkage.
2. To critically analyse and evaluate the existing financial management practices of the sampled University Institutions and to suggest and recommend remedial measures for effective and efficient financial management of the Universities in India.
3. To analyse and evaluate the existing sources of finances, grants-in-aid rules, criteria for fixation of grants-in-aid, pattern of expenditure and financial health of the University Institutions in

India, and to suggest model grants-in-aid rules, model criteria for fixation of grants-in-aid and a normative pattern of expenditure.
4. To critically analyse and evaluate the existing budgeting and planning systems and suggest measures for their improvement.
5. To critically analyse and evaluate the existing accounting and auditing system of universities in India and suggest measures for their improvement.

Utility of the Study

The Universities in India are facing allocative inefficiency, distributive inequality and a financial crisis. The study will throw light on the existing financial management practices of universities and will suggest and recommend remedial measures for effective and efficient financial management. The study will also help in understanding some of the achievements, successes, and problems of financial management.

Methodology

There is a network of University Institutions in India, presently numbering 176 (1987).[21] This study cannot cover all University Institutions but by random selection of small representative groups of universities conclusions can be derived and practical suggestions made for improvement. Throughout the study, the common term 'University Institution(s)' has been used to refer to different types of universities. Samples of Central Universities, Institutions recognised as 'Deemed Universities', Institutions of National Importance and State Agricultural Universities have been drawn through the technique of random sampling from the list of the total number of universities in each category. The selection of State General Universities has been made on the basis of five zones of the country, namely: Northern Zone, Central Zone, Western Zone, Southern Zone and Eastern Zone. Each zone has been taken as a strata and the States of the Union within a zone as sub-strata. The technique of stratified random sampling was applied for selection of State General Universities from the sub-strata in such a manner as that at least one or two universities are sampled from each State. Table 1.1 gives the percentages of the sampled universities for the purpose of the study.

TABLE 1.1: Sampled University Institutions

Sr. No.	Type of the University Institution	Total Number	Number Sampled	Percentage Sampled
1.	Central Universities	10	3	30.00
2.	Institutions recognised as 'Deemed Universities'	22	2	9.09
3.	Institutions of National Importance	10	2	20.00
4.	State General Universities	109	21	19.27
5.	State Agricultural Universities	25	8	32.00
	Total	176	36	20.45

The primary data has been collected through an opinion survey with the help of pre-tested questionnaires, designed separately for the three major functionaries, viz., Vice-Chancellors/Directors, Finance Officers/Comptrollers/Registrars and Professors and Heads of the Departments. The salient parameters of primary data are: (i) existing financial organisational set up, (ii) representation of teachers, students and non-teaching employees on the fiscal policy laying authorities/bodies, (iii) powers and functions and status of such authorities, (iv) grants-in-aid rules, nature and periodicity of grants, (v) financial autonomy, (vi) financial control, (vii) decentralization and delegation of powers, (viii) system of budgeting and planning, (ix) system of accounting and auditing, (x) composition, powers and functions of the Finance Committee, and (xi) status, powers and functions of the Finance Officers/Comptrollers/Treasurers. The opinion of one hundred and eighty (180) respondents has been used for the purpose of this study, as per position given in Table 1.2.

TABLE 1.2: Responses of Primary Data

Sr. No.	Functionaries	Responses
1.	Vice-Chancellors/Directors	28
2.	Finance Officers/Comptrollers/Registrars	46
3.	Professors and Heads of the Departments	106
	Total	180

The secondary data had been collected through correspondences, giving the purpose and objective of the study and through personal visits (Table 1.3).

TABLE 1.3: Secondary Data

Sr. No.	Agency/Sources	Documents, Publications and Statistical Data
1.	University Institutions	Acts, Statutes, Ordinances, Memorandum of Association, Rules and Regulations; Grants-in-Aid rules, criteria for fixation of grants-in-aid; Budgets, Accounts compiled, Audit Reports.
2.	University Grants Commission	Annual Reports, Proceedings of conferences of Vice-Chancellors, Reports of Review Committees on University Grants Commission Programmes, Reports of the Committee to enquire into the working of Central Universities, Income and Expenditure data of Universities for the years 1982-1985.
3.	Association of Indian Universities	Minutes of the meetings of the Conferences of the Vice-Chancellors and their annual meets, minutes of Standing Committees of the Vice-Chancellors, Recommendations of the Committee on Model Act, University Institutions in India.
4.	Indian Council of Agricultural Research	Revised Model Act for State Agricultural Universities.

Analytical Procedures

The primary data was tabulated item-wise in terms of parameters. Only affirmative responses in respect of each parameter have been taken into account. The affirmative responses have been further worked out in terms of percentages in respect of each type of University Institution by taking into account the total number of University Institutions sampled under each type. The parameters of the financial management system have been analysed in terms of percentage responses to arrive at conclusions and to make recommendations.

The secondary data of income and expenditure in respect of Central Universities, Institutions recognised as 'Deemed Universities', and State General Universities were tabulated on a comparative basis for different parameters under study. The statistical data regarding the income and expenditure, both recurring and non-recurring have been further processed State-wise in respect of State General Universities and Institutions recognised as 'Deemed Universities' for drawing comparisons of source position, pattern of expenditure and financial health of the University Institutions State-wise. This was done by aggregating the income and expenditure figures both recurring and non-recurring for the three different years, that is, 1982-83, 1983-84 and 1984-85. The proportion of income and expenditure on different items was computed for the respective total figures.

The income and expenditure, both recurring and non-recurring for the University Institutions including sampled University Institutions have been examined and surplus or deficit has been estimated by taking the difference of total income (recurring and non-recurring) and total expenditure (recurring and non-recurring). The percentages in respect of different items for income and expenditure and surplus or deficit have been accordingly worked cut. The percentage surplus or deficit was further classified into four ranges viz., surplus during all the three years, deficit during one year, deficit for two years and deficit during all the three years to assess the financial health of all types of sampled University Institutions. Various reports like the Report of the Committee on Model Act and the Revised Model Act of the Indian Council of Agricultural Research (ICAR) have been utilized to arrive at the extent to which their recommendations have been implemented by the Union or State Governments or the University Grants Commission and the Indian Council of Agricultural Research at the time of revising the existing Acts, Statutes and framing the Acts and Statutes for the establishment of new University Institutions. The use of all data from different places has been made in the light of the nature and suitability of the data available and the requirement of analysis, to make the analysis and interpretation more authentic.

PEFERENCES

1. Report of the Committee on Model Act for Universities, 1961, pp.42-43.
2. Report of the Committee on the Governance of Universities, 1971, p.15.
3. James Maynard, Some Micro Economics of Higher Education, Economics of State University of Nebraska Press Uncooin, XIX, 1971, p.186.
4. CERI (Centre for Education Research and Innovations), Costs and Potential Economics OECD, 1972.
5. Coombs, Phillip, H. and Hallak Jacques, *Managing Educational Costs*, Oxford University Press, New York, 1972.
6. Lakdawala, D.T. & Shah, K.R., Optimum Utilization of Educational Expenditure

in Gujarat and Financing of Universities in Gujarat, *Economic and Political Weekly*, X(20), 1975.

6a. Nigam, M.S., Study of the Finance of the University of Rajasthan, *Journal of Higher Education*, 1(3), Spring 75, pp.400-402.

7. Azad, J.L. State Grants to Collegiate Institutions: A Study of Patterns and Procedures, *Journal of Higher Education*, 1976, pp.243-52.
8. Mukerji, Kshitimohan, Study of the Finances of Calcutta University, Calcutta, Firma K.L.M., 1976, p.87.
9. Nanjundappa, D.M., *Working of University Finances*, New Delhi, Sterling, 1976.
10. Panchamukhi, P.R., Economics of University Finances. Centre for Multi-Disciplinary Research, Dharwar, 1977.
11. Sharma, G.D., Unit Cost of Education in a College of Delhi University, *University News*, Vol. 17(8), 1979, pp.212-17.
12. Sharma, G.D., Institutional Costs of University Education, Association of Indian Universities, 1980.
13. Balbir Singh and Satya Paul, Delhi University Finances. University College Finances, Seminar Papers, Association of Indian Universities, 1981, pp.134-147.
14. Garg, V.P. Finances of University of Punjab: A Trend Analysis. University and College Finances. Seminar Paper, Association of Indian Universities, 1981, pp.148-169.
15. Ruddar Datt, Costing of Corresponding Education. Need for Rational Policy. University and College Finances. Seminar Paper. Association of Indian Universities, 1981, pp.170-190.
16. Ghosh, D.K., *University System in India*. Rahul Publications, 1983.
17. Balachandran, K.K., Government Grants and Higher Educational Development (with special reference to Indian experience since Independence). Thesis Ph.D. (Economics), 1984.
18. Balachandran, K.K., Government and Higher Education. Need for Realistic Grant, Article published in *Economics Times*, 1986.
19. Bhardwaj and Balachandran, Higher Educational Planning and Administration. The Challenge of Change. Indian Institute of Education, Pune, 1985, (unpublished).
20. Group Discussion-cum-Orientation Programme on Financial Administration in Universities. Association of Indian Universities, 1988.
21. University Institutions in India, Association of Indian Universities, December, 1987.

2

UNIVERSITY INSTITUTIONS IN INDIA AND THEIR LINKAGE

Concept of University Institution

A UNIVERSITY is a social institution which has to interact with society. The word 'University' connotes the existence of a corporate body of teachers and scholars, a place where students would be attracted to drink freely from the fountain of knowledge, provided by teachers and, of course, the students for whom the former exists. The universities, should be permanent bodies and have the freedom to select their teachers to teach those students whom they decide to admit to the different courses of studies and finally grant 'licenses' to the worthy students at the end of the successful completion of the course of studies, According to Nehru, (1947)[1] "A university stands for humanism, for tolerance, for reasons, for the adventure of ideas, and for the search of truth. It stands for the onward march of the human race towards even higher objectives. If the universities discharge their duties adequately, then it is well with the nation and the people". These great words highlight the basic truth that universities have a crucial part to play in the life, welfare and strength of a nation. They can, however, justify this role only if they owe uncompromising loyalty to certain fundamental values of life. They are essentially a community of students and teachers, where in some way, all learn from one or another or at any rate strive to do so. Their principal object is to deepen man's understanding of the universe and of himself in body, mind and spirit, to disseminate his understanding throughout the society and to apply it in the service of mankind. They are the dwelling places of ideas and idealism and expect high standards of conduct and integrity from all their members.

Functions of a University Institutions

According to a report of the Education Commission (1964-66)[2] university education should have a three-fold emphasis, that is, (1) internal transformation so as to relate it to the life, needs and aspirations of the nation, (2) qualitative improvement so that the standards achieved are adequate, keep continually rising and atleast in a few sections, become internationally comparable, (3) expansion of educational facilities broadly on the basis of manpower needs with emphasis on equalisation of educational opportunities.

Development of Universities in India

Education imparted at a high level of abstractions and sophistication has an unbroken tradition in India that can be traced back to ancient times when the guru would impart the principles of the *Vedas* to pupils selected from princely and ruling classes. *Gurukuls* were expanded to Parishads and the Parishads stabilised into residential schools. At Nalanda, "The Buddhist Monastic Community Viharas" was one of the largest and earliest of such centres, where 10,000 students received instruction, ranging from Metaphysics to Astronomy. Buddhist Monastic Community Viharas were followed by Muslim Institutions – Madarashas which offered instruction in Logic, Astronomy, Mathematics and Arabic.

The establishment of three universities in the year 1857, viz., the University of Calcutta, the University of Bombay and the University of Madras marks the genesis of an organised system of higher education in India. The University of Panjab at Lahore was established in the year 1882 and Allahabad University in 1887. On the recommendations of the Education Commission (1902)[3] the 'Indian Universities Act, 1904' was enacted which was a land mark for transferring the Indian Universities from just affiliating and examining bodies to those of centres of teaching and research. The said Act provided for changes in the organisation and administration of universities, viz., empowering the universities to appoint teachers, limiting the size and fixing a tenure of five years for the members of the Syndicate, representation of Professors on the Syndicate, powers to the Government to over-rule the Senate and to fix territorial jurisdictions of the universities. The said Act created much dissatisfaction amongst the people and was considered a design to officialise the universities so that they did not become a medium of nationalism. With the said Act, the Government control was imposed heavily on the universities and that is why the Calcutta University Commission (1917-18)[4] described Indian Universities as the "most completely government universities in the world". The Education Policy in 1917 recommended the creation of teaching and residential universities for each of the leading provinces. Consequently, the Banaras Hindu University in 1915, Mysore University in 1916, Patna University in 1917 and Osmania University in 1918 were established in quick succession. The Third Education Commission in 1917 examined the position and power of Calcutta University and the problems of secondary education in the country. The Commission recommended lessening of the government control on the universities, appointing of a whole time salaried Vice-Chancellor and the establishment of an Inter-university Board for coordinating the activities of the universities. During the period from 1921-29, the University of Aligarh in 1920, Lucknow in 1920, Dacca in 1920, Delhi in 1922, Nagpur in 1922, Andhra Pradesh in 1926, Agra in 1927, and Annamalai in 1929 were established. The Hartog Committee (1929)[5] recommended the establishment of affiliating, unitary residential and teaching universities for honours and pass courses and opening of employment bureaus for students. During the period from 1937 till independence, i.e., 1947, Kerala University in 1937, Utkal University in 1943, Sagar University in 1946 and Rajasthan University in 1947 were established. The Sargeant Report on Education (1944)[6] recommended admission to courses on the basis of merit, competent teachers, with better pay scales and establishment of Grants Committee on the lines of the University Grants Committee of the United Kingdom.

The recommendations of Commission, Committees and constituted bodies/Institutions appointed by the Government of India after independence for suggesting measures for the improvement of higher education, in general and university education in particular are briefly given as under:

The First University Education Commission (1948)[7] recommended the establishment of the University Grants Commission, new universities to be established on the recommendation of the University Grants Commission, establishment of rural universities, education to be on the concurrent list of the constitution and coordination of finances on All India basis by the Central Government. Consequently, the University Grants Commission was established in 1956, one

Agricultural University was established in each State of Union and Education was included in the concurrent list.

On the recommendation of Mudaliar Commission (1952-53)[8] intermediate courses were abolished and a three-year degree programme was started by most of the States in India. The Committee on Model Act (1961-62)[9] for the universities made recommendations that the Court/Senate, Executive Council/Syndicate/Board of Management/Governors and the Academic Councils would be the main authorities of the university. The membership of the Court/Senate should not exceed 100, of which fifty should be external ones. For effective management of the universities, the three sections of the University, viz., teachers, students and non-teachers should be represented on the Court/Senate. The Court/Senate should operate as a body for laying down general policy for the well being of the university. The membership of the Executive Council/Syndicate/Board of Management should not exceed 20 and due representation on it should be given to teachers, elected members of the court, students and the Government. Fifty per cent of its membership should constitute academicians and it should be the principal executive body of the university for the management of its affairs. On the Academic Council, representation should be given only to academicians and its decisions except for financial reasons should not be subject to modification or approval by any one else. The Finance Committee should be a sub-committee of the Executive Council/Syndicate/Board of Management. On its membership there should exist provision for an ex-officio member of the Executive Council and representation of the State Government.

The Finance Committee should have effective control on all the financial transactions of the University and it should frame financial and budgetary rules. The audit of the University should be conducted by a recognised audit agency and the audit report should be sent to the Government and in order to honour autonomy and the standard of internal discipline it should not be placed on the table of Parliament/State Legislative Assembly. The Treasurer/Finance Officer should be a whole time officer of the University instead of an elected one.

The Kothari Commission (1964-66)[10] advised the Government on the national pattern of education and the general principles for the development of education at all stages and in all other aspects. This Commission recommended that if education was to develop adequately, expenditure on education in the next twenty five years should rise from Rupees 12 per capita in 1965-66 to Rupees 54 in 1985-86. This implies that the educational expenditure which increased from Rupees 1144 million in 1950-51 to Rupees 6000 million in 1955-56 will further rise to Rupees 40,364 million in 1985-85 and that the proportion of GNP allocated to education will rise from 2.9 per cent in 1965-66 to 6 per cent in 1985-86.

The Gajendragadkar Committee (1969)[11] recommended, (i) a flexible pattern of organisation which is responsive to the changing needs of society as well as knowledge, (ii) autonomy of the universities to be maintained by all sections of society, (iii) effective participation of all members of the University in the governance of the University, (iv) role of the University Grants Commission in advising the State Government for the fixation of quantum of grants to the universities and (v) setting up of suitable machineries to look into the grievances of the university community.

Coordinating Bodies for University Institutions

The Association of Indian Universities established in the year 1925, coordinates the work of the University Institutions, acts as a bureau of information, establishes equivalance of degrees awarded, promotes sports and cultural activities, promotes research on universal development and represents the universities at national and international forums. Some other coordinating bodies for University Institutions are briefly described as under:

University Grants Commission

The University Grants Commission (UGC) established in the year 1956 is both a grant giving and a coordinating body for academic purposes. The Commission in consultation with the universities and other bodies takes all such steps as it may think fit for the promotion and coordination of university education and for the determination and maintenance of standards of teaching, examination and research in universities. The Commission also clears/consents the establishment of new universities in the country and also declares a university fit to receive central assistance for development in terms of University Grants Commission Act of 1956.

Indian Council of Agricultural Research

The Council which is almost half a century old, is the central coordinating agency on agricultural education in research and extension education. Like the University Grants Commission, it provides central assistance to the Agricultural Universities for their development activities. It also finances research and extension education projects of the universities through a net work of All India Coordinated Research Projects and other *ad hoc* Research Projects under the Cess Fund Aid Scheme. The Council has formulated a 'Model Act' (1987)[12] for the governance of Agricultural Universities in the country. Provision exists in the 'Model Act' for the creation of a foundation fund and non-lapsable grants to the universities annually, thus ensuring sufficiency of funds for the universities.

Council of Scientific and Industrial Research

The Council of Scientific and Industrial Research (CSIR) established in the year 1942 is the premier organisation for promotion of scientific and industrial research in the country. The primary objectives of the Council is to establish a sound base of scientific capabilities and excellence over a wide spectrum of science and technology. The Council also provides funds for scientific research, which is being carried out in various universities. As of April, 1984, the Council had 38 National Laboratories/Institutions all over the country. In addition to industrial research associations there are 138 extension centres/field stations.

Central Advisory Board of Education

At the policy-making level, the Central Advisory Board of Education (CABE) has been functioning for almost half a century. Ministers of Education in States and Union Territories of the country sit on this Board. The meeting is presided over by the Union Minister of Education. On an average the Board meets once in two or three years.

Number of University Institutions

The total number of University Institutions in the country, as it stood on December 1987, was 176, out of which 130 are traditional

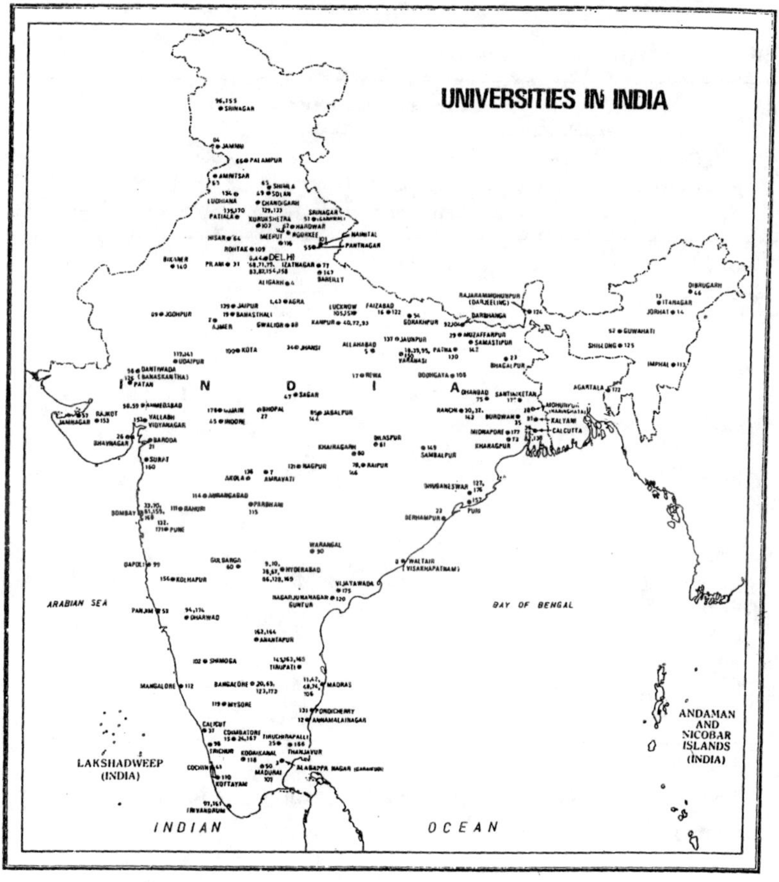

FIG. 2.1: Map of University Institutions in India

Source: University Institutions in India, Association of Indian Universities; December, 1987.

universities, 26 are Agricultural Universities, 6 Medical Institutions and 14 Technical Institutions (1987).[13] The map (Fig.2.1) gives the description/locations of University Institutions all over India. Table 2.1 presents the growth of the University Institutions from the year 1857 to 31st December, 1987.

TABLE 2.1: Growth of University Institutions

Period	University Institutions					
	Central Universities	Deemed Universities	Institutions of National Importance	State General Universities	State Agricultural Universities	Total
1857-1947	3	5	2	18	—	28
1948-1950	—	—	1	6	—	7
1951-1956 (1st Plan)	1	1	1	7	—	10
1956-1961 (2nd Plan)	—	3	4	10	1	18
1961-1966 (3rd Plan)	1	2	1	15	5	24
1967-1969 (Plan inter-regnum)	1	—	—	9	3	13
1969-1974 (4th Plan)	2	—	—	8	10	20
1974-1979 (5th Plan)	—	1	—	8	1	10
1980-1985 (6th Plan)	2	5	1	16	3	27
1986-1987	—	5	—	12	2	19

The maximum number of University Institutions of all types were established after independence and during the Five-Year Plans.

Enrolment of Students

The year-wise enrolment of students in the University has been graphically described in Fig. 2.2 for the period from 1966-67 to 1985-86.

The enrolment of students rose at the compound rate of 2.4 per cent per annum during the period from 1966-67 to 1985-86. The compound growth rate was found statistically significant ($p < 0.05$) as indicated by its standard error.

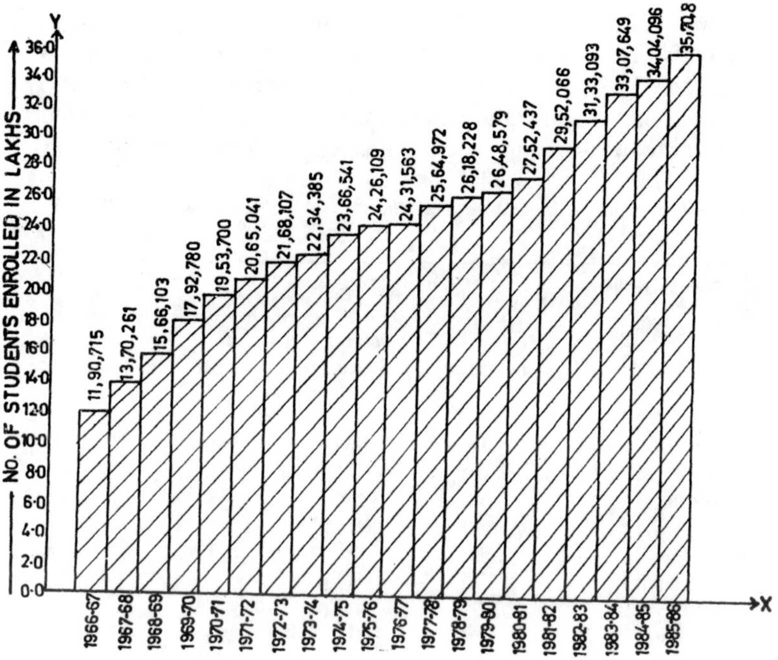

FIG. 2.2: Number of Students Enrolment during 1966-67 to 1985-86

Pattern of Expenditure on Higher Education

The growth of higher education, particularly university education has been phenomenal in terms of the number of universities established, students enrolled and the amount allocated under the various Five-Year Plans (1985).[14] Table 2.2 gives the pattern of expenditure on university education and education as a whole in the Five-Year Plans. The proportion of expenditure of total education on plan outlay decreased from 7.6 per cent in 1951-56 to 2.6 per cent in 1980-85. As against this the expenditure on university education has increased from 9.0 per cent to 19 per cent during the corresponding period. In terms of absolute figures on expenditure on the total education had increased from Rs.

153 crores in 1951-56 to Rs. 2,524 crores in 1985-86. The expenditure on university education has increased from Rs. 14 crores in 1951-56 to Rs. 486 crores in 1985-86. This increase did not commensurate with the rise in the price index and establishment of new University Institutions. The compound growth rate on university education was estimated at 71.2 per cent per annum for the period from 1951 to 1985 and was found statistically significant ($p < 0.05$). The corresponding figures for total education were estimated at 52.38 per cent ($p < 0.05$).

TABLE 2.2: Expenditure in the Five-Year Plans — University Education and Total Plan

(Rupees in crores)

Sr. No.	Five-Year Plans	Sectors			
		University Education	Total Education	Total Plan	Education as percentage of total plan
1.	1st Plan (1951-56)	14 (9)	153 (100)	1946	7.6
2.	2nd Plan (1956-61)	48 (18)	273 (100)	4680	5.8
3.	3rd Plan (1961-66)	87 (15)	589 (100)	8572	6.8
4.	Plan regnum	77 (24)	322 (100)	—	—
5.	4th Plan (1969-74)	195 (25)	786 (100)	15224	5.0
6.	5th Plan (1974-79)	292 (23)	1285 (100)	39322	3.2
7.	6th Plan (1980-85)	486 (19)	2524 (100)	97500	2.6

The diagrammatic representation of the expenditure on university education and education sector as a whole under plan during the period from 1951 to 1985 has been given in Figs. 2.3 and 2.4, respectively.

On the whole, the pattern of expenditure on general education and university education showed a smooth growth. Education expenditure increased by about 130 times from Rs. 550 million in 1947 to Rs. 71,740 million in 1985. In per capita terms the increase during 1950-51 to 1977-78 has been 13 times only. Starting from a very low figure of Rs. 3.2 per capita in 1950-51, a figure of Rs. 41 per capita in 1977-78 was reached. In contrast, the expenditure per pupil increased only by about 8 times during the period from 1950-51 to 1977-78, that is, from Rs. 35.6 to Rs. 384.4.

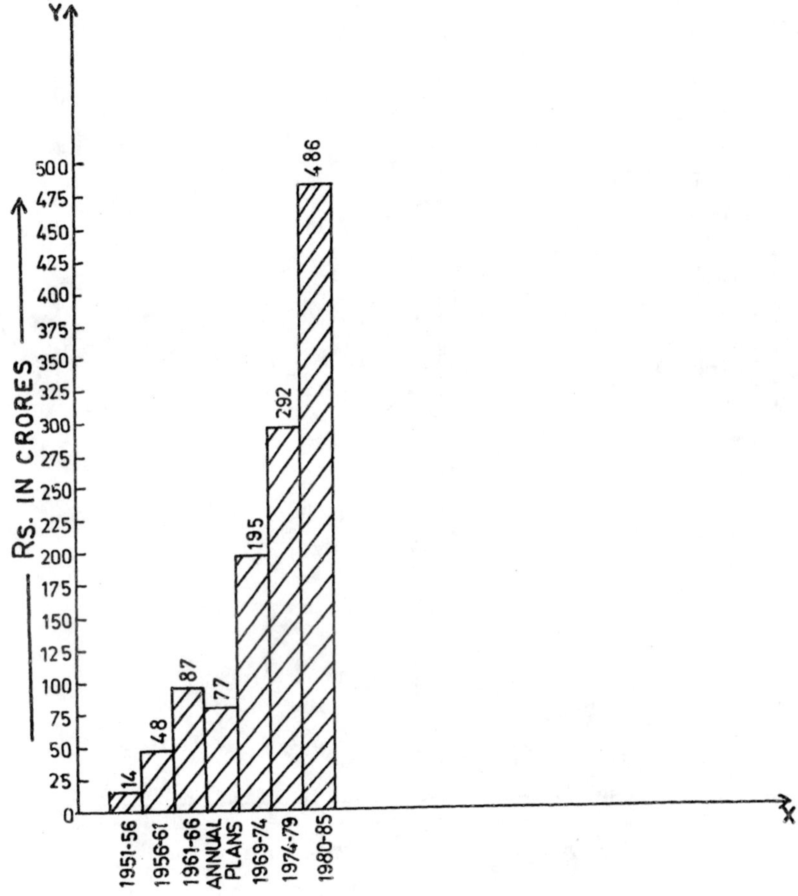

FIG. 2.3: Expenditure on University Education in the Five-Year Plans

The percentage of education expenditure to total budget (Revenue Accountant) during 1981-82 both for State/Union Territory and Central Government is given in Table 2.3.

The Government expenditure on education has not increased significantly while the growth of expenditure has been fluctuating. It decreased form 11.9 per cent in 1967-68 to less than 11.0 per cent in 1985-86 with an all time high proportion of 14.1 per cent reaching in 1970-71 and 1974-75.

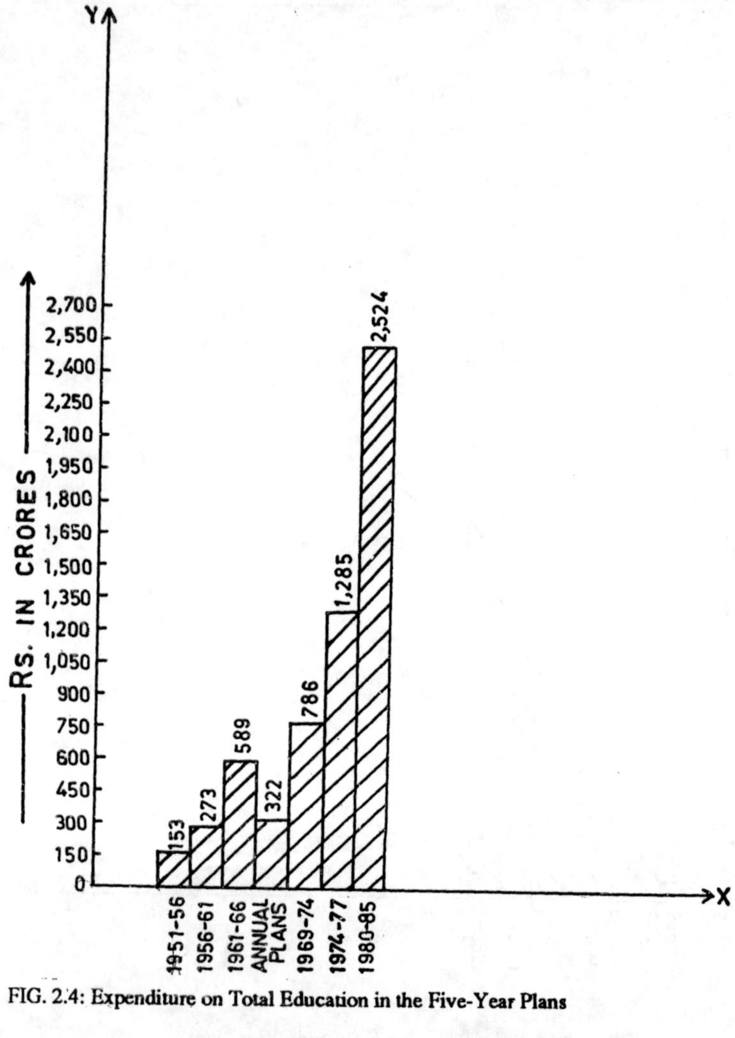

FIG. 2.4: Expenditure on Total Education in the Five-Year Plans

Education expenditure as a proportion of Gross National Product showed an increase from 1.2 per cent in 1950-51 to about 4.0 per cent in 1984-85. This share is quite low. When these figures are compared with those of other less developed countries, it is found to be 4.9 per cent in African countries and 5.1 per cent in Asian countries. In some of the developed countries like Netherlands and Sweden it is as high as 9 per cent to 10 per cent (1984).[15] Moreover, these proportions at the national level are far below the threshold of 6 per cent (1986).[16] In 1980-81, both Central and State Governments contributed 80.5 and 15 per cent (fees 12 per cent, endowment 3 per cent) respectively to finance higher education (1980-81).[17]

TABLE 2.3: Percentage of Education Expenditure to Total Budget (Revenue Account)

Year	State/Union Territory	Centre	Total
1967-68	19.8	1.6	11.9
1968-69	20.2	2.0	12.5
1969-70	20.5	2.3	13.0
1970-71	21.4	2.8	14.1
1971-72	20.3	2.5	13.4
1972-73	19.8	2.4	12.6
1973-74	20.6	2.0	13.0
1974-75	23.2	2.1	14.1
1975-76	22.9	2.0	13.7
1976-77	22.7	2.3	13.8
1977-78	21.4	2.1	12.7
1978-79	21.8	2.2	13.1
1979-80	21.6	2.0	13.1
1980-81	20.9	2.0	12.8
1981-82	20.8	1.9	12.5
1982-83	21.3	1.3	10.8
1983-84	20.8	1.5	11.4
1984-85*	20.5	1.6	11.2
1985-86#	20.1	1.5	10.8

* Revised Estimates

\# Budgeted Estimates

Types of University Institutions in India

The University Institutions in India are of following types: (i) Affiliating and Teaching, (ii) Unitary, (iii) Affiliating, Teaching and Unitary, (iv) Agricultural Universities, (v) Technical Universities, (vi) Institutions of National Importance and (vii) Institutions recognised as 'Deemed Universities".

Funding of University Institution in India

A University Institution in India is an innovation of law and it comes into official being by an Act of either the Central or the State Government. Education being a concurrent subject and as such the universities in India are established with the prior concurrence of the Central Government, which accords the same on the advice of the University Grants Commission and the Indian Council of Agricultural

Research (for Agricultural Universities). Thus all the University Institutions have to begin after an official sanction, public definitions, and with a sober character.

The University Institutions established through enactment of Parliament are classified as Central Universities and are mainly funded both for maintenance and development by the University Grants Commission. The Institutions recognised as 'Deemed Universities' are recognised by the Government of India on the recommendations of University Grants Commission in terms of its Act of 1956. The main source of their funding both for maintenance and development is again the University Grants Commission. The Institutions of National Importance, created by an Act of Parliament are mainly funded by the Central Government through its ministries. The State multi-faculty universities, technical universities and agricultural universities are creations of an Act of the State Legislation and the main source of their funding is the State Government. However, the University Grants Commission and the Indian Council of Agricultural Research also provide funds for the development and conduct of specific research. The other source of funding the universities is the domestic income which does not contribute much to the exchequer of the universities.

Governance of University Institutions in India

The University Institutions in India are autonomous in character and are governed through their Acts, Statutes, Ordinances and Regulations. The Acts of the University Institutions have the legal identity and Statutes of the University have the official sanction of the Government. The executive authority of the university is vested with powers for effecting additional and repealing existing Statutes with the consent of the Chancellor/Visitor of the university. The Ordinances and Regulations of the University Institutions can be framed, approved and amended or repealed by the principal executive authority of the University Institutions. Normally, the Governors are Chancellors of the University Institutions in the concerned States through in some of the universities, the Chief Minister is the Chancellor of the university. The Chancellor or Visitor is the Head of the University and is vested with the power to appoint the Vice-Chancellor, the Pro-Vice-Chancellor and in some universities, he also appoints the Registrar and the Treasurer/Finance Officer. The Vice-Chancellor is the principal executive and academic officer of the university responsible for the effective and efficient management of the affairs of the university. Provisions exist in the Act in most of the universities for the representation of the State Governments on most of the authorities/bodies of the university. For uniform governance of the University Institutions some of the State Governments have promulgated common Acts as per details given in Table 2.4.

TABLE 2.4: States having Common Act for the Governance of Universities in India

Sr. No.	Name of the State	Name of the Common Act
1.	Uttar Pradesh	The Uttar Pradesh State Universities Act 1973 (Act No. 10 of 1973).
2.	Bihar	The Bihar State Universities Act, 1976 (Act No. 23 of 1976).
3.	Karnataka	The Karnataka State University Act 1976 (Act No. 28 of 1976).
4.	Jammu & Kashmir	The Kashmir and Jammu Universities Act, 1969 (Act No. XXIV of 1969).
5.	Madhya Pradesh	The Madhya Pradesh Viswa Vidyalaya Adhiniyam (No. 22 of 1973).
6.	Himachal Pradesh	The Himachal Pradesh Universities of Agriculture, Horticulture and Forestry Act 1986 (Act No. 4 of 1987).
7.	Maharashtra	The Maharashtra Agricultural Universities (Krishi Vidyapeeths) Act, 1983 (Act No. XLI of 1983).
8.	Karnataka	The Karnataka Universities of Agricultural Sciences Act, 1987 (Act No. 40 of 1987).
9.	Haryana and Punjab	The Haryana and Punjab Agricultural Universities Act, 1970 (Act No. 16 of 1970).
10.	Uttar Pradesh	The Uttar Pradesh (Krishi Evam Prodyogik Viswa Vidyalaya Adhiniyam Act 1958 (U.P. Act XIV of 1958).
11.	Bihar	The Bihar Agricultural Universities (Ordinance No. 5, 1987).

Through the network of University Institutions the country is producing the third largest scientific manpower in the world and the top level of this category is comparable with the best talents amongst the leading countries of the world. The technical know-how is today in demand in West Asia, Africa, Europe and America which are amongst the ten top most industrial countries of the world.

REFERENCES

1. Convocation address of Jawaharlal Nehru, the Prime Minister of India at Allahabad University in December, 1947, University Grants Commission Report on the Governance of Universities and Colleges, Part I, 1971.
2. Report from the summary of the recommendations of the Education Commission Report (or Kothari Commission) published by the NCERT, 1967.
3. Report of the Indian Universities Commission (Government of India), 1902.
4. Report of the Calcutta University Commission (or Commission) Government of India, 1917.
5. Report of the Hartog Committee (Government of India), 1929.
6. Report of the Sargeant Committee, (Government of India), 1944.
7. Report of Radhakrishnan Commission (or University Education Commission), Government of India, 1948-49.
8. Report of Mudaliar Commission (Government of India), 1952-53.
9. Report of the Committee on Model Act for Universities, University Grants Commission, 1961-62.
10. Report of the Kothari Commission, Government of India, 1964-66.
11. Report of the Gajendragadkar Committee on the Governance of Universities, University Grants Commission, 1969-70.
12. The Indian Council of Agricultural Research 'Model Act', circulated vide letter No. F. 17-6/86-Edn. II, 13th July, 1987.
13. University Institutions in India, Association of Indian Universities, December, 1987.
14. Saraf, S.N., 'Financial Resources: Dimensions and Dilemmas', *University News*, 1985.
15. Statistical Year Book, 1984, (UNESCO, Paris).
16. Orivel, F. (1986), Economic Crisis and Education Crisis Looking Ahead Project 16(2), pp.197-204, a norm also recommended by the Kothari Commission and non-impartiality adopted by Government of India in the National Policy Resolution of Education (1968), a goal research in the New National Policy on Education (1986).
17. Education in India, Vol. I (various years) and Planning Commission, for 1980-81.

3

FINANCIAL MANAGEMENT PRACTICES OF SAMPLED UNIVERSITY INSTITUTIONS

For effective and efficient management of an organisation, Financial Management Practices/Systems, play a predominant role. Proven and good practices help in its speedier development and growth, free it from both internal and external criticism and undue interference from the Government and other funding agencies. They also create a healthy atmosphere and feeling of security in the university community. The Financial Management Systems of University Institution can be known from its Acts, Statutes, Ordinances, Rules and Regulations. The shortcomings in the existing systems/practices can be identified and suggestions based on the recommendations of various committees/ commissions constituted by the Government and co-ordinating bodies, can be made to improve it further. An attempt in his direction has been made in this chapter. Some of the provisions in the Acts of University Institutions which do not conform to the recommendations of committee/commission are briefly given as under:

The Kothari Commission (1964-66)[1] suggested that the Senate (Court/Council) of the University Institutions should have lay representation and should not be concerned with the day-to-day administration of the University. It should advise the University in laying down general policies and programmes. The Senate has been vested with executive powers for the management of University Institutions by the Acts of some of the Universities. In spite of this fact the 'Model Act' of Indian Council of Agricultural Research (1987)[2] does not provide for a Senate. Provision for this authority exists in some of the Acts of State Agricultural Universities.

Provision exists for a 'Council' in the Central Government Act for coordinating the activities of Indian Institutes of Technology. The said Council is vested with some of the financial powers, which are normally exercised by a Court/Syndicate.

The Common Acts for governance of Agricultural Universities in the States of Himachal Pradesh, and Maharashtra provide for a State Council, an authority, vested with financial powers. New Colleges and Departments can be established with the approval of the State Council in the State of Himachal Pradesh and the State Council in Maharashtra has also been vested with powers to accord financial sanctions beyond certain limits and to approve the budget. In terms of the Uttar Pradesh State Universities Act 1973 as amended upto 1987; the Chancellor (Governor) in emergent circumstances can supersede the existing Executive Council of a University and constitute an adhoc Executive Council consisting of the Vice-Chancellor and ten other members. The Karnataka State Universities Act 1976 (Amended upto 1986) has provision for the Chancellor to constitute the 'University Review Commission' once atleast in every five years. The recommendations of the said Commission along with a memorandum indicating the actions to be taken are laid before both Houses of the State Legislature. The Madhya Pradesh Viswa Vidyalaya Adhiniyam 1973, provides the Madhya Pradesh Uch Shiksha Anudan Ayog with powers for the coordination of activities and release of grants to the State General Universities (other than Agricultural Universities). The State Government can also assume financial control of a University in case of maladministration, financial mismanagement and financial instability. The acts of the Telugu University and the University of Health Sciences in Andhra Pradesh direct that the Chief Minister of the State is the Chancellor of these Universities. Provisions exist in the Acts of the University of Kerala and the University of Calicut in Kerala State, for the State Education Minister to be the pro-Chancellor of these universities. He performs all functions of the Chancellor in his absence. The Chancellor of these universities in emergent circumstances can dismiss any authority of the University and can take measures for the interim administration of the University. He can also annul any proceedings of an authority of the University which is not in accordance with Act, Statutes, and Rules and Regulations.

The parameters of paramount importance for the financial management of Universities are discussed as given hereinafter.

Powers and Functions of Fiscal Policies Laying Authorities

Central Universities

The Senate (Court/Council) of Delhi University is the supreme authority and can review the acts of the Executive Council and Academic Council, which is not the position in the case of North Eastern Hill and Visva Bharti Universities (Table 3.1). The limits for recurring and non-recurring expenditure are fixed by the Executive Council in the case of North Eastern Hill and Visva Bharti Universities, whereas this power is vested in the Finance Committee of the University of Delhi. The Finance Committees of the University of Delhi and Visva Bharti are also vested with the power to allow expenditure in excess of budget provisions.

Institutions Recognised as 'Deemed Universities'

In the case of sampled institutions recognised as 'Deemed Universities', the Senate (Court/Council) of Jamia Millia Islamia is vested with powers to review the decisions of the Executive Council, and Academic Council which is not so in the case of the Thaper Institute of Engineering and Technology. The Board of Governors of the Thaper Institute of Engineering and Technology is vested with powers to review the decisions of Senate (Academic Council). The Finance Committee of Thaper Institute of Engineering and Technology is also vested with the powers to confirm the appropriation approved by the Vice-Chancellor from one head to another (Table 3.2).

Institutions of National Importance

Board of Governors (Executive Council) of the Indian Statistical Institute is the highest decision-making authority whereas the Board of Governors of Indian Institute of Technology is a recommendatory authority in respect of most of the financial matters (Table 3.3).

State General Universities

The Universities in the States of Uttar Pradesh, Bihar, Karnataka, Jammu and Kashmir and Madhya Pradesh are governed through Common Acts so promulgated by the concerned State Governments (Table 3.4). Except for two State Universities in Andhra Pradesh, viz. Telugu University and University of Health Sciences, Senate (Court/Council) exists as one of the authorities in the rest of the universities. The Senate (Court/Council) is the supreme authority in respect of universities in the States of Bihar, Karnataka and Jammu and

TABLE 3.1: Powers and Functions of Fiscal Policy Laying Authorities of Central Universities

Sl. No.	Universities	Senate (Council/Court)	Syndicate (Board of Management/ Board of Governors)	Academic Council	Finance Committee/Board
1	2	3	4	5	6
1.	University of Delhi	(i) Review of the acts of other authorities;	(i) Creating of posts, managing finances, accounts, investment and property;	Teaching posts are recommend for creation	(i) Recommending budget and annual accounts to Executive Council;
		(ii) Budget, annual report, annual accounts presented for passing resolutions	(ii) Approving of annual accounts and budget;		(ii) Fixing annual 'imit of recurring and non-recurring expenditure;
			(iii) Amending or repealing statutes		iii) Allowing expenditure in excess cf budget.
2.	North-Eastern Hill University, Shillong	(i) Reviewing of broad policies and programmes;	(i) Amending or repealing statutes; (ii) Fixing limit of annual expenditure;	-do-	-do- except (iii)
		(ii) Passing resolutions on budget, annual accounts and audit reports	(iii) Delegating powers		
3.	Visva Bharti	-do-	-do-	-do-	As in the case of University of Delhi.

TABLE 3.2: Powers and Functions of Fiscal Policy Laying Authorities of Deemed Universities

Sl. No.	Universities	Senate (Council/Court)	Syndicate (Board of Management/ Board of Governors)	Academic Council	Finance Committee/Board
1	2	3	4	5	6
1.	Jamia Millia Islamia	(i) Reviewing acts of authorities; (ii) Passing resolution on budget, annual accounts and audit report	(i) Creating posts, managing finance, accounts and investment of property; (ii) Approving budget and annual accounts.	Creating and abolishing academic posts	(i) Recommending budget and annual accounts; (ii) Fixing annual limits of recurring and non-recurring expenditure; (iii) Allowing expenditure true not provided in the budget; (iv) Appropriations made by Vice-Chancellor are confirmed.
2.	Thaper Institute of Engineering & Technology, Patiala	(i) Reviewing broad policies and programmes; (ii) Passing resolutions on budget, annual accounts and audit report	-do- (iii) Reviewing decisions of the Senate (Academic Council); (iv) Delegating of powers	-do-	-do- except (iv)

TABLE 3.3: Powers and Functions of Fiscal Policy Laying Authorities of Institutions of National Importance

Sl. No.	Universities	Senate (Council/Court)	Syndicate (Board of Management/ Board of Governors)	Academic Council	Finance Committee/Board
1	2	3	4	5	6
1.	Indian Institute of Technology, Kanpur	(i) Supervision, Direction & Control; (ii) Starting new Courses and making Statutes; (iii) Passing resolutions on budget, annual accounts; (iv) Instituting and appointing persons	(i) Creating posts, managing finances, accounts and investment of property; (ii) Approving budget and annual accounts; (iii) Reviewing decisions of the Senate (Academic Council); (iv) Delegating of powers	No financial powers	(i) Examining and scrutinizing annual budget; (ii) Rendering advice on financial matters
2.	Indian Statistical Institute, Calcutta	-	(i) Adopting budget; (ii) Managing university property and administering funds; (iii) Delegating of powers	No financial powers	

Note: Council is common authority in respect of all the Institutions of National Importance (Indian Institute of Technology).

TABLE 3.4: Powers and Functions of Fiscal Policy Laying Authorities of State General Universities

Sl. No.	Universities	Senate (Council/Court)	Syndicate/Executive Council/ Board of Management/Board of Governors)	Academic Council	Finance Committee/Board
1	2	3	4	5	6
1.	Kanpur University	(i) Reviewing broad policies and programmes;	(i) Managing property and administering funds;	Advising on all academic matters	(i) Advising on financial matters;
2.	University of Allahabad	(ii) Passing resolutions on annual accounts, budget and audit report	(ii) Creating posts with the approval of Government;		(ii) Fixing limit for total recurring and non-recurring expenditure
3.	Meerut University (Common Act)		(iii) Preparing budget for sanction of Government; (iv) Making and repealing statutes		
4.	Patna University	(i) Supreme Governing Body;	(i) Decision on financial matters on the advice of Financial Adviser;	-do-	(i) Advising on all financial matters;
5.	Magadh University (Common Act)	(ii) Passing resolutions on budget and annual accounts; (iii) Amending and repealing statutes	(ii) Making, amending and repealing ordinances; (iii) Approving and submitting budget for financial approval of the Government; (iv) Creating posts with the prior approval of the Government		(ii) Formulating budget; (iii) Scrutinizing new items of expenditure not provided in the budget

(Contd.)

TABLE 3.4 *Contd.*

1	2	3	4	5	6
Karnataka					
6.	Bangalore University	(i) Creating teaching posts with the approval of the State Government; (ii) Making, amending and repealing statutes; (iii) Considering the budget so prepared by the Syndicate; (iv) Reviewing policies and suggesting measures for improvement	(i) Managing property and administering funds; (ii) Preparing budget; (iii) Delegating its powers to the Vice-Chancellor	Proposing creation of posts	(i) Scrutinizing and recommending budget; (ii) Examining annual accounts and reviewing audit reports; (iii) Examining proposals for which no provision in the budget exists
Jammu & Kashmir					
7.	University of Jammu	(i) Approving budget and development plans; (ii) Making, amending or repealing statutes	(i) Managing property and administering funds; (ii) Making draft statutes; (iii) Formulating budget; (iv) Delegating financial powers to various functionaries	Decisions on academic matters involving finanaces with prior approval of Syndicate or Council	(i) Scrutinising budget and recommending it to Syndicate; (ii) Reviewing financial position; (iii) Examining new proposals for which no provision exists

(Contd.)

TABLE 3.4 *Contd.*

1	2	3	4	5	6
Madhya Pradesh					
8.	Jiwajee University	(i) Advisory Body for reviewing broad policies and programmes; (ii) Passing resolutions on the budget, annual accounts, and audit report	(i) Managing property and administering funds; (ii) Adopting annual accounts, budget and audit report; (iii) Fixing limits for recurring and non-recurring expenditure; (iv) Creating teaching posts with prior approval of Madhya Pradesh Uch Anudan Ayog	Making proposals for creation of teaching posts	N.A.

(Contd.)

TABLE 3.4 *Contd.*

1	2	3	4	5	6
Andhra Pradesh					
9.	Telugu University	No such authority exists	(i) Managing property and administering funds; (ii) Delegating its powers; (iii) Creating teaching and non-teaching posts with prior approval of Government; (iv) Approving annual accounts and budget	Recommending institution of academic posts	(i) Examining annual accounts and budget; (ii) Recommending limits for recurring and non-recurring expenditure; (iii) Recommending to Syndicate new proposals for which no provision exist in in the budget and make recommendations on all financial matters
10.	University of Health Sciences	-do-	-do- (v) Making, amending or repealing statutes	-do-	-do-
11.	Osmania University	(i) Creating/instituting teaching posts; (ii) Delegating its powers; (iii) Considering budget and passing resolutions; (iv) Making, amending or repealing statutes	(i) Managing property and administering funds; (ii) Making, amending or repealing statutes; (iii) Delegating its powers to Committees; (iv) Formulating annual accounts and budget	-do-	-do- except (ii)

(*Contd.*)

TABLE 3.4 *Contd.*

1	2	3	4	5	6
Kerala					
12.	University of Kerala	(i) Reviewing acts of the Syndicate and Academic Council; (ii) Making, amending or repealing statutes; (iii) Creating teaching and other academic posts; (iv) Considering and passing budget	(i) Managing property and administering funds; (ii) Making, amending or repealing ordinances; (iii) Considering and examining budget and recommending to Senate; (iv) Creating non-teaching posts	Proposing creation of posts	(i) Examining annual accounts and budget and recommending to Syndicate; (ii) Advising limits on recurring and non-recurring expenditure; (iii) Allowing expenditure not provided in the budget; (iv) All posts with maximum pay of Rs.700.00 p.m. or above, to be created with the prior approval of the Finance Committee
13.	University of Calicut	-do-	-do-	-	-do-
Punjab					
14.	Punjabi University	(i) Reviewing broad policies and programmes; (ii) Passing resolutions on annual accounts and budget	(i) Managing property and administering funds; (ii) Making, amending or repealing statutes and ordinances; (iii) Creating teaching and other posts; (iv) Approving budget	Recommending creation of academic posts	(i) Advising the Syndicate on all financial matters; (ii) Recommending the budget estimates

(Contd.)

TABLE 3.4 *Contd.*

1	2	3	4	5	6
Haryana					
15.	Maharshi Dayanand University	(i) Reviewing broad policies and programmes; (ii) Passing resolutions on annual accounts, audit report and budget	(i) Managing property and administering funds; (ii) Creating teaching and other posts; (iii) Making, amending or repealing statutes; (iv) Approving annual accounts and budget	Recommending creation of posts	(i) Examining annual accounts, scrutinizing budget and recommending to the Executive Council; (ii) Fixing limits for recurring and non-recurring expenditure; (iii) Allowing expenditure not provided in the budget
Rajasthan					
16.	University of Rajasthan	(i) Making, amending or repealing statutes and cancelling ordinances; (ii) Passing resolutions on accounts and budget	(i) Raising loans with concurrence of Government; (ii) Managing property and and administering funds	Recommending creation of teaching and academic posts	(i) Examining the budget and advising Syndicate thereon; (ii) Reviewing accounts, audit objections; (iii) Recommending all matters relating to finances

(Contd.)

TABLE 3.4 *Contd.*

1	2	3	4	5	6
Himachal Pradesh					
17.	Himachal Pradesh University	(i) Reviewing broad policies and programmes; (ii) Passing resolutions on budget, annual accounts and audit report	(i) Creating all types of posts; (ii) Managing property and administering funds; (iii) Making, amending and repealing statutes and ordinances	-do-	(i) Considering and examining annual accounts and budget; (ii) Fixing limit for the recurring and non-recurring expenditure; (iii) All new proposals of expenditure can be considered if recommend by the Finance Committee
West Bengal					
18.	University of Calcutta	(i) Creating and instituting posts with the approval of the Government; (ii) Passing resolutions on annual accounts, audit report and budget; (iii) Modifying budget so approved with majority of votes; (iv) Making, amending or repealing statutes	(i) Recommending creation of posts with the approval of Government; (ii) Approving annual accounts and budget; (iii) Managing property and administering funds; (iv) Proposing formulation of statutes	Proposing establishment of Colleges and Departments, and recommending creation of teaching posts	(i) Considering and recommending budget, annual accounts and audit reports; (ii) Preparing financial and accounts rules; (iii) Allowing expenditure; not provided in the budget; (iv) Regulating income and expenditure
19.	Rabindra Bharti University	-do-	-do-	-do-	-do-

(Contd.)

TABLE 3.4 *Contd.*

1	2	3	4	5	6
Maharashtra					
20.	University of Bombay	(i) Making, amending or repealing statutes and refer back to Syndicate ordinances if not approved; (ii) Passing resolutions on annual accounts and audit report; (iii) Passing budget; (iv) Reviewing policies and programmes	(i) Producing draft statutes; (ii) Managing property and administering funds: (iii) Delegating powers with the approval of the Chancellor; (iv) Recommending budget; (v) Making, amending, repealing ordinances	-do-	(i) Considering and examining annual accounts and budget; (ii) Examining proposals for fresh expenditure; (iii) Recommending limit for recurring and non-recurring expenditure
Gujarat					
21.	Sardar Patel University	(i) Making, amending or repealing statutes; (ii) Establishing and Managing university colleges and departments; (iii) Instituting and managing teaching and academic posts; (iv) Passing annual accounts and budget	(i) Managing property and administering funds; (ii) Recommending annual accounts and budget estimates	Proposing establishment of university departments and creation of teaching and other academic posts	(i) Advising on all financial matters; (ii) Preparing budget and annual accounts

Kashmir, Osmania University in Andhra Pradesh, Universities of Kerala and Calicut in Kerala, Calcutta University in West Bengal, University of Bombay in Maharashtra, and Sardar Patel University in Gujarat.

The Senate (Court/Council) of the University of Kerala, the University of Calicut (in Kerala State) is vested with the powers to review the Acts of Syndicate (Executive Council) and the Academic Council. The budget of the universities namely, Bangalore University, Jammu University, Osmania, University, University of Kerala, University of Calicut, University of Calcutta, University of Bombay and Sardar Patel University is approved by the Senate, whereas in the case of other universities the same is approved by the Syndicate (Executive Council). It is also pertinent to note that in the case of universities in the States of Uttar Pradesh, Bihar and Jammu and Kashmir, the budget is sent to the Government for approval. Posts are created with the approval of the Senate (Court) in the case of Bangalore University, University of Calcutta, Rabindra Bharti University, Osmania University, University of Kerala, University of Calicut and Sardar Patel University. For the creation of posts in Calcutta University and Rabindra Bharti, prior approval of the Government is essential. The Syndicate is vested with powers for the creation of posts in the case of universities in the States of Uttar Pradesh, Bihar, Madhya Pradesh and Telugu University, University of Health Sciences in Andhra Pradesh, Punjabi University in Punjab, Maharshi Dayanand University in Haryana, University of Calcutta and Rabindra Bharti in West Bengal. Prior approval of the Government is requisite for the creation of posts by Syndicate in respect of these universities except those in Madhya Pradesh (Uch Shiksha Anudan Ayog), Punjabi University, Maharshi Dayanand University, Calcutta University and Rabindra Bharti.

The Senate (Court) is vested with the powers to make, amend and repeal statutes in the case of most of the universities, excepting universities in the States of Uttar Pradesh, University of Health Sciences in Andhra Pradesh, Punjabi University in Punjab, Maharshi Dayanand University in Haryana and Himachal Pradesh University in Himachal Pradesh. The Syndicate is vested with the powers of fixing limits of recurring and non-recurring expenditure in the case of Jiwajee University in Madhya Pradesh. In most of the universities the Finance Committee/Board is vested with the powers to fix/recommend limits for recurring and non-recurring expenditure and to allow expenditure above the budget provision

State Agricultural Universities

The States of Himachal Pradesh, Maharashtra, Karnataka, Uttar Pradesh and Bihar, which have more than one Agricultural University have promulgated Common Acts for the governance of Agricultural Universities.

From the perusal of Table 3.5, it can be seen that the Senate (Court/Council) exists as one of the authorities in Himachal Pradesh Krishi Vishva Vidyalaya, Bidhan Chandra Krishi Vishwa Vidyalaya, Rajindra Agricultural University and Kerala Agricultural University. The Senates of Himachal Pradesh Krishi Vishwa Vidyalaya and Rajindra Agricultural University are vested with powers to review broad policies and programmes, and thus play advisory roles. The Senate (Court/Council) of Bidhan Chandra Krishi Vishwa Vidyalaya can review the acts of the Executive Council (Syndicate), whereas the Senate (Court/Council) of Kerala Agricultural University besides reviewing the acts of the Executive Council and the Academic Council is vested with powers to approve the budget, to create teaching and academic posts, and to make, amend or repeal statutes.

Financial powers like creation of posts, approval of the budget, management of university property, and administering funds and farming of statutes are vested with the Syndicate (Board of Management/Regent/Executive Council) in almost all the Agricultural Universities of the country, excepting Kerala Agricultural University where these powers are vested with the Senate (Council/Court) of the University. The Finance Committee of all Agricultural Universities is a recommendatory body in respect of all financial matters and it also exercises independent powers of allowing expenditure where expenditure is in excess of budget provision or for which no budget provision exists.

There is no uniformity in the existence and nomenclature of the University Institutions in India. (Tables 3.1 to 3.5). The powers and functions of various authorities also differ from university to university. The Kothari Commission has expressed the role and functions of the Senate (Council/Court) in the following words:

> The Court (Senate) should be the policy-making body of the university with a lay element and should not be concerned with the details of academic matters or day-to-day administration of the university.

TABLE 3.5: Powers and Functions of Fiscal Laying Authorities of State Agricultural Universities

Sl. No.	Universities	Senate (Council/Court)	Syndicate (Board of Management/ Board of Regent/Executive Council)	Academic Council (Faculties)	Finance Committee/Board
1	2	3	4	5	6
1.	Himachal Pradesh Krishi Vishva-vidyalaya, Palampur (Common Act)	(i) Reviewing broad policies and programmes; (ii) Passing resolutions on annual accounts, financial estimates and audit report	(i) Managing property and administering funds; (ii) Approving budget and annual accounts; (iii) Proposing establishment of new colleges and departments; (iv) Creating teaching/academic and other posts; (v) Making, amending or repealing statutes	Recommending creation of teaching and other academic posts	(i) Examining annual accounts, budget and audit report and advising the Board thereon; (ii) Reviewing financial position of the university from time to time
2.	Mahatma Phule Agricultural University (Common Act)	No such authority exists	(i) Making, amending or repealing statutes; (ii) Delegating its powers; (iii) Considering and farming the budget for the approval of State Council	Recommending creation of teaching and other academic posts	N.A.

(Contd.)

TABLE 3.5 *Contd.*

1	2	3	4	5	6
3.	University of Agricultural Sciences, Bangalore (Common Act)	No such authority exists	(i) Managing property and administering funds; (ii) Making, amending or repealing statutes; iii) Approving budget	-do-	(i) Examining annual accounts and budget and advising the Board thereon; (ii) Examining all proposals for which no budget exists or expenditure is in excess of amount provided
4. 5.	Punjab Agricultural University Haryana Agricultural University (Common Act)	-do-	(i) Managing property and administering funds; (ii) Approving budget; (iii) Creating academic and other posts; (iv) Making, amending or repealing statutes	Recommending creation of teaching and other academic posts.	(i) Reviewing financial position from time to time; (ii) Recommending to the Board proposals for which no funds exist and expenditure is in excess of budget; (iii) Examining budget and annual accounts.
6.	Gobind Ballabh Pant University of Agriculture & Technology, Pant-nagar (Common Act)	-do-	-do-	Recommending the establishment and amalgamation of Divisions or abolition of Facul-ties of Departments	Finance Committee under composition

(Contd.)

TABLE 3.5 *Contd.*

1	2	3	4	5	6
7.	Bidhan Chandra Krishi Vishva Vidyalaya	Reviewing the actions of Executive Council	(i) Approving budget; (ii) Managing property and administering funds; (iii) Creating teaching and academic posts; (iv) Making, amending or repealing statutes	Recommending teaching and other academic posts	(i) Scrutinizing audited annual accounts and budget; (ii) Controlling expenditure and watch income
8.	Tamil Nadu Agricultural University	No such authority exists	(i) Approving budget; (ii) Managing property and administering funds; (iii) Creating and establishing colleges and Departments; (iv) Making, amending or repealing statutes	-do-	(i) Examining annual accounts, budget and advising the Board thereon; (ii) Recommending proposals for which no provision exists in the budget; (iii) Reviewing financial position from time to time

(*Contd.*)

TABLE 3.5 *Contd.*

1	2	3	4	5	6
9.	Rajindra Agricultural University (Common Act)	(i) Reviewing broad policies and programmes; (ii) Passing resolutions on annual accounts, audit report and budget	(i) Approving budget; (ii) Managing property and administering funds; (iii) Making, amending or repealing statutes	Recommending creation of teaching and other academic posts	(i) Examining annual accounts, budget advising the Board thereon; (ii) Making recommendations on all financial matters; (iii) Recommending to the Board proposals for which budget proposal does not exist; (iv) Reviewing financial position from time to time
10.	Gujarat Agricultural University	No such authority exists	-do-	-do-	-do-

(Contd.)

TABLE 3.5 *Contd.*

1	2	3	4	5	6
11.	Kerala Agricultural University	(i) Supreme authority, Reviewing the acts of Executive Council/ Committee and Academic Council; (ii) Approving budget; (iii) Making, amending or repealing statutes; (iv) Creating teaching and other academic posts	(i) Examining budget and submitting it to the Council; (ii) Managing property and administering funds; (iii) Making, amending or repealing ordinances; (iv) Creating non-teaching posts	-do-	-do-

In sharp departure from the above opinion of the Education Commission, the Senates of some of the universities have been vested with the powers of reviewing acts of other authorities, approving the budget, creating posts, making, amending or repealing statutes.

The Senate (Court) is intended to function as a policy-making authority and on it various sections of society are represented. It is desirable that such powers should not be vested in the Senate (Court). Moreover, a smaller group of members of the Syndicate (Executive Council/Board) can appreciate the problems of University Institutions in a better way and suggest measures on the basis of consensus decisions after deliberating the issues.

The Syndicate (Executive Council/Board) should be the principal executive body/authority in respect of fiscal policies and programmes and all financial powers and functions should be vested in it. It should be advised in all financial matters by the Finance Committee. The Finance Committee being a statutory authority in respect of all University Institutions in India and as such it should be vested with the powers like fixing of limits for expenditure, allowing expenditure over and above the budget provisions, examination of annual accounts, budget and audit reports of the university. The advice of the Finance Committee should be mandatory on the Syndicate (Executive Council/Board) and in case the Syndicate does not agree to the recommendations of the Finance Committee, it should be referred back to the Committee for review/re-examination.

Representation of Teachers, Students and Non-Teachers on the Authorities of the University Institutions

The university community mainly comprises teachers, students and non-teaching employees. The policies and programmes formulated by the authorities for the governance are mainly to the advantage of the university community. They can be better planned and executed if all sections of university community are actively associated in the deliberations of the authorities of the University Institutions. This can be achieved by giving them due representation on such authorities. Participation in management helps to redress grievances and gives a look of democratic decision making instead of the taking of decisions by one or two administrators. It also creates a feeling of satisfaction and belongingness in the university community. The Gajendragadkar Committee (1969-70)[3] in its report has recommended the effective participation of all the members of University as an essential element of the concept of university autonomy. This Committee has not only strongly favoured participation by students in the governance of the university, it has also recommended such participation as an integral part of the system, for it is only through their participation in the syllabi framing and co-curricular activities etc. that the functioning of the academic system becomes meaningful. As such the representation of university community on the authorities of University Institutions has been studied and information contained in Table 3.6 reveals the position as given hereafter.

Representation exists for all sections of the university community on the Senate in respect of North Eastern Hill University, Visva Bharti, Jamia Millia Islamia, Patna University, Magadh University, Osmania University, University of Kerala, University of Calicut, Himachal Pradesh University, University of Calcutta, Rabindra Bharti, University of Bombay, Sardar Patel University, Bidhan Chandra Krishi Vishwa Vidyalaya, Rajindra Agricultural University and Kerala Agricultural University. Two sections of the University Community, i.e. teachers and students find representation on the Senate in case of Kanpur University, University of Allahabad, Meerut University, Bangalore University, Jiwajee University, Punjabi University, Maharshi Dayanand University and the University of Rajasthan. It is only in the case of Himachal Pradesh Krishi Vishva Vidyalaya where representation exists for teachers and non-teachers on the Senate. Only teachers are represented on the Senate in case of the University of Delhi.

It is only in the case of University of Kerala, State General Universities in Uttar Pradesh, Himachal Pradesh University, Rabindra Bharti, University of Calcutta and Bidhan Chandra Krishi Vishva Vidyalaya where all sections of the university community are represented on the Syndicate. In the case of the Indian Statistical Institute representation exists for teachers and non-teachers on the Syndicate whereas in the University of Calicut and the University of Rajasthan both teachers and students are represented. No representation exists on the Syndicate in the University of Health Sciences and most of the Agricultural Universities. Teachers and students are represented on the Academic Council in the case of all Central Universities, Patna University, Magadh University, Osmania University, University of Kerala, University of Calicut and Kerala Agricultural University.

TABLE 3.6: Representation of Teachers, Students and Non-teachers on the Authority of the University Institutions

Sl. No.	University/ Institution	Senate (Council/Court)	Syndicate (Executive Council/ Board of Management/Governors)	Academic Council (Faculties)	Finance Committee/Board
1	2	3	4	5	6
A.	*Central Universities*				
1.	University of Delhi	Teachers	Teachers	Teachers and students	None
2.	North-Eastern Hill University	Teachers, students, and non-teaching employees	Teachers	-do-	-do-
3.	Visva Bharti	-do-	-do-	-do-	Teachers (Head of Department)
B.	*Deemed Universities*				
4.	Thaper Institute of Engineering & Tech-nology	Teachers	Teachers	Teachers	None
5.	Jamia Millia Islamia	Teachers, students and non-teaching employees	Teachers	Teachers	Teachers (Dean)
C.	*Institutions of National Importance*				
6.	Indian Institute of Technology	-	Teachers	Teachers	None
7.	Indian Statistical Institute	-	Teachers and non-teachers	Teachers	N.A.
D.	*State General Universities*				

(Contd.)

TABLE 3.6 *Contd.*

1	2	3	4	5	6
(a)	*Uttar Pradesh*				
8.	Kanpur University	Teachers and students	Teachers, non-teachers and students	Teachers	None
9.	University of Allahabad				
10.	Meerut University (Common Act)				
(b)	*Bihar State*				
11.	Patna University	Teachers, students and non-teachers	Teachers	Teachers and students	None
12.	Magadh University (Common Act)				
(c)	*Karnataka*				
13.	Bangalore University (Common Act)	Teachers and students	Teachers	Teachers	None
(d)	*Jammu & Kashmir*				
14.	University of Jammu (Common Act)	Teachers	Teachers	Teachers	None
(e)	*Madhya Pradesh*				
15.	Jiwajee University (Common Act)	Teachers and students	Teachers	Teachers	N.A.
(f)	*Andhra Pradesh*				
16.	Telugu University	—	Teachers	Teachers	Teachers (Deans, Directors and Professors)
17.	University of Health Sciences	—	None	Teachers	-do-
18.	Osmania University	Teachers, students and non-teachers	Teachers	Teachers and students	None

(Contd.)

TABLE 3.6 *Contd.*

1	2	3	4	5	6
(g)	*Kerala*				
19.	University of Kerala	Teachers, students and non-teachers	Teachers, students and non-teachers	Teachers and students	None
20.	University of Calicut	-do-	Teachers and students	-do-	None
(h)	*Punjab*				
21.	Punjabi University	Teachers and students	Teachers	Teachers	Teachers (Dean)
(i)	*Haryana*				
22.	Maharshi Dayanand University	Teachers and students	Teachers	Teachers	Teachers (Two Deans)
(j)	*Rajasthan*				
23.	University of Rajasthan	-do-	Teachers and students	-do-	Teachers (Two Heads)
(k)	*Himachal Pradesh*				
24.	Himachal Pradesh University	Teachers, students and non-teachers	Teachers, students and and non-teachers	Teachers	Teachers (Dean)
(l)	*West Bengal*				
25.	University of Calcutta	-do-	-do-	-do-	None
26.	Rabindra Bharti	-do-	-do-	-do-	Teachers (Three Deans)
(m)	*Maharashtra*				
27.	University of Bombay	-do-	Teachers	-do-	-do-
(n)	*Gujarat*				
28.	Sardar Patel University	-do-	-do-	-do-	Teachers (One Dean, One Head and one Principal)

(Contd.)

TABLE 3.6 *Contd.*

1	2	3	4	5	6
E.	*State Agricultural Universities*				
29.	Himachal Pradesh Krishi Visva Vidyalaya (Common Act)	Teachers and non-teachers	One Dean/ Director	Teachers	None
30.	Mahatma Phule Agricultural University (Common Act)	No such body exists	None	Teachers	N.A.
31.	University of Agricultural Sciences	-do-	-do-	-do-	None
32.	Haryana Agricultural University	-do-	-do-	-do-	-do-
33.	Punjab Agricultural University	No such body exists	None	Teachers	None
34.	Gobind Ballabh Pant University of Agriculture & Technology, Pantnagar	-do-	-do-	-do-	No such Committee exists
35.	Bidhan Chandra Krishi Vishwa Vidyalaya	Teachers, students and non-teachers	Teachers, students and non-teachers	-do-	None
36.	Tamil Nadu Agricultural University	No such body exists	None	-do-	-do-
37.	Rajindra Agricultural University	Teachers, students and non-teachers	Teachers	-do-	Teachers (Dean, Director and Head of Department)
38.	Kerala Agricultural University	-do-	-do-	Teachers and students	None
39.	Gujarat Agricultural University	No such body exist	None	Teachers	None

Teachers are mostly involved in the capacity of Deans of the Faculty and Professor and Heads of the Departments on the Finance Committee in respect of Visva Bharati, Jamia Millia Islamia, Telugu University, University of Health Sciences, Punjabi University, Maharshi Dayanand University, University of Rajasthan, Himachal Pradesh University, Rabindra Bharti, University of Bombay, Sardar Patel University and Rajindra Agricultural University.

From the facts given above, it can be deduced that there is no uniformity on the issue of representation of the university community to various authorities of the University. All sections of the university community should be represented on the Senate (Court/Council) where the general policy and programmes of the University are discussed and resolutions on the budget, annual accounts, audit report and annual reports are passed. The participation of all sections of the university community in the Senate acquaints them with the general climate of the University. The Syndicate being the principal executive authority of the university and as such the representation on it should be restricted to elected members of the teachers and non-teachers. The representation of students is not desirable since administrative matters pertaining to students are discussed and may influence the decisions. Non-teachers should not be represented on the Academic Council and participation of students in the Academic Council should be confined only to matters concerning syllabi framing, co-curricular activities for matters where their welfare is concerned. Teachers should be represented on the Finance Committee as they can safeguard the interests of Faculties/Colleges and Departments.

Composition of Finance Committee

Among the various authorities, the Finance Committee/Board plays a very important role. It functions through 'formal resolution', duly recorded in accordance with the provisions laid down in constitution. The Finance Committee/Board distinctively functions in the system for all financial matters of the university. It examines the budget and annual accounts and audit report of the university and advises thereon. It fixes limits of expenditure and considers new proposals for which no provision exists in the budget. All financial matters in the university system are decided on the recommendation of the Finance Committee/Board. As such the composition of the Finance Committee/Board matters considerably in the Financial Management

System of the University Institution. The Vice-Chancellor/Director of the University Institution is the ex-officio Chairman of the Finance Committee/Board. Exceptions are there in respect of the Thaper Institute of Engineering and Technology and Indian Institute of Technology where the Chairman of the Finance Committee/Board is other than the Director. The Committee on 'Model Act' (1961-62) has recommended the representation of the Government on the Finance Committee/Board. The Gajendragadkar Committee (1969-70) has recommended the representation of the members of the University on the authorities of the University Institution. Various experts in the field of university administration have expressed their views in favour of nomination of financial experts to the Finance Committee/Board. The constitution of the University Institution should provide for representation of university official, Government/U.G.C. official, nominee of the university authorities and nominee of the Chancellor (Visitor) on the Finance Committee/Board. Broadly, the position of representation of various sections on the Finance Committee/Board is shown in Table 3.7.

Analysed position of the composition of the Finance Committee/Board reveals that the Dean/Directors are representatives on the Finance Committee/Board in respect of Jamia Millia Islamia, Telugu University, University of Health Sciences, Punjabi University, Maharshi Dayanand University, Himachal Pradesh University, Rabindra Bharti, University of Bombay, Sardar Patel University and Rajindra Agricultural University. The Head/Chairman of the Department/Institutions are represented on it in the case of Visva Bharti, University of Health Sciences, University of Rajasthan, Sardar Patel University and Rajindra Agricultural University. The Finance Officer is not the Secretary of the Finance Committee in the University of Jammu, Punjabi University and Sardar Patel University whereas the Registrar is the Secretary of the Committee in the Punjabi University and Sardar Patel University and the Member Secretary in the University of Jammu. The Treasurer/Finance Officer is the Member-Secretary of the Finance Committee in the case of University of Delhi, Jamia Millia Islamia, Thaper Institute of Engineering and Technology, Kanpur University, University of Allahabad, Meerut University, Himachal Pradesh University, Rabindra Bharti and in most of the Agricultural Universities. A post of Financial Adviser exists in the two universities in Bihar State and University of Jammu, who is also the Member-Secretary of the Finance Committee.

TABLE 3.7: Comparative Position of Representation on the Finance Committee/Board

Sr. No.	University/Institution	The University official	The Government/ U.G.C. official	Nominee of University authorities	Nominee of the Chancellor (Visitor)/Government etc.
1	2	3	4	5	6
A.	*Central Universities*				
1.	University of Delhi	1. Pro-vice-Chancellor 2. Treasurer (Convener)	None	Two elected members of the Court (not employees)	Two nominees of the visitor
2.	Visva Bharati,	1. Head of the Department/Institution 2. Finance Officer Non-member Secretary	None	One nominee of Executive Council (not employee)	Three nominees of the Visitor
3.	North Eastern Hills University	1. Pro-Vice-Chancellor 2. Finance Officer Non-member Secretary	None	Three nominees of the Executive Council	Three nominees of the Visitor
B.	*Deemed Universities*				
4.	Jamia Millia Islamia	1. Two Deans as Member of Executive Council 2. Treasurer	One nominee of of U.G.C.	One nominee of Court	Two nominees of Central Government
5.	Thapar Institute of Engineering & Technology	1. Director 2. Treasurer	Secretary, Finance & Technology, Punjab Government	Two nominees of Board	One nominee of Chancellor

(Contd.)

TABLE 3.7 *Contd.*

1	2	3	4	5	6
C.	*Institutions of National Importance*				
6.	Indian Institute of Technology, Kanpur	1. Director	None	Two nominees of Board	Two nominees of the Central Government
D.	*State General Universities*				
7. 8. 9.	Kanpur University University of Allahabad Meerut University	1. Pro-Vice-Chancellor 2. Finance Officer (Member Secretary)	None	One nominee of the Executive Council	None
10. 11.	Patna University Magadh University	1. Financial Advisor 2. Finance Officer ex-Officio Secretary	One Officer of the State Government not below the Deputy Secretary	Four nominees of Senate	None
12.	Bangalore University	1. Finance Officer (Non-Member Secretary) 2. Registrar (Permanent Invitee)	Two Officers nominated by the State Government	One each nominee of Senate and Syndicate	None
13.	University of Jammu	1. Pro-Vice-Chancellor 2. Financial Advisor 3. Registrar (Member-Secretary)	Additional Secretary Higher and Technical Education	Two nominees of Syndicate	None
14.	Telugu University	1. One Dean, one Director and one Professor as nominee of Syndicate 2. Finance Officer (Non-Member-Secretary)	1. Secretary, Finance and Planning Department 2. Secretary dealing with University	Three nominees of Syndicate (one Dean, one Director and one Professor)	None

(Contd.)

TABLE 3.7 *Contd.*

1	2	3	4	5	6
15.	University of Health Sciences	1. One Dean, one Director and one Professor so nominated by the Executive Council. 2. Finance Officer (Non-Member Secretary)	1. -do- 2. Secretary, Medicine and Health	-do-	None
16.	Osmania University	1. Finance Officer (Can attend the meeting, but cannot vote on the issues) 2. Registrar (Secretary)	Secretary to the State Finance Department	Two nominees each of Syndicate and Senate	None
17. 18.	University of Kerala University of Calicut	1. Pro-Vice-Chancellor 2. Finance Officer (Non-Member Secretary)	1. State Finance Secretary 2. State Secretary Higher Education	One elected member each of Senate, Syndicate and Academic Council	None
19.	Punjabi University	1. Pro-Vice-Chancellor 2. Dean, Academic Affairs 3. Registrar (Secretary)	1. State Finance Secretary 2. State Secretary Education	1. Two elected Members of Senate 2. Two elected Members of Syndicate	None
20.	Maharshi Dayanand University	1. Two Deans of Faculties 2. Finance Officer (Non-Member Secretary)	1. State Finance Secretary 2. State Education Secretary	None	One nominee of Chancellor out of four nominated members of Executive Council

(Contd.)

TABLE 3.7 *Contd.*

1	2	3	4	5	6
21.	University of Rajasthan	1. Two Heads of Departments 2. Finance Officer (Non-Member Secretary)	1. State Financial Commissioner or his nominee 2. State Education Commissioner or his nominee	Four nominees of Syndicate	None
22.	Himachal Pradesh University	1. One Dean of Faculty 2. Registrar 3. Finance Officer (Member-Secretary)	1. State Finance Secretary 2. State Education Secretary	One nominee of Executive Council	One nominee of Chancellor
23.	University of Calcutta	1. Pro-Vice-Chancellor for Business Affairs and Finance (Vice-Chairman) 2. Pro-Vice-Chancellor Academic Affairs 3. Registrar (Non-Member Secretary)	None	1. One nominee of Senate 2. One nominee of Syndicate	One expert nominee of the State Government
24.	Rabindra Bharti University	1. Three Deans of Faculties 2. Finance Officer 3. Registrar (Secretary)	None	1. One Member of Court 2. One Member of Executive Council	-do-
25.	University of Bombay	1. Two Deans of Faculties 2. Registrar 3. Finance Officer (Non-Member Secretary)	None	1. Three nominees of Executive Council 2. Two nominees of Senate	One nominee of State Government

(Contd.)

ABLE 3.7 *Contd.*

1	2	3	4	5	6
26.	Sardar Patel University	1. One Dean of Faculty 2. One Head of Department 3. One Principal of Degree College 4. Registrar (Secretary)	None	Three members of Syndicate	None
E.	*State Agricultural Universities*				
27.	Himachal Pradesh Krishi Vishva Vidyalaya	Comptroller (Non-Member Secretary)	1. State Finance Secretary 2. Director of Agri-culture Animal Husbandry and Chief Warden of Fisheries	One non-official member of Board	None
28.	University of Agricul-tural Sciences, Bangalore	-do-	1. State Agriculture and Horticulture Secretary 2. State Finance Secretary	Two nominees of Board	None
29.	Haryana Agricultural University	Comptroller (Member-Secretary)	None	1. One non-official Member of Board 2. One Official Member of Board	None
30.	Bidhan Chandra Krishi Vishva Vidyalaya	Comptroller (Member-Secretary)	1. State Secretary of Finance 2. State Secretary, Agriculture and Animal Husbandry	Three nominees of Executive Council	One expert nominee of of Chancellor

(Contd.)

TABLE 3.7 *Contd.*

1	2	3	4	5	6
31.	Tamil Nadu Agricultural University	Comptroller (Ex-officio Secretary)	1. State Secretary Finance 2. State Secretary Agriculture	One non-official Member of Board	None
32.	Rajendra Agricultural University	1. One Dean or Director 2. One Chairman of the Department 3. Comptroller (Secretary)	1. One Officer of State Finance Department 2. One Officer of State Agriculture Department	-do-	None
33.	Gujarat Agricultural University	Comptroller (Member-Secretary)	State Finance Secretary	-do-	None
34.	Kerala Agricultural University	Comptroller (Member-Secretary)	-do-	Two Nominees of Executive Council (one Non-official and one Ex-officio)	None

There is no representation to the State Government/University Grants Commission official on the Finance Committee/Board in respect of University of Delhi, Visva Bharti. North Eastern Hill University, Indian Institute of Technology, State General Universities in the State of Uttar Pradesh, University of Calcutta, Rabindra Bharti University, University of Bombay, Sardar Patel University. The Government is fully represented on the Finance Committee/Board in almost all the State Agricultural Universities. Nomination exists for the authorities of the University in all types of universities covered under they study, excepting in the case of Maharshi Dayanand University.

Provisions exist for the nominee of the Chancellor (Visitor)/Government on the Finance Committee in respect of Central Universities, Deemed Universities and Institutions of National Importance covered under the study. It is only in the case of a few State General Universities, viz. Bangalore University, Maharshi Dayanand University, Himachal Pradesh University, University of Calcutta, Rabindra Bharati and University of Bombay where such nomination exists on the Finance Committee/Board. Amongst the State Agricultural University, it is only in the case of Bidhan Chandra Krishi Vishva Vidyalaya where such nomination exists.

It can be conferred that variation exists with regard to the representation on the Finance Committee and as such there is no uniformity in its composition. The constitutional structure of authorities of the University Institution determines its character which, in turn, controls its functioning. The Finance Committee plays a predominant role and as such representation of the officials of the University, who matter a lot in the planning and utilization of funds, plays a pivotal role in deciding the issue like allocation of funds and in the realisation of the financial constraints and financial health of the university. This can serve a better purpose if some Heads of the Departments/College are represented on it which will give them a comprehensive idea about the funds available and their effective utilization.

The main source of funds to the University is the Government/University Grants Commission and as such their representation on it is in the greater interest of the University Institution and they will better appreciate the needs/requirements and the difficulties encountered by the University Institution for the management of the University finances. The representation of nominee(s) or even members elected by the authorities of the

University to the Finance Committee/Board will help in taking prompt and realistic decisions on the recommendations of the Finance Committee. They can better explain the spirit behind the recommendations so made. The nominee of outside expert(s) by the Chancellor/Government will help in the deliberation of intricate financial matters and in the formulation of financial policies and procedures.

The following model composition of the Finance Committee/Board is suggested for adoption in the Act/Statutes of the University Institutions.

1.	Vice-Chancellor/Director	... Chairman
2.	Secretary Finance, Department of the Government or his nominee not below the rank of Joint Secretary	... Member
3.	Secretary of the Government dealing the subject of University Education (representative of the U.G.C. in the case of Central Universities or Deemed Universities)	... "
4.	Two Deans of the Faculty according to seniority by rotation	... "
5.	Three Professors according to seniority by rotation	... "
6.	Two nominees of the Syndicate (Board/ Executive Council)	... "
7.	One expert nominee of the Chancellor (visitor) Government	... "
8.	Treasurer/Comptroller/Finance Officer	... Member-Secretary

The Registrar should be a permanent invitee to the Finance Committee.

Besides other financial powers, the Finance Committee should be vested with the following specific powers to be laid in the Act and Statutes of the University Institution:

1. Fixing limits for the total recurring and non-recurring expenditure based on the domestic income and other resources, no expenditure will be incurred in excess of limit so fixed and not provided in the budget without the prior approval of the

Finance Committee.

2. All matters regarding creation of new posts and incurring expenditure on new schemes as on the lines of Government should be first placed before the Finance Committee and with the recommendations of the Finance Committee, the same shall be placed before the Syndicate (Executive Council/Board).

Status, Powers and Functions of the Treasurer/Financial Advisor/Finance Officer/Comptroller of Universities

Financial administration is a complex problem for state control, statutory requirements and administrative needs, all of which are 'constraints' to the administrators. It plays a vital role in the functioning of the University and its autonomy, the slightest mishandling of which may lead to serious consequences. All financial matters and fiscal policy programmes are approved by the authorities of the University Institutions on the recommendations of Finance Committee/Board. The Finance Committee/Board is assisted by an expert officer in financial management, who produces/formulates the agenda for its consideration. The commonly used nomenclature for this expert is Finance Officer in most of the universities. Its variant nomenclature is Chief Accounts Officer, Audit and Finance Officer in some of the universities and Comptroller in almost all the Agricultural Universities. In some of the universities, a higher post exists than that of Finance Officer named as Treasurer of Financial Advisor. As the Treasurer/Financial Advisor and Finance Officer/Comptroller are required to deal with the financial and service problems of the academicians and other personnel engaged in the services of institutions, it is desirable that they should have a suitable understanding of the needs and problems of the universities. They should also possess long experience and technical training in Finance and Accounts and Management. The assessed position reveals that the overall performance of the administrative staff in the proper perspectives aims at meeting the needs of the socio-economic goals of the country through teaching and research which has been far from satisfactory. Recognising this need, the Kothari Commission (1964-66) observed. "Administration is essentially a matter of faith and vision, bold and courageous leadership and proper handling of human relations. The importance of securing the right type of personnel for it cannot therefore be over emphasised". In such a background it is all the more desirable that the Finance Officer/Comptroller should possess sound technical background and vision and enjoy due status in the University hierarchy. He should be vested with adequate powers and functions for effective and efficient management of university finances. The Association of Indian Universities has deliberated on the issue of the status of the Finance Officer/Comptroller in the Group Discussion-cum-Orientation Programme on Financial Administration in the Universities in 1988 and has recommended the redesignation of the post of Finance Officer to that of Controller of Finances with the same status as that of Registrar and his membership to the authorities of the University. The status, powers and functions of Treasurer/Financial Advisor and Finance Officer/Comptroller in respect of surveyed universities is given in Table 3.8.

From the perusal of Table 3.8, it can be observed that there a post of pro-Vice-Chancellor of Business Affairs and Finance exists in the University of Calcutta, Treasurer in the case of University of Delhi, Jamia Millia Islamia and Thaper Institute of Engineering and Technology and Financial Advisor in the surveyed Universities of Bihar and University of Jammu. The Treasurer/Financial Advisor in all these universities, excepting that of Thaper Institute of Engineering and Technology is assisted by the Finance Officer. In the case of the University of Jammu, the Financial Advisor is Secretary to State Finance Department and the Registrar assists him in day-to-day transactions of all financial matters. The post of Finance Officer is provided in the Act/Statutes in almost all the universities excepting that of Jiwajee University and the University of Rajasthan. The Finance Officer/Chief Accounts Officer in the case of Punjabi University, Patiala, Sardar Patel University and the University of Bombay is the rank of Deputy Registrar and works under the control of the Registrar.

The Treasurer in most of the universities, where such posts exist, is appointed by election on a tenure basis. The Financial Advisor is appointed on deputation for a specific period. Out of twenty six universities, other than Agricultural Universities, this is in the case of nine university institutions where the Finance Officer is appointed on deputation from the Government (Table 3.8). It is only in the case of two Agricultural Universities, viz. Mahatma Phule Agricultural University and Gobind Ballabh Pant University of Agriculture and Technology that the comptroller is taken on deputation from the State Government.

TABLE 3.8: Comparative position of Status, Power and Functions of the Treasures/Finance Officer/Comptroller of University Institutions in India

Sr. No.	University/ Institution	Status and mode of appointment	Representation on the University/ Institution	Powers and functions
1	2	3	4	5
A.	*Central Universities*			
1.	University of Delhi	The Treasurer is Statutory Officer appointed by the Executive Council by election for five years. Finance Officer also taken on deputation	Member, Senate (Court)/ Executive Council and Member Convener Finance Committee	The Treasurer advises on financial policy. Manages and administers University funds and property. Responsible for preparation of budget, annual accounts.
2.	North Eastern Hill University	The Statutory Officer from IAAS service. Executive Council appoints by selection	Member Senate (Court) and Non-Member Secretary Finance Committee	- do - (ii) Calls for explanation for unauthorised expenditure
3.	Visva Bharati	- do -	Non-Member Secretary of Finance Committee	- do -
B.	*Deemed Universities*			
4.	Jamia Millia Islamia	The Statutory Treasurer Senate (Court) appoints on the recommendation of Vice-Chancellor	Member Senate (Court) Executive Council & Finance Committee	The Financial Advisor manages and administers University finances and proproperty. Prepares annual account and budget and ensures that expenditure is incurred on approved items only.

Contd.

TABLE 3.8 *Contd.*

1	2	3	4	5
5.	Thapar Institute of Engineering and Technology	The Statutory Treasurer for a tenure of three years	Member Council and Finance Committee	Custodian of funds and ensures that expenditure is incurred on approved items
6.	Kanpur University	The Statutory Finance Officer from State Government on deputation	Member Court and Finance Committee. Can participate in Executive Council proceedings without voting right.	Ensures authorised expenditure and disallows unauthorised one. Manages and administers University funds and property. Ensures no financial irregularity. Difference of opinion between Vice-Chancellor and Finance Officer decided by the State Government.
7.	University of Allahabad	- do -	- do -	- do -
8.	Meerut University	- do -	- do -	- do -
9.	Patna University	The Chancellor appoints Statutory Financial Advisor from Indian Audit & Accounts Service for three years. Vice-Chancellor on the recommendation of Syndicate appoints Statutory Finance Officer on deputation from Government. Works under the control of Financial Adviser.	The Financial Adviser Member Finance Committee and the Finance Officer Secretary of the said Committee.	Advice of Financial Adviser is mandatory on all financial matters. Difference of opinion between the Financial Adviser and Vice-Chancellor referred to Chancellor for decision. The Finance Officer is responsible to Treasurer for preparation of budget and annual accounts.

Contd.

TABLE 3.8 *Contd.*

1	2	3	4	5
10.	Magadh University	- do	- do -	- do -
11.	University of Jammu	The State Finance Secretary ex-officio Financial Adviser. No post of Finance Officer. Registrar performs day-to-day functions.	Financial adviser Member Senate (Council) Syndicate and Finance Committee.	Financial Adviser advises on financial policy. Prepares budget and annual accounts.
12.	Bangalore University	The Statutory Finance Officer appointed on deputation from State/Central Accounts Service by Vice-Chancellor with the approval of Syndicate.	Permanent invitee to the meeting of Senate. Ex-officio Secretary of Finance Committee.	Advises on financial matters and fiscal policy. Keeps liaison with State Government and other funding agencies.
13.	Jiwajee University	The Non-Statutory Finance Officer on deputation from State Government.	Secretary Finance Committee	Advises on financial matters and prepares budget and annual accounts.
14.	Telugu University	The Statutory Finance Officer on deputation from State Government.	- do - (Non-Member)	Advises on financial matters and fiscal policy. Prepares budget and annual accounts. Ensures observance of expenditure limits and authorised expenditure. Points out financial irregularities and suggests action there against.
15.	University of Health Science	- do -	- do -	- do -
16.	Osmania University	The Statutory Finance Officer on deputation from State Government	Permanent invitee to Finance Committee	Maintains accounts, advises on all financial matters.

Contd.

TABLE 3.8 *Contd.*

1	2	3	4	5
17.	University of Kerala	The Statutory Finance Officer appointed by Syndicate	Secretary Finance Committee	Advises on financial matters and fiscal policy. Advice mandatory. Ensures observance of expenditure limits and authorised expenditure. Prepares annual accounts and budget.
18.	University of Calicut	- do -	- do -	- do -
19.	Punjabi University	The Finance Officer of the rank of Deputy Registrar appointed by Syndicate.	None	Works under the control of Registrar.
20.	Maharshi Dayanand University	The Statutory Finance Officer appointed by Executive Council.	Member Court and Secretary Finance Committee.	Advises on financial matters and fiscal policy. Manages and administers funds and property. Ensures observance of expenditure limits and authorised expenditure. Brings financial irregularities to the notice of Vice-Chancellor.
21.	University of Rajasthan	The non-Statutory Finance Officer appointed on deputation from State Government.	Secretary to Finance Committee	Advises on financial matters and fiscal policy. Prepares annual accounts and budget.
22.	Himachal Pradesh University	The Statutory Finance Officer. Appointed by Executive Council either on deputation or through direct recruitment.	Member-Secretary Finance Committee	Advises on financial matters and fiscal policy. Prepares annual accounts and budget. Manages and administers university funds and property. Ensures observance of expenditure limits and authorised expenditure.

Contd.

TABLE 3.8 *Contd.*

1	2	3	4	5
23.	University of Calcutta	Senior post of the rank of Pro-Vice-Chancellor Business Affairs and Finances who is assisted by Audit and Finance Officer.	Pro-Vice-Chancellor is Member of Senate, Syndicate and Finance Committee.	Managers and administers funds and property. Prepares budget, annual accounts and audit report. Submits annual accounts and budget and annual report to the Government through Syndicate.
24.	Rabindra Bharati University	The Statutory Finance Officer appointed by the Executive Council.	Member Finance Committee. Invitee to the meeting of Court and Executive Council.	Advises on financial matters and fiscal policy. Assists the Vice-Chancellor in general administration and organization. Responsible for finances, preparation of budget and annual report.
25.	University of Bombay	The Statutory Finance Officer under the control of Registrar appointed by direct recruitment or deputation by the Executive Council.	Secretary of Finance Committee.	Advises on financial matters and fiscal policy. Ensures observance of expenditure limit and authorised expenditure. Prepares annual accounts and budget.
26.	Sardar Patel University	The Chief Accounts Officer of the rank of Deputy Registrar under the control of Registrar.	None	Assists the Registrar on financial matters matters and fiscal policy.
E.	*State Agricultural Universities*			
27.	Himachal Pradesh Krishi Vishvavidyalaya	The Statutory Comptroller appointed by Board by selection or on deputation.	Member Senate and Secretary Finance Committee.	Ensures authorised expenditure and disallows expenditure not warranted. Prepares budget, annual accounts. Points out financial irregularities. Purchase and Planning Officer.

Contd.

TABLE 3.8 *Contd.*

1	2	3	4	5
28.	Mahatma Phule Agricultural University	The Statutory Comptroller appointed on deputation.	Member Secretary Finance Committee.	Advises on financial matters; ensures authorised expenditure and disallows expenditure not warranted. Points out financial irregularities.
29.	University of Agricultural Sciences, Bangalore	The Statutory Comptroller appointed by Chancellor in consultation with Board.	Coopted Member Academic Council. Secretary Finance Committee	Responsible for all accounts matters. Ensures authorised expenditure and disallows expenditure not warranted.
30.	Haryana Agricultural University	The Statutory Comptroller appointed by Vice-Chancellor with the approval of Board.	Member Secretary Finance Committee	Responsible for all accounts matters. Ensures authorised expenditure and disallows expenditure not warranted.
31.	Punjab Agricultural University	- do -	- do -	- do -
32.	Gobind Ballabh Pant University of Agriculture and Technology	The Statutory Comptroller appointed by Government	Ex-officio Secretary of Board of Management	Advises on fiscal policy; ensures authorised expenditure and disallows expenditure not warranted.
33.	Bidhan Chandra Krishi Vishva Vidyalaya	The Statutory Comptroller appointed by Vice-Chancellor with the approval of Board and Chancellor	Member-Secretary Finance Committee	Prepares budget and annual accounts; ensures authorised expenditure and disallows expenditure not warranted.
34.	Kerala Agricultural University	The Statutory Comptroller appointed by Government	- do -	Advises on fiscal policy; ensures authorised expenditure and disallows expenditure not warranted.
35.	Rajindra Agricultural University	The Statutory Comptroller appointed by Vice-Chancellor with the approval of Board.	- do -	- do -
36.	Tamil Nadu Agricultural University	- do -	- do -	- do -
37.	Gujarat Agricultural University	- do -	- do -	- do -

The Treasurer of the University of Delhi, Jamia Millia Islamia and Thapar Institute of Engineering and Technology is a Member of all the authorities whereas the Financial Advisor of two Universities in Bihar is only a member of the Finance Committee. The Finance Advisor of the University of Jammu is a member of all the authorities of the university. It is only in the case of the North Eastern Hill University, Kanpur University, University of Allahabad and Meerut University that the Finance Officer is a member of the Senate (Court) and Finance Committee. In the case of Maharshi Dayanand University and Himachal Pradesh Krishi Visva Vidyalaya the Finance Officer/Comptroller is a member of the Senate (Court) and Secretary of the Finance Committee. The Finance Officer of Jiwajee University, Telugu University, University of Health Sciences, University of Kerala, University of Calicut, University of Rajasthan, University of Bombay, Bidhan Chandra Krishi Visva Vidyalaya is a Non-Member Secretary of the Finance Committee. The Finance Officer of Osmania University attends the meetings of the Finance Committee as a permanent invites whereas in the case of Punjabi University and Sardar Patel University he is not represented on it.

The Finance Officer of Punjabi University, University of Bombay and Chief Accounts Officer of Sardar Patel University work under the control of the Registrar. The Finance Officer of the University of Delhi, and the Audit and Finance Officer of the University of Calcutta work under the control of Treasurer and Pro-Vice-Chancellor Business Affairs and Finance, respectively. No post of Finance Officer exists in the case of Jammu University and the Registrar performs all financial functions of the University. Besides performing functions like advice in laying fiscal policies, and preparation of annual accounts and budget etc., the Finance Officer of the universities in Uttar Pradesh, Telgu University, University of Health Sciences, University of Kerala, University of Calicut, Punjabi University, Himachal Pradesh University, University of Bombay, and the Comptroller of almost all agricultural universities are vested with specific powers of ensuring that expenditure is within the prescribed limits and disallowing unwarranted expenditure. The advice of the Financial Adviser in the case of the universities in Bihar is mandatory. It has been specifically provided in the case of three universities in Uttar Pradesh and two Universities in Bihar, that in the case of difference of opinion between the Finance Officer/Financial Adviser and the Vice-Chancellor, the matter shall be referred to the State Government (Uttar Pradesh

Universities) and the Chancellor (Bihar Universities) for decision.

From the above description, it can be gathered that there is no uniformity in the Statutes, Powers and Functions of Treasurer/Financial Adviser and Finance Officer/Comptroller of University Institutions in India.

The Head of the Finance Department of University Institutions has to play a vital role in the management of university finances. Its growth and development depends mainly upon sound fiscal policies and programmes. It is, therefore, imperative that the Finance Officer/ Comptroller should enjoy a good status in the hierarchy of university administration. He should be a statutory officer of the rank of Registrar and other statutory officers and should be directly responsible to the Vice-Chancellor in the field of his functioning. The post should be designated as Controller of Finance in all types of universities. There should be no posts like Treasurer and Financial Adviser, which is an outdated concept. The Finance Officer/Comptroller should be appointed by the Vice-Chancellor on the recommendations of the Syndicate (Executive Council/Board) through direct selection, for which the Government officers can also compete. This will give the Vice-Chancellor an opportunity to select the right type of person for the post. The person so selected can be appointed on a tenure basis for a period of five years, which can be extended on the recommendation of the Vice-Chancellor by the Syndicate. The Finance Officer/ Comptroller should be a Member-Secretary of the Finance Committee/ Board, Member of the Senate (Court/Council) and Syndicate (Executive Council/Board). He should also be a co-opted member of the Academic Council. He should not be vested with unfettered powers like disagreeing with the decisions of the Vice-Chancellor and making references to the Chancellor/State Government in case of difference of opinion.

The management system of an University Institution can be known from the various provisions in the Act, Statutes, Rules and Regulations. The provisions in the Act and Statutes is a testimony to the seriousness of the legislators in planning for the efficient and effective management of such institutions and also speak of their concern for granting functional and financial autonomy to such institutions. We have discussed some of the parameters of paramount importance as per the provisions in the Act and Statutes which play an effective role in the management of the university finances. The shortcomings in the financial management of University Institutions and suggestions for its improvement can be best known from its three major functionaries i.e. Vice-Chancellor/Director, Finance Officer/Comptroller/Registrar and Professors and Heads of Departments. Their opinion on some parameters of importance was obtained through an opinion survey and the opinion so expressed by them is discussed as under:

Existing Powers and Functions of Finance Officer/Comptroller

The existing status of the Fiance Officer/Comptroller has been reported to be 'exactly what it should be' by the Finance Officer/Comptroller of all types of surveyed universities, except in the case of institutions of national importance, which have reported it to be 'lower than what it should be' (Table 3.9). The Finance Officers/Comptrollers of Central Universities, Deemed Universities and State General Universities expressed the opinion that the functions and duties be restricted only to financial matters. In almost all types of universities, the Finance Officers/Comptrollers have been reported to be directly responsible to the Vice-Chancellor/Director, excepting that in some of the State General Universities, it has been reported that the Finance Officer would report to the Vice-Chancellor through the Registrar. The Finance Officer/Comptroller in respect of all types of universities has to keep liaison with grant-in-aid agencies and he discusses with them the requirements of grants and provisions of Five-Year/Annual Plans.

Keeping in view the important role of the Finance Officer/Comptroller in the management of the university finances, it is highly desirable that he should enjoy the same status as that of the Registrar in the university hierarchy and he should be directly responsible to the Vice-Chancellor/Director. Besides performing financial functions and responsibility, he should be actively associated in the formulation of development plans and other matters of general administration and advice rendered by him on all financial matters of policy nature, should be mandatory.

Decentralisation and Delegation of Financial Powers to Various Functionaries of University Institutions

The examination of the Acts and Statutes and on the spot study of the Financial Management Systems of some of the Universities revealed that the Acts and Statutes of some of the University Institutions

TABLE 3.9: Existing Status, Powers and Functions of Finance Officers/Comptrollers

(Percentage responses)

Sr. No.	Particulars/ Description	Central Universities	Deemed Universities	Institutions of National Importance	State General Universities	State Agricultural Universities
Finance Officers/Comptrollers/Registrars						
1.	Status is					
1.1	Higher than it should be	0.00	0.00	0.00	20.00	7.69
1.2	Exactly what it should be	66.66	66.66	0.00	52.00	61.54
1.3	Lower than what it should be	33.33	33.33	50.00	36.00	0.00
2.	Functions and duties should be restricted to finance only	100.00	66.66	0.00	68.00	30.77
3.	Secretary to Finance Committee	66.66	0.00	0.00	44.00	76.92
4.	Member Secretary to Finance Committee	0.00	33.33	0.00	40.00	76.92
5.	Directly responsible to Vice-Chancellor/Director	66.66	66.66	100.00	48.00	92.31
6.	Responsible to the Vice-Chancellor/Director through Registrar	0.00	33.33	0.00	40.00	7.69
7.	Advises the Vice-Chancellor and authorities	100.00	33.33	100.00	76.00	100.00
8.	Keeps liaison with grants-in-aid agencies	100.00	66.66	100.00	64.00	100.00
9.	Participates in discussion with funding agencies					
9.1	Grants-in-aid to University	100.00	66.66	100.00	76.00	92.31
9.2	Five-Year/Annual Plan	100.00	66.66	100.00	68.00	100.00

provide powers to various authorities and further delegation of powers by these authorities to the Vice-Chancellors/Directors and other statutory officers. But it has been observed that in the case of Central Universities, Deemed Universities and Institutions of National Importance and State General Universities, the financial powers are mainly vested with the Vice-Chancellors, Deans and Finance Officers/Comptrollers/Registrars. The Heads of the Departments and other functionaries have been delegated limited powers just to meet the petty contingent expenditure out of the limited amount of imprest money sanctioned to the Departments in some of the University Institutions. The centralized system of payments and accounting is followed in most of these University Institutions. Salary bills and other payments are centrally processed and payments accordingly released. In some of the University Institutions the powers are decentralized to the extent of preparation of budget of the Department and placing orders to the suppliers for effecting purchases by the various Heads of the Department and other units of the University Institutions. Almost all the State Agricultural Universities are functioning on the system of decentralization. Salary bills and other contingent bills of suppliers are processed and passed by the Heads of the Departments and sent to the Finance Department of the University Institutions for release of cheques and their inclusion in the university accounts. The Heads of the Departments and other functionaries have been delegated adequate power in most of the Agricultural Universities for all the financial transactions pertaining to the Departments.

In the case of Central Universities, Deemed Universities, State Agricultural Universities, Professors and Heads of Departments are delegated power to draw the salary and personal claims of the staff. It is however not so in the case of Institutions of National Importance and most of the State General Universities (Table 3.10). As regards the contingent expenditure, the Professors and Heads of Departments in all types of Universities/Institutions have delegated powers. It is further observed that excepting some State General Universities, the payments in respect of bills and personal claims are passed and made by the Finance Wing. The Professors and Heads of Departments of the Deemed Universities, Institutions of National Importance and State General Universities are satisfied with the existing delegation of powers whereas in the case of Central Universities and State Agricultural Universities, the staff is not satisfied with the existing delegation of powers. It is interesting to note that the Professors and

TABLE 3.10: Delegation of Financial Powers

(Percentage responses)

Sr. No.	Particulars/ Description	Central Universities	Deemed Universities	Institutions of National Importance	State General Universities	State Agricultural Universities
Professors and Heads of Departments						
1.	Department is Drawing and Disbursing for					
1.1	Salary and personal claims of staff	66.66	100.00	0.00	33.33	60.53
1.2	Other contingent expenditure	66.66	100.00	66.66	78.33	71.05
2.	Bills and personal claims passed and payments made by					
2.1	Finance Wing	66.66	50.00	66.00	30.00	84.21
2.2	Department itself	0.00	100.00	33.33	75.00	44.74
3.	Satisfied with existing delegation of financial powers	33.33	100.00	100.00	43.33	39.47
4.	Power delegated are inadequate	33.33	50.00	66.66	61.67	50.00
5.	Power delegated put great set-back to academic functions of Department.	66.66	50.00	0.00	58.33	39.47

Heads of Departments of Deemed Universities, Institutions of National Importance and State General Universities have also expressed that the powers delegated are inadequate. In the case of Central Universities and State Agricultural Universities partial adequacy in the powers is reported. It is only the Professors and Heads of Departments of the Central Universities, Deemed Universities and the State General Universities who expressed the opinion that the powers delegated put a great set back to the academic functions of the departments whereas partial satisfaction has been reported by the Institutions of National Importance and the State Agricultural Universities. The Vice-Chancellors of all types of universities have expressed their opinion in favour of the delegation of financial powers to the Deans/Directors, Finance Officer/Comptroller/Registrar and other statutory officers. They have also favoured the delegation of financial powers to the Professors and Heads of Departments. It is only the Vice-Chancellors of the Central Universities and the State Agricultural Universities who have favoured the delegation of powers to the other functionaries as well (Table 3.11). The decentralisation and delegation of powers to various functionaries of an organisation like University/ Institution is highly desirable for the speedier execution of programmes/activities. The non-delegation of powers to the Heads of the Departments/functionaries for payments of personal claims of the staff and bills of the suppliers results in undue inconvenience and may tarnish the credibility of the University/Institution. It may also entail the risk of timely execution of the programmes and shifting the responsibility and may even result in frustration and discontentment. As such the effective and efficient financial management of University/Institution can be ensured to a great extent through adequate schedule of delegation of financial powers.

Financial Control and Interference by Government and Others Funding Agencies

The Central Government/University Grants Commission exercises broad general control over the affairs of Central Universities through built-in provisions in the Acts and Statutes with regard to submission of audited annual accounts to the Visitor (President of India in respect of University of Delhi and Jamia Millia Islamia), Prime Minister, in case of Visva Bharti and thereafter publishing the same in the Gazette of India. It is only in the case of Visva Bharti that audited annual

TABLE 3.11: Delegation of Financial Powers (Proposed)

(Percentage responses)

Sr. No.	Particulars Description	Central Universities	Deemed Universities	State General Universities	State Agricultural Universities
	Vice-Chancellors/Directors				
1.	Financial Powers should be delegated to				
1.1	Deans/Directors/Finance Officers/Comptrollers/Registrars and other statutory officers only	100.00	100.00	87.50	88.88
1.2	Professors and Heads of Departments also	50.00	100.00	81.25	100.00
1.3	All Drawing and Disbursing Officers.	50.00	0.00	18.75	66.66

accounts are laid before both Houses of Parliament. Financial discipline is also exercised through the process of internal audit and statutory powers to the Finance Committee and Syndicate (Executive Council) to ensure that the expenditure does not exceed the limits fixed for recurring and non-recurring expenditure vis-a-vis the available resources. The Treasurer/Finance Officer exercises financial control over the finances of the universities and ensure that the limit so fixed for expenditure is not exceeded and expenditure is incurred on approved items only.

The broad general control over the affairs of two sampled. Deemed Universities is exercised in the same manner as described above for Central Universities. Financial control is exercised in the two sampled Institutions of National importance through the process of internal audit. The Central Government finally approves the budget and the audited annual accounts are laid on the table of Parliament. The extent of financial control exercised by the state governments in respect of the State General Universities.can be observed in Table 3.12. In almost all the Agricultural Universities in India, the State Governments are adequately represented on the authorities, in particular on the Finance Committee. As such there exists adequate financial control of the State Government in framing the fiscal policies of the Agricultural Universities. The Acts and Statutes of almost all the State Agricultural Universities prohibit incurring expenditure where it is not provided for in the budget and the Comptrollers are empowered to disallow any expenditure which may contravene any provisions of the Acts and Statutes. The systems of pre-audit and internal audit are prevailing in most of the State Agricultural Universities which have an effective check/control over the management of university finances.

The Vice-Chancellors/Directors of Central Universities, Deemed Universities and Institutions of National Importance have stated that there is no day-to-day interference of the Government/Funding Agencies, whereas the Vice-Chancellors of some of the State General and Agricultural Universities have observed otherwise. The Finance Officer/Comptroller/Registrar of State General Universities and State Agricultural Universities have reported control of Government/Funding Agencies 'more than appropriate', whereas it is 'appropriate' in case of Central Universities, Deemed Universities and Institutions of National Importance (Table 3.13).

TABLE 3.12: Extent of Control Exercised by the State Government on Universities

Sr. No.	State(s)	Extent of Financial Control
1.	Uttar Pradesh, Bihar, Karnataka, and Madhya Pradesh State Universities	Financial Advisor/Finance Officer appointed on deputation from the State Government. State Government approves the budget. Posts created with the prior approval of the Government, payscales and other fringe benefits with the approval of Government. Difference of opinion between the Vice-Chancellor and Finance Officer/Financial Advisor is resolved at the level of Chancellor or the State Government. Finance Officer can disallow any expenditure not provided in the budget or is not in deference to Act & Statues. Submission of annual accounts and audited report to the Government. Internal Audit.
2.	Kerala State Universities	Governance of service conditions and regulation of emoluments with the approval of State Government.
3.	West Bengal Universities	Creation of posts with the approval of Government; approval of the budget by the State Government; submission of annual accounts alongwith the audited report to State Government.

TABLE 3.13: Financial Control/Interference of the Government/Funding Agencies

(Percentage responses)

Sr. No.	Particulars/ Description	Central Universities	Deemed Universities	Institutions of National Importance	State General Universities	State Agricultural Universities
Vice-Chancellors/Directors						
1.	Interference in day-to-day day-to-day matters	0.00	0.00	0.00	12.05	11.11
Finance Officers/Comptrollers/ Registrars						
1.	Control of the Government/ Funding Agencies is					
1.1	More than appropriate	0.00	0.00	0.00	52.00	53.84
1.2	Appropriate	66.66	66.00	100.00	28.00	23.08
1.3	Less than appropriate	0.00	0.00	0.00	4.00	15.38

The representation of the Government to the Senate (Court/Council) has been favoured by all the Vice-Chancellors of Deemed Universities and most of the Vice-Chancellors of State General and Agricultural Universities. The Vice-Chancellors of Central Universities have not favoured this representation. All the Vice-Chancellors/Directors of Deemed Universities and State General Universities, most of the Vice-Chancellors of Agricultural Universities and some of the Vice-Chancellors of Central Universities have favoured the representation of the State Government on the Syndicate (Executive Council/Board) (Table 3.14).

It is only the Vice-Chancellors/Directors of the Deemed Universities who have favoured the representation of the State Government on the Academic Council, whereas some of the Vice-Chancellors of the Central Universities have also favoured this representation. The representation of State Government to the Finance Committee/Board has been favoured by all the Vice-Chancellors of Central Universities, Deemed Universities and most of other universities. Most of the Vice-Chancellors of State General Universities and State Agricultural Universities have favoured the representation of the State Government on budget finalisation Committee/Board, whereas representation to the Planning Board/Committee has been favoured by some of the Vice-Chancellors of the Central, State Government and Agricultural Universities. They are of the opinion that representation of the Government on the authorities of the University Institution is helpful in its management.

From the foregoing description, it can be inferred that there are mixed opinions of the university administrators on various issues relating to financial control. Despite the fact that there exist inbuilt provisions for effective financial control in the Acts and Statutes of the University Institutions, yet the management of university finances particularly in the State General Universities is not satisfactory. Appointment of person on deputation by the Government of their own as Finance Officer/Comptroller, the prior approval of the Government for the creation of posts, approval of the budget of the University by the Government are against the functional and financial autonomy of the University Institutions. The non-representation of the Government/University Grants Commission on the authorities of the University Institutions may create misunderstanding between the University and Government in the implementation of various educational programmes envisaged for the nation. The

TABLE 3.14: Representation of State Government on University Authorities

(Percentage responses)

Sr. No.	Particulars/ Description	Central Universities	Deemed Universities	State General Universities	State Agricultural Universities
Vice-Chancellors/Directors					
1.	State Government should be represented on				
1.1	Court/Senate	0.00	100.00	93.75	77.77
1.2	Syndicate/Executive Council/ Board of Management	50.00	100.00	100.00	88.88
1.3	Academic Council	50.00	100.00	25.00	11.11
1.4	Finance Committee/Board	100.00	100.00	93.75	77.77
1.5	Budget finalisation Committee/Board	0.00	0.00	81.25	66.66
1.6	Planning Board/Committee	50.00	0.00	62.50	55.55
2.	Representation of Government is				
2.1	Helpful in the management	50.00	100.00	93.75	77.77
2.2	Stands in the way of autonomy	50.00	0.00	0.00	44.44

non-representation of the Government/University Grants Commission on the Finance Committee/Board may entail the risk of proper understanding of the requirement of the University Institutions in terms of funds and related matters.

It is, therefore, suggested that the Government should not exercise the powers to approve the budget and allow creation of posts in respect of University Institutions once the quantum of the financial assistance is determined by the Government and the University Institutions should thus be in a position to bear additional liability from its existing resources. The Government/University Grants Commission should be represented on these authorities of the University Institutions which lay down fiscal policies. Financial control can be exercised by the Government through the process of internal and statutory pre-audit. The financial status of the University Institution can be assessed by the Government from the perusal of the audited annual accounts, audit report and annual report so submitted to them.

Functional and Financial Autonomy

The examination of the Acts, Statutes, Memorandum of Association, Rules and Regulations of all types of surveyed University Institutions (1946 to 1987)[4 to 38] reveals the following facts with regard to the present status of their functional and financial autonomy.

The Central Government or University Grants Commission does not directly interfere and control the management of university finances of Central Universities, except that in the case of Visva Bharti, the audited annual accounts and the audit report are laid on the table of the both the Houses of Parliament, which is against the principle of autonomy as envisaged in the recommendations of Committee on Model Act (1961-62).[39] Financial autonomy in the management of university finances exists in the case of Deemed Universities to the extent that there is no direct control and interference of the Central Government/State Governments/University Grants Commission. A similar situation prevails in the case of Institutions of National Importance.

Thus in the case of State General Universities wherein prior approval of the Government is required for the creation of posts, payment of fringe benefits to the employees and budget estimates are approved by the Government, there exists no financial autonomy. Rather such University Institutions are under the direct control of the Government for the management of their finances. It is interesting to note that in some of the universities in the State of Andhra Pradesh, the Chief Minister is the Chancellor, whereas in respect of universities in the State of Jammu and Kashmir, the Chief Minister is the Pro-Chancellor. The State Education Minister is Pro-Chancellor in some of the universities in the State of Kerala. The Secretary to the State Finance Department or an officer of the State Government, so appointed by the Government is the Financial Advisor in the case of universities in the State of Jammu and Kashmir. The Chancellor, in some of the universities, has been vested with unfettered powers to dismiss the authorities of the universities and constitute adhoc authorities to run the affairs of the universities.

The Acts of some of the universities provide powers to Chancellors even to annual the proceedings of such authorities. All this does not speak well about autonomy of the institutions. Taking over day-to-day control of some of the universities by the Government and the Chancellor, is against the recommendations of the Committee on 'Model Act' and various recommendations of the Committees/Commissions so constituted by the Government of India, and the University Grants Commission for the improvement of the governance of universities in India.

The State Governments are exercising effective control for the management of the finances in most of the Agricultural Universities through its effective representation on the authorities of universities and various other provisions in the Acts of such universities which stand in the way of functional and financial autonomy to such University Institutions. The glaring provisions against the autonomy of Agricultural Universities are the submission of annual accounts and audit report to the State Government for laying on the table of the House which is against the recommendations of the Committee on 'Model Act'. The provisions in the Act of Himachal Pradesh Krishi Vishva Vidyalaya for delegating the powers to the State Councils for Education and Research to grant permission to start new courses or disciplines, departments, schemes or projects, to be financed out of the state exchequer and provisions in the Maharashtra Agricultural University Act that the State Government shall exercise powers to grant administrative approval for construction of buildings, purchase of equipment, reappropriation of the budgeted grants and approval of the annual plan and the budget estimates of the universities, are glaring examples of Government interference in the financial autonomy of the concerned universities.

Although the foregoing description gives the status of functional and financial autonomy as laid down in the Acts, Statutes, Memorandum of Association, Rules and Regulations of University Institutions, yet in practice it may not be so and the important functionaries in the university administration may be having altogether different opinions on this important aspect of financial management. The opinion so expressed by various functionaries is discussed as given hereinafter.

It is evident from Table 3.15 that all the Vice-Chancellors of Central Universities and Deemed Universities have stated that functional and financial autonomy exists in such institutions, whereas some of the State General and Agricultural Universities have also reported this in the affirmative. Most of the Finance Officers/Comptrollers/Registrars of Institutions of National Importance, Deemed Universities and State Agricultural Universities have stated that they enjoy functional and financial autonomy to plan action for raising funds.

Finance Officer/Comptroller/Registrar of surveyed Institutions of National Importance and State General Universities in divided opinion have reported that financial autonomy exists to plan pattern of expenditure. All the Finance Officers/Comptrollers/Registrars of Institutions of National Importance and State Agricultural Universities have expressed that realisation of grants is mainly dependent on the discretion of granting authorities whereas most of the Central Universities State General Universities and some of the Deemed Universities have also confirmed this. It is only in the case of half of the Institutions of National Importance that it has been reported that funds are made available to them whenever needed. Half of the sampled Institutions of National Importance have expressed that funds are made available to them when demanded whereas such response in the case of State Agricultural Universities and Central Universities is nearly one third.

From the above analysis of functional and financial autonomy, it can be said that variation exists amongst them. The various Committees/Commissions of University Institutions so appointed by the Government of India or University Grants Commission from time to time have recommended functional and financial autonomy to University Institutions. Such autonomy is needed to enable them to discharge their functions and obligations more effectively to society and to contribute fully in the development and progress of the country. Autonomy is much more essential to free such institutions from external control as well as from autocratic or bureaucratic authorities and insensitiveness to the real needs and interests of the academic community (staff and students). The absence of autonomy, both external and internal to University Institution defeats the very purpose for which it is established and also adversely affects its functioning.

TABLE 3.15: Functional and Financial Autonomy

(Percentage responses)

Sr. No.	Particulars/ Description	Central Universities	Deemed Universities	Institutions of National Importance	State General Universities	State Agricultural Universities
Vice-Chancellors/Directors						
1.	Functional and Financial autonomy exists	100.00	100.00	N.A.	37.05	55.55
Finance Officers/Comptrollers/ Registrars						
1.	Financial autonomy exists to plan					
1.1	Action for raising funds	33.33	66.66	100.00	40.00	61.54
1.2	Pattern of expenditure	33.33	33.33	50.00	52.00	30.77
2.	*Built-in-flexibility in management of finance exists*					
2.1	Raising more funds when needed	33.33	0.00	50.00	16.00	23.08
2.2	No increase in funds with changed enrolment	33.33	0.00	50.00	36.00	46.15
3.	Realisation of grants mainly at the discretion of granting authorities	66.66	33.33	100.00	84.00	100.00
4.	Funds are made available when need is put forth	33.33	22.33	50.00	24.00	38.46

It is, therefore, recommended that the 'autonomous' character of University Institutions should be maintained. They should enjoy full freedom for raising funds and planning the expenditure there against. The availability of funds should proportionately increase with the increase in enrolment and the start of new programmes/projects. The release of grants should not be at the sole discretion of granting authorities, rather it should be released as per time schedule mutually agreed upon between the University Institutions and funding agencies, once its quantum is fixed/earmarked.

Participation of Professors and Heads of the Departments in Policy Matters

The Professors and Heads of the Departments play a vital role in the management of university finances. The available funds are planned at the level of Heads of the Departments/Officers/Institutions/Units for effective utilisation and as such their participation in policy matters is essential.

It can be observed (Table 3.16) that Professors and Heads of the Departments are consulted in most of the sampled university institutions, except the Deemed Universities in the preparation of development plans for financial assistance from funding agencies. They are associated in most of the University Institutions in specification and purchase of foreign equipments; purchase of books and journals; training and development of faculty and scholarships to students. The participation in research policy framework; preparation of agenda for Academic Council/Board of Studies and Budget formulation exist in most of the universities, except that it is nearly fifty per cent in the case of Deemed Universities. Very little participation exists for preparation of agenda for Senate (Court) and Syndicate (Executive Council/Board) in case of Institutions of National Importance, State General and Agricultural Universities, whereas it does not exist in Central Universities and Deemed Universities. Nearly in fifty per cent of the Deemed Universities and State Agricultural Universities, Professors and Heads of the Departments are associated in Professional Consultancy Service, whereas it is so in the case of one third of Central Universities and Institutions of National Importance. The Professors and Heads of the Departments are consulted for provision of physical facilities in most of the universities except in the case of State General Universities where it is nearly forty eight per cent.

TABLE 3.16: Participation of Heads of Departments in Policy Matters

(Percentage responses)

Sr. No.	Particulars/ Description	Central Universities	Deemed Universities	Institutions of National Importance	State General Universities	State Agricultural Universities
1	2	3	4	5	6	7
	Professors and Heads of the Departments					
1.	University Institute associates/ consults the Departments for					
1.1	Development proposals for financial assistance from funding agencies	100.00	0.00	66.66	85.00	86.84
1.2	Research policy framework	100.00	50.00	100.00	81.67	71.05
1.3	Professional consultancy service	33.33	50.00	33.33	46.67	57.89

(Contd.)

TABLE 3.16 *Contd.*

1	2	3	4	5	6	7
2.	Agenda preparation and papers for					
2.1	Senate/Court	0.00	0.00	33.33	30.00	18.42
2.2	Syndicate/Executive Council/ Board of Management	0.00	0.00	33.33	26.67	26.32
2.3	Academic Council/Board of Studies	100.00	50.00	100.00	76.67	84.21
2.4	Finance Committee/Board	33.33	50.00	66.66	31.66	31.58
3.1	Budget formulation	66.66	50.00	66.67	66.67	81.58
3.2	Budget allocation	66.66	0.00	66.66	58.33	42.10
3.3	Specification and purchases of foreign equipments	100.00	100.00	66.66	66.33	84.21
3.4	Purchase of chemicals and other equipments	100.00	100.00	33.33	60.00	89.47
3.5	Purchase of books and journals	100.00	100.00	100.00	93.33	92.11
3.6	Training and Development of Faculty	66.66	100.00	100.00	86.67	71.05
3.7	Provision of physical facilities	100.00	100.00	66.66	48.33	71.05
3.8	Staff benefits or fringe benefits	66.66	100.00	33.33	36.67	44.74
3.9	Scholarships for students	66.66	100.00	100.00	71.67	63.16

From the above analysis of opinion survey on the issue of participation of Heads of Departments in policy matters, it can be inferred that variation exists amongst the surveyed universities. The Professors and Heads of the Departments are most vital and integral part of the university administration and most of the financial matters are initiated at the level of this basic unit of administration. They are executors of the academic policies of the university who feed back the difficulties encountered by them and the staff in their implementation. Their active association/consultancy is essential for the development and growth of the University Institutions, and as such they should be involved in all matters, specifically in academic matters, concerning policy framing.

Satisfaction with the Existing Financial Management Practices/Systems

The management system of an organisation exists for its development and growth with the prime objectives of satisfying and meeting the requirements of the community being served through it. It is also one of the established truths that the productivity of an organisation increases manifold if its community is satisfied with its policies and programme. It is, therefore, necessary to know the opinion of major functionaries, viz. Vice-Chancellors/Directors, Finance Officers/ Comptrollers/Registrars and Professors and Heads of the Departments with regard to their satisfaction with the prevailing financial management systems in their institutions. The opinion expressed by them in terms of affirmative percentage responses is given in Table 3.17.

All the Vice-Chancellors/Directors of Central Universities and Deemed Universities have reported that they are satisfied with the existing financial management systems, whereas fifty per cent and sixty six per cent of the Vice-Chancellors of State General Universities and Agricultural Universities, respectively, reported satisfaction. The Finance Officers/Comptrollers/Registrars of surveyed Institutions of National Importance and Central Universities expressed satisfaction with the existing financial management systems, whereas 48 per cent and 60 per cent cases of dissatisfaction have been reported in the case of State General Universities and State Agricultural Universities respectively.

All Professors and Heads of the Department of the Institutions of National Importance and most of the Central Universities are satisfied with the existing financial management system, whereas satisfaction in respect of State General Universities, State Agricultural Universities and Deemed Universities has been reported in 35, 47 and 50 per cent cases. The reasons for dissatisfaction with the existing financial management systems were also ascertained from Finance Officers/Comptrollers/Registrars through an opinion survey. The opinion so expressed by them in terms of affirmative responses is given in Table 3.18.

It is observed from the above table that 48 per cent of the Finance Officers/Comptrollers/Registrars of the sampled State General Universities and 46 per cent of State Agricultural Universities have expressed their dissatisfaction with the existing Financial Management Systems on account of lack of funds. But the financial position is better in case of Deemed Universities as only one third of the respondent Finance Officers/Comptrollers/Registrars recorded lack of funds as one of the reasons. Delay of funds has also been reported as one of the reasons for dissatisfaction by 44 per cent and 54 per cent of Finance Officers/Comptrollers/Registrars of State General Universities and State Agricultural Universities, respectively. Rigid allocation has also been reported to be one of the reasons for dissatisfaction by some of the Finance Officers/Comptrollers/Registrars of Deemed Universities, State General Universities and State Agricultural Universities. Fifty per cent of the Professors and Heads of the Departments of Deemed Universities have expressed lack of funds, rigid allocation, delay of allocation, delayed passing of bills and release of payments and system of auditing contribute to dissatisfaction. More than 50 per cent Respondents Professors and Heads of the Departments of Central Universities, Deemed Universities and State General Universities have expressed dissatisfaction with the existing financial management systems on account of delayed passing of bills and release of payments. The response in respect of dissatisfaction, both from the Finance Officers/Comptrollers/Registrars and Professors and Heads of Departments of State General Universities and State Agricultural Universities ranges between 15 to 38 per cent, is in respect of items of system of auditing and rigid allocations.

It is, therefore, suggested that adequate funds, flexibility in allocation, timely allocation and release of funds by the Government/funding agencies, and efficient system of auditing be ensured for running the activities of various Units/Departments of a University Institution.

TABLE 3.17: Level of Satisfaction with Existing Financial Management Systems

(Percentage responses)

Sr. No.	Particulars/ Description	Central Universities	Deemed Universities	Institutions of National Importance	State General Universities	State Agricultural Universities
I.	Vice-Chancellors/Directors					
1.	Satisfaction with existing financial management	100.00	100.00	N.A.	50.00	66.66
II.	Finance Officers/ Comptrollers/Registrars					
1.	Level of satisfaction					
1.1	Very much satisfied	0.00	0.00	100.00	8.00	0.00
1.2	Satisfied	100.00	33.33	0.00	40.00	38.46
1.3	Undecided	0.00	0.00	0.00	4.00	0.00
1.4	Not satisfied	0.00	33.33	0.00	48.00	61.54
1.5	Not at all satisfied	0.00	0.00	0.00	0.00	0.00
III.	Professors and Heads of Departments					
1.	Level of satisfaction					
1.1	Very much satisfied	33.33	—	—	3.33	5.26
1.2	Satisfied	66.66	50.00	100.00	35.00	47.37
1.3	Undecided	—	—	—	6.67	5.26
1.4	Not satisfied	—	50.00	—	33.33	21.05
1.5	Not at all satisfied	—	—	—	11.67	15.79

TABLE 3.18: Reasons for Dissatisfaction

(Percentage responses)

Sr. No.	Particulars/ Description	Central Universities	Deemed Universities	Institutions of National Importance	State General Universities	State Agricultural Universities
I.	Finance Officers/Comptrollers/ Registrars					
1.	Reasons for dissatisfaction					
1.1.	Lack of funds	0.00	33.33	0.00	48.00	46.15
1.2	Rigid allocation	0.00	33.33	0.00	36.00	38.46
1.3	Late receipt of funds	33.33	33.33	0.00	44.00	53.85
1.4	System of auditing	0.00	0.00	0.00	20.00	15.38
II.	Professors and Heads of Departments					
1.	Reasons for dissatisfaction					
1.1	Lack of funds	0.00	50.00	0.00	33.31	34.21
1.2	Rigid allocation	0.00	50.00	0.00	35.00	28.95
1.3	Late receipt of allocation	0.00	50.00	0.00	30.00	28.95
1.4	Delayed passing of bills and release of payments	66.66	50.00	0.00	51.67	28.95
1.5	System of auditing	0.00	50.00	0.00	23.33	21.05

REFERENCES

1. Report of the Kothari Commission, Government of India (1964-66) (University Education Commission).
2. The Indian Council of Agricultural Research 'Model Act' circulated vide letter No.I. 17-6/86-Edn.II, 13th July, 1987.
3. Report of the Gajendragadkar Committee on the Governance of Universities, U.G.C. 1969-70
4. The University of Delhi, Act No. VII of 1922 (amended upto Feb., 1987).
5. The North Eastern Hill University, Act No. 24 of 1973 (amended upto March, 1985).
6. The Visva Bharti, Act No. XXIX of 1951 (amended upto May, 1984).
7. The Jamia Millia Islamia, Memorandum of Association and Rules (amended upto Feb., 1984).
8. The Thaper Institute of Engineering and Technology, Memorandum of Association and Rules (amended upto Jan., 1986).
9. The Indian Institute of Technology, Act No. 59 of 1961 (amended upto 1985).
10. The Indian Statistical Institute, Memorandum of Association and Regulations (amended upto 1986).
11. The Uttar Pradesh State Universities Act No. 10 of 1973 (amended upto Feb., 1987).
12. The Bihar State Universities Act, No. XXIII of 1976 (amended upto April, 1986).
13. The Karnataka State Universities Act No. 28 of 1976 (amended upto May, 1986).
14. The Kashmir and Jammu Universities Act No. XXIV of 1969 (amended upto 1972).
15. The Madhya Pradesh Visva Vidyalaya Adhiniyam Act No. 22 of 1973 (amended upto 1986).
16. The Telugu University Act. No. 27 of 1985.
17. The University of Health Sciences Act No. 6 of 1986.
18. The Osmania University Act No. IX of 1959 (amended upto Feb., 1988).
19. The Kerala University Act No. 17 of 1974 (amended upto Dec., 1984).
20. The Calicut University Act No. 5 of 1975 (amended upto 1980).
21. The Punjabi University Act No. 35 of 1961 (amended upto June, 1985).
22. The Maharshi Dayanand University Act No. 25 of 1975 (amended upto Oct., 1984).
23. The University of Rajasthan Act 1946 (amended upto Aug., 1985).
24. The Himachal Pradesh University Act No. 17 of 1970 (amended upto March, 1986).
25. The Calcutta University Act No. XXXVIII of 1979 (amended upto Oct., 1983).
26. The Rabindra Bharti Act. No XXXVI of 1981 (amended upto Jan., 1983).
27. The University of Bombay Act No. XXII of 1974 (amended upto May, 1983).
28. The Sardar Patel University Act No. XL of 1955 (amended upto July, 1978).
29. The Himachal Pradesh Universities of Agriculture, Horticulture and Forestry Act No. 4 of 1987.
30. The Maharashtra Agricultural Universities (Krishi Vidyapeeths) Act, 1983 (Act No. XLI of 1983).
31. The Karnataka University of Agricultural Sciences Act, No. 40 of 987.
32. The Haryana and Punjab Agricultural Universities Act, No. 16 of 1970.
33. The Uttar Pradesh Krishi Evam Prodyogik Vishva Vidyalaya Adhiniyam, Act No. XIV of 1958 (amended upto 1974).
34. The Bidhan Chandra Krishi Vishva Vidyalaya Act,No. 49 of 1974.
35. The Tamil Nadu Agricultural Universities Act,No. 8 of 1971.
36. The Gujarat Agricultural Universities Ordinance No. 13 of 1969.
37. The Rajindra Agricultural University Ordinance No. 5 of 1987.
38. The Kerala Agricultural University Act,No. 33 of 1971.
39. Report of the Committee on 'Model Act' for Universities, U.G.C., 1961-62.

4

SOURCE OF FINANCES, GRANTS-IN-AID RULES AND CRITERIA OF FIXATION OF GRANTS

THE PROBLEMS faced by university administration in the management of university finances are: sources of funding, the criteria/formulae for determination of grants and rules prescribed, that is 'Grants-in-aid Rules' for release of grants. The adequacy of funds from various sources, normal periodical increase in grants and timely release and utilization of funds play a pivotal role in the effective and efficient management of university finances. This can be achieved through tapping various sources of funding, sound criteria/formulae for periodical determination and fixation of grants and sound 'Grants-in-aid Rules' for release and utilisation of funds/grants. In this chapter existing sources of finances, criteria/formulae for fixation of grants and grants-in-aid rules have been analysed in respect of University Institutions sampled for the study. An attempt has been made to suggest measures for further augmentation of sources of income, model grants-in-aid rules for release of grants and their utilisation and model criteria/formulae for fixation of grants in respect of University Institutions in India.

Sources of Finances

The main sources of funding the University Institutions in India are: the Central Government, the State Governments, the University Grants Commission, the Indian Council of Agricultural Research and other public and private agencies. The funds are made available to the University Institutions in the form of grants-in-aid, development assistance, from the University Grants Commission and the Indian Council of Agricultural Research, fees, domestic income from sale/ hiring of movable and immovable property, hostels, and sale of university publications and farm produce. The endowments and benefactions are also sources of finance to the University Institutions. The available funds are utilised for the running of the existing activities/programmes and for taking up new activities/programmes including development activities.

The available data on funding of the University Institutions as obtained from the University Grants Commission (1987)[1] have been analysed and given hereafter.

Central Universities

The percentage share of recurring income from the University Grants Commission was the highest (96.1 per cent) for the year 1982-83 in the case of the University of Hyderabad and the lowest (75.4 per cent) in respect of the Banaras Hindu University for the same year. The next highest source of funds was 'other sources'; the highest (22.6 per cent) in the case of the Banaras Hindu University 1982-83 and the lowest (1.8 per cent) in that of the North Eastern Hill University 1984-85. The highest income from fees (22.2 per cent) 1982-83 was that of Visva Bharti (Table 4.1).

The major sources of non-recurring funds (more than 55 per cent) was from the University Grants Commission for almost all the universities except that of the Banaras Hindu University (2.02 per cent) in 1984-85. The highest share (13.43 per cent) in 1984-85 was for North Eastern Hill University from the Central Government and the lowest (2.67 per cent) in 1982-83 was for Visva Bharti from the State Government. The highest income from other sources was in respect of the Banaras Hindu University (100 per cent) and the lowest (15.4 per cent) in case of Visva Bharti (Table 4.2).

Deemed Universities

The University Grants Commission is the major source of recurring income for all Deemed Universities, except for such institutions in the State of Rajasthan, where the main source is fees and endowments taken together. The highest assistance (98.19 per cent) from the University Grants Commission has been reported in respect of Deemed Universities in Karnataka State and the lowest (0.22 per cent) in respect of such institutions in the State of Rajasthan followed by Uttar Pradesh (30.06 per cent). The income from fees has been reported the

TABLE 4.1: Recurring Income (Plan and Non-plan) of Central Universities (1982-85)

(Amount in '00 rupees)

Sr. No. University Institution and year	Sources of Recurring Income								
	Central Government	University Grants Commission	State Government	Local Bodies	Other sources (including Management Societies)	Fees (including Hostels, Exams., lab. fees etc.)	Endowments	Other Sources	Total
1	2	3	4	5	6	7	8	9	10
1. University of Hyderabad									
1982-83	—	1,71,246 (96.1)	—	—	—	3,305 (1.9)	—	3,649 (2.0)	1,78,200 (100.0)
1983-84	—	2,01,309 (96.1)	—	—	—	3,864 (1.8)	—	4,420 (2.1)	2,09,593 (100.0)
1984-85	—	2,41,526 (95.9)	—	—	—	4,471 (1.8)	— —	5,763 (2.3)	2,51,760 (100.0)
2. North Eastern Hill University									
1982-83	—	1,765,00 (87.8)	—	—	—	19,458 (9.7)	46	5,114 (2.5)	2,01,118 (100.0)
1983-84	—	1,92,000 (88.5)	—	—	—	19,675 (9.1)	50	5,280 (2.4)	2,17,005 (100.0)
1984-85	—	3,09,012 (92.8)	—	—	—	18,075 (5.4)	47	5,917 (1.8)	3,33,051 (100.0)

(Contd.)

TABLE 4.1 *Contd.*

1	2	3	4	5	6	7	8	9	10
3. Aligarh Muslim University									
1982-83	11,166	11,23,638	1,855	—	—	26,924	6,993	64,005	12,34,581
	(0.9)	(91.0)	(0.1)			(2.2)	(0.6)	(5.2)	(100.0)
1983-84	18,385	13,38,493	464	—	299	33,664	2,700	58,024	14,52,529
	(1.3)	(92.2)			Negligible	(2.3)	(0.2)	(4.0)	(100.0)
1984-85	16,125	15,32,668	1,723	—	36,176	29,090	8,713	74,931	16,99,426
	(1.8)	(90.2)	(0.1)		(2.1)	(1.7)	(0.5)	(4.4)	(100.0)
4. Banaras Hindu University									
1982-83	22	15,20,827	2,584	43	—	31,341	5,680	4,55,632	20,16,134
		(75.4)	(0.1)			(1.6)	(0.3)	(22.6)	(100.0)
1983-84	—	19,09,114	163	—	48	37,349	5,047	36,889	23,22,078
		(82.2)	(0.1)		Negligible	(1.6)	(0.2)	(15.9)	(100.0)
1984-85	—	20,28,264	2,865	—	48	32,120	5,821	4,93,378	25,62,496
		(79.2)	(0.1)		Negligible	(1.2)	(0.2)	(19.3)	(100.0)
5. Visva Bharti									
1982-83	—	3,44,449	2,030	—	—	99.374	—	—	4,45,853
		(77.3)	(0.5)			(22.2)			(100.0)
1983-84	1,299	3,92,077	7,122	—	88,266	3,806	—	—	4,92,570
	(0.3)	(79.6)	(1.4)		(17.9)	(0.8)			(100.0)
1984-85	—	4,43,825	14,010	—	—	3,943	—	78,438	5,27,606
		(84.1)	(0.3)			(0.7)		(14.9)	(100.0)

(Contd.)

TABLE 4.1 *Contd.*

1	2	3	4	5	6	7	8	9	10
6. Delhi University									
1982-83	—	7,82,288 (89.8)	—	—	—	88,962 (10.2)	—	—	8,71,250 (100.0)
1983-84	—	9,20,930 (88.8)	—	—	—	1,20,606 (11.6)	—	—	10,41,536 (100.0)
1984-85	—	11,00,643 (89.1)	—	—	—	1,31,795 (10.7)	2,555 (0.2)	—	12,34,813 (100.0)
7. Jawaharlal Nehru University									
1982-83	—	4,07,000 (93.8)	—	—	—	7,795 (1.8)	—	19,275 (4.4)	4,34,070 (100.0)
1983-84	—	4,84,432 (95.4)	—	—	—	5,607 (1.1)	—	17,683 (3.5)	5,07,722 (100.0)
1984-85	—	5,12,735 (94.8)	—	—	—	6,730 (1.2)	—	21,499 (4.0)	5,40,964 (100.0)

Source: University Grants Commission

Note: Figures in parenthesis are proportion of income in terms of percentage

TABLE 4.2: Non-recurring Income (Plan and Non-plan) of Central Universities (1982-85)

(Amount in '00 rupees)

Sr. No.	University Institution and year	Sources of Non-Recurring Income					
		Central Govern-ment	University Grants Commission	State Govern-ment	Local Boards	Other Sources	Total
1	2	3	4	5	6	7	8
1.	University of Hyderabad						
	1982-83	—	56,358 (100.00)	—	—	—	56,358 (100.00)
	1983-84	—	33,950 (100.00)	—	—	—	33,950 (100.00)
	1984-85	—	1,64,390 (100.00)	—	—	—	1,64,390 (100.00)
2.	North Eastern Hill University						
	1982-83	—	44,028 (100.00)	—	—	—	44,028 (100.00)
	1983-84	—	1,20,898 (100.00)	—	—	—	1,20,898 (100.00)
	1984-85	55,000 (13.47)	3,53,387 (86.53)	—	—	—	4,08,387 (100.00)
3.	Aligarh Muslim University						
	1982-83	—	1,77,268 (100.00)	—	—	—	1,77,268 (100.00)
	1983-84	—	1,87,877 (100.00)	—	—	—	1,87,877 (100.00)
	1984-85	7,100 (2.30)	3,02,246 (97.70)	—	—	—	3,09,346 (100.00)
4.	Banaras Hindu University						
	1982-83	—	—	—	—	1,75,311 (100.00)	1,75,311 (100.00)
	1983-84	—	—	—	—	3,12,757 (100.00)	3,12,757 (100.00)
	1984-85	—	8,000 (2.02)	—	—	3,88,237 (97.98)	3,96,237 (100.00)
5.	Visva Bharti						
	1982-83	9,375 (3.02)	29,172 (9.36)	8,315 (2.67)	—	2,64,868 (84.95)	3,11,730 (100.00)

(Contd.)

1	2	3	4	5	6	7	8
	1983-84	—	70,378 (84.60)	—	—	12,808 (15.40)	83,186 (100.00)
	1984-85	11,254 (12.48)	49,767 (55.20)	4,194 (4.65)	—	24,936 (27.67)	90,151 (100.00)
6.	Delhi University						
	1982-83	—	47,302 (100.00)	—	—	—	47,302 (100.00)
	1983-84	—	56,393 (100.00)	—	—	—	56,393 (100.00)
	1984-85	—	3,41,125 (100.00)	—	—	—	3,41,125 (100.00)
7.	Jawaharlal Nehru University						
	1982-83	—	45,061 (100.00)	—	—	—	45,061 (100.00)
	1983-84	—	1,44,964 (100.00)	—	—	—	1,44,964 (100.00)
	1984-85	—	2,43,007 (72.98)	—	—	90,000 (27.02)	3,33,007 (100.00)

Source: University Grants Commission
Note: Figures in parenthesis are proportion of Income in terms of percentages.

highest (50.14 per cent) for such institutions in Rajasthan State and the lowest (1.02 per cent) in Karnataka State. The highest share (56.09 per cent) of the State Governments is in Uttar Pradesh, whereas the lowest has been reported in Karnataka and Delhi. The income from other sources has been reported the highest (47.07 per cent) in the State of Rajasthan and the lowest (0.26 per cent) in the State of Uttar Pradesh. The institutions recognised as 'Deemed Universities' in Rajasthan are getting income from endowments ranging from 20.24 per cent to 40.31 per cent whereas in other cases it is negligible (Table 4.3).

The percentage share of non-recurring income from the University Grants Commission is the highest (100 per cent) in consecutive (1982-85) years for the institutions in the State of Tamil Nadu, Maharashtra, Bihar and Gujarat and the lowest in Karnataka (28.41 per cent). The other sources of non-recurring income has been reported the highest (71.59 per cent) for Deemed Universities in Karnataka State and the lowest (1.82 per cent) in Uttar Pradesh. The State Government also provided funds to the institutions located in Andhra Pradesh, Rajasthan and Uttar Pradesh which was highest (14.43 per cent) in Uttar Pradesh and the lowest (0.06 per cent) in Andhra Pradesh (Table 4.4).

TABLE 4.3: Recurring Income (Plan and Non-plan) of Deemed Universities (1982-85)

(Amount in 00's rupees)

Sr. No. University Institutions/ States and year	Sources of Recurring Income								
	Central Government	University Grants Commission	State Government	Local Bodies	Other sources (including Management Societies)	Fees (including Hostels, Exams., lab. fees etc.)	Endowments	other Sources	Total
1	2	3	4	5	6	7	8	9	10
1. Andhra Pradesh									
1982-83	—	51,700 (57.86)	—	—	24,513 (27.43)	7,272 (8.14)	773 (0.87)	5,090 (5.70)	89,348 (100.00)
1983-84	—	82,780 (86.27)	—	—	47 (0.05)	4,135 (4.31)	129 (0.13)	8,865 (9.24)	95,956 (100.00)
1984-85	3,000 (3.06)	78,076 (79.55)	—	—	—	5,165 (5.26)	2,765 (2.82)	9,139 (9.31)	98,143 (100.00)
2. Bihar									
1982-83	—	1,44,360 (88.46)	—	—	—	6,620 (4.06)	7,830 (4.80)	4,380 (2.68)	1,63,190 (100.00)
1983-84	—	1,62,980 (88.50)	—	—	—	21,170 (11.50)	—	—	1,84,150 (100.00)
1984-85	—	1,80,020 (87.96)	—	—	—	24,650 (12.04)	—	—	2,04,670 (100.00)
3. Gujarat									
1982-83	—	51,547 (91.37)	2,596 (4.60)	—	—	1,617 (2.87)	—	657 (1.16)	56,417 (100.00)
1983-84	—	65,559 (91.44)	3,657 (5.10)	—	—	2,480 (3.46)	—	—	71,696 (100.00)
1984-85	—	75,200 (90.27)	6,110 (7.33)	—	—	1,996 (2.40)	—	—	83,306 (100.00)

(Contd.)

TABLE 4.3 *Contd.*

1	2	3	4	5	6	7	8	9	10
4. Karnataka									
1982-83	—	4,35,870	150	—	—	5,830	3,700	1,06,630	5,52,180
		(78.94)	(0.03)			(1.06)	(0.67)	(19.30)	(100.00)
1983-84	—	5,17,360	1,230	—	—	6,670	3,540	1,24,190	6,52,990
		(79.23)	(0.19)			(1.02)	(0.54)	(19.02)	(100.00)
1984-85	—	6,78,793	1,130	—	—	7,853	3,503	—	6,91,279
		(98.19)	(0.16)			(1.14)	(0.51)		(100.00)
5. Maharashtra									
1982-83	37,000	—	875	2,000	—	1,201	—	2,289	43,305
	(85.32)		(2.02)	(4.61)		(2.77)		(5.28)	(100.00)
1983-84	—	44,760	—	1,750	895	1,371	—	2,363	51,139
		(87.53)		(3.42)	(1.75)	(2.68)		(4.62)	(100.00)
1984-85	—	57,000	849	1,750	—	1,350	—	2,041	62,990
		(90.49)	(1.35)	(2.78)		(2.14)		(3.24)	(100.00)
6. Rajasthan									
1982-83	—	443	—	313	1,423	40,987	26,724	62,155	1,32,045
		(0.33)		(0.24)	(1.08)	(31.04)	(20.24)	(47.07)	(100.00)
1983-84	967	520	26,986	—	9,025	62,720	74,985	10,802	1,86,005
	(0.52)	(0.28)	(14.51)		(4.85)	(33.72)	(40.31)	(5.81)	(100.00)
1984-85	1,567	521	32,459	—	859	1,17,998	72,302	9,634	2,35,340
	(0.67)	(0.22)	(13.79)		(0.37)	(50.14)	(30.72)	(4.09)	(100.00)

(Contd.)

TABLE 4.3 *Contd.*

1	2	3	4	5	6	7	8	9	10
7. Tamil Nadu									
1982-83	—	32,999	—	—	—	4,984	—	—	37,983
		(86.88)				(13.12)			(100.00)
1983-84	—	45,060	—	—	—	2,643	—	2,324	50,027
		(90.07)				(5.28)		(4.65)	(100.00)
1984-85	—	65,400	—	—	—	2,989	—	2,748	71,137
		(91.94)				(4.20)		(3.86)	(100.00)
8. Uttar Pradesh									
1982-83	—	20,800	38,813	—	2,084	7,228	92	192	69,199
		(30.06)	(56.09)		(3.01)	(10.45)	(0.13)	(0.26)	(100.00)
1983-84	—	30,770	37,642	500	—	7,795	163	3,107	79,977
		(38.47)	(47.07)	(0.63)		(9.75)	(0.20)	(3.88)	(100.00)
1984-85	—	39,030	40,501	—	545	8,028	—	2,698	90,802
		(42.98)	(44.60)		(0.60)	(8.84)		(2.98)	(100.00)
9. Delhi									
1982-83	70,250	96,400	50	—	—	4,965	—	3,641	1,75,306
	(40.07)	(54.99)	(0.03)			(2.83)		(2.08)	(100.00)
1983-84	85,750	1,11,450	20	—	—	12,960	—	1,610	2,11,790
	(40.49)	(52.62)	(0.01)			(6.12)		(0.76)	(100.00)
1984-85	66,660	1,56,568	784	9,255	—	6,297	1,010	11,967	2,53,220
	(26.32)	(61.83)	(0.31)	(3.65)		(2.75)	(0.40)	(4.74)	(100.00)

Source: University Grants Commission

Note: Figures in parenthesis are proportion of Income in terms of percentages.

TABLE 4.4: Non-recurring Income (Plan and Non-plan) of Deemed Universities (1982-85)

(Amount in '00 rupees)

Sr. No.	University Institution/ State and year	Central Govern-ment	University Grants Commission	State Govern-ment	Local Boards	Other Sources	Total
		Sources of Non-Recurring Income					
1	2	3	4	5	6	7	8
1.	Andhra Pradesh						
	1982-83	—	38,340	1,085	—	—	39,425
			(97.25)	(2.75)			(100.00)
	1983-84	—	40,650	56	—	60,188	1,00,894
			(40.29)	(0.06)		(59.65)	(100.00)
	1984-85	—	41,170	—	—	61,026	1,02,196
			(40.29)			(59.71)	(100.00)
2.	Bihar						
	1982-83	—	14,000	—	—	—	14,000
			(100.00)				(100.00)
	1983-84	—	24,000	—	—	—	24,000
			(100.00)				(100.00)
	1984-85	—	16,130	—	—	—	16,130
			(100.00)				(100.00)
3.	Gujarat						
	1982-83	—	17,345	—	—	—	17,345
			(100.00)				(100.00)
	1983-84	—	18,447	—	—	—	18,447
			(100.00)				(100.00)
	1984-85	—	47,081	—	—	—	47,081
			(100.00)				(100.00)
4.	Karnataka						
	1982-83	—	75,000	—	—	1,89,010	2,64,010
			(28.41)			(71.59)	(100.00)
	1983-84	—	3,59,390	—	—	—	3,59,390
			(100.00)				(100.00)
	1984-85	2,08,220	2,77,176	—	—	9,578	4,94,974
		(42.07)	(56.00)			(1.93)	(100.00)
5.	Maharashtra						
	1982-83	—	13,018	—	—	—	13,018
			(100.00)				(100.00)
	1983-84	—	8,884	—	—	—	8,884
			(100.00)				(100.00)
	1984-85	—	16,285	—	—	—	16,285
			(100.00)				(100.00)

(Contd.)

TABLE 4.4 *Contd.*

1	2	3	4	5	6	7	8
6.	Rajasthan						
	1982-83	—	3,483 (42.97)	—	4,623 (57.03)	—	8,106 (100.00)
	1983-84	—	8,948 (100.00)	—	—	—	8,948 (100.00)
	1984-85	7,817 (11.98)	38,000 (58.23)	7,500 (11.49)	—	11,945 (18.30)	65,262 (100.00)
7.	Tamil Nadu						
	1982-83	—	14,400 (100.00)	—	—	—	14,400 (100.00)
	1983-84	—	20,361 (100.00)	—	—	—	20,361 (100.00)
	1984-85	—	7,127 (100.00)	—	—	—	7,127 (100.00)
8.	Uttar Pradesh						
	1982-83	—	14,373 (89.27)	1,728 (10.73)	—	—	16,101 (100.00)
	1983-84	450 (1.49)	25,455 (84.08)	4,369 (14.43)	—	—	30,274 (100.00)
	1984-85	25,581 (55.90)	19,346 (42.28)	—	—	832 (1.82)	45,759 (100.00)
9.	Delhi						
	1982-83	—	90,120 (100.00)	—	—	—	90,120 (100.00)
	1983-84	—	39,290 (100.00)	—	—	—	39,290 (100.00)
	1984-85	34,000 (26.14)	96,070 (73.86)	—	—	—	130,070 (100.00)

Source: University Grants Commission
Note: Figures in parenthesis are proportion of Income in terms of percentages.

State General Universities

On an average, sixty per cent or more funds are provided to State General Universities by the State Governments. The percentage share of States in highest (88.40 per cent) in Jammu and Kashmir, whereas it is lowest (31.56 per cent) for universities in the State of Tamil Nadu. Thus the share of the State Government is less than fifty per cent in the case of universities in Tamil Nadu and Kerala. The second major source of income is 'Fees', which varies from 4.52 per cent in universities of West Bengal to 49.45 per cent in Kerala. It can be seen that the universities in Tamil Nadu are getting more income from 'Fees' than the State Government grants. Since the universities situated in Tamil Nadu sizeably mobilised their resources through 'Fees', there is a strong case for the State Governments to enhance their share of grants to the universities as a measure of incentive, for the speedier development and growth of the universities. The universities in the State of West Bengal are generating income from 'Fees' ranging from 4.52 to 6.62 per cent, which is much below the country's average (9.7 per cent). The income from 'Local Boards' and 'Endowments' to State General Universities is not significant. The income of 'Local Boards' varies from 0.03 per cent in Kerala State universities to 2.30 per cent in Haryana State Universities, whereas 'Endowments' income varies from 0.01 per cent in the universities in Kerala to 7.30 per cent in Karnataka State Universities. It is interesting to note that 'Endowments' and contribution of Local Boards, are declining year by year. The figures in the table further reveal that the income from 'Other Sources' was less than 12 per cent in most of the State General Universities. But the universities of Kerala and Karnataka can be highlighted due to their income from other sources which is 28.86 per cent in Karnataka and 21.83 per cent in Kerala. The income from other sources ranked third after the contribution of the State Government and the collection from fees in the State General Universities in the country as a whole (Table 4.5).

The major source of non-recurring income has been reported to be the University Grants Commission in respect of almost all State General Universities. The highest (86.74 per cent) non-recurring income provided by the said agency was for the universities of Madhya Pradesh, followed by 79.96 per cent in the universities of West Bengal. The lowest non-recurring income (3.28 per cent) has been reported from State Universities in Karnataka followed by Tamil Nadu (4.91 per cent). The States of Haryana followed by Jammu and Kashmir provided 100 per cent and 93.45 per cent non-recurring income to the universities, respectively. The lowest share of the State Governments for the non-recurring income was in the case of universities in Himachal Pradesh (6.55 per cent), followed by Punjab (8.72 per cent) and Madhya Pradesh (10.06 per cent). The non-recurring income from Central Government to State General Universities varies from 0.41 per cent to 66.97 per cent. The non-recurring income from 'Local Boards' was only in the case of universities in the State of Andhra Pradesh, Maharashtra, Uttar Pradesh, Orissa and Punjab. The highest percentage

TABLE 4.5: Recurring Income (Plan and Non-plan) of State General Universities (1982-85)

(Amount in '00 rupees)

Sr. No. University Institutions/ States and year	Sources of Recurring Income								
	Central Government	University Grants Commission	State Governments	Local Bodies	Other sources (including Management Societies)	Fees (including Hostels, Exams., lab. fees etc.)	Endowments	other Sources	Total
1	2	3	4	5	6	7	8	9	10
1. Andhra Pradesh									
1982-83	—	92,952	16,04,532	10,000	—	3,71,685	2,609	116,992	21,98,770
		(4.30)	(72.84)	(0.55)		(16.87)	(0.13)	(5.31)	(100.00)
1983-84	—	95,581	20,59,132	15,000	21,653	5,03,419	10,589	111,814	28,17,188
		(3.38)	(72.90)	(0.61)	(0.87)	(17.86)	(0.42)	(3.96)	(100.00)
1984-85	—	32,675	9,22,994	15,000	—	2,46,251	9,571	29,935	12,56,726
		(2.60)	(73.45)	(1.20)		(19.60)	(0.76)	(2.38)	(100.00)
2 Assam									
1982-83	—	—	2,07,000	—	—	1,12,917	—	34,181	3,54,098
			(58.46)			(31.89)		(9.65)	(100.00)
1983-84	—	—	2,55,000	—	—	1,30,551	—	44,677	4,30,228
			(59.27)			(30.35)		(10.38)	(100.00)
1984-85	—	—	—	—	—	—	—	—	—
3. Bihar									
1982-83	1,440	1,710	20,90,996	—	65,229	3,37,882	—	250	24,99,007
	(0.06)	(0.07)	(83.69)		(2.64)	(13.53)		(0.01)	(100.00)
1983-84	1,004	50,400	30,22,730	—	—	5,32,650	—	1,583	36,10,358
	(0.02)	(1.45)	(83.73)			(14.76)		(0.04)	(100.00)
1984-85	—	5,636	10,89,853	—	—	2,67,602	—	38,756	14,01,747
		(0.40)	(77.75)			(19.09)		(2.76)	(100.00)

(Contd.)

TABLE 4.5 *Contd.*

1	2	3	4	5	6	7	8	9	10
4. Gujarat									
1982-83	15,791	21,574	4,16,058	—	9,909	2,20,340	4,012	10,269	6,96,864
	(2.27)	(3.09)	(59.56)		(1.42)	(31.60)	(0.57)	(1.47)	(100.00)
1983-84	14,230	50,350	4,52,254	2,386	10,952	2,34,261	3,036	12,279	7,79,757
	(1.82)	(6.46)	(58.00)	(0.31)	(1.40)	(30.04)	(0.39)	(1.58)	(100.00)
1984-85	15,018	73,511	5,96,392	—	14,076	2,44,467	2,719	13,026	9,50,008
	(1.58)	(7.75)	(62.82)		(1.48)	(25.75)	(0.29)	(0.32)	(100.00)
5. Haryana									
1982-83	1,100	35,876	4,63,020	8,973	13,639	1,25,398	1,402	89,429	7,28,837
	(0.15)	(4.92)	(62.16)	(1.23)	(1.87)	(17.21)	(0.19)	(12.27)	(100.00)
1983-84	1,014	84,079	4,13,835	16,809	9,675	1,17,722	973	87,485	7,31,592
	(0.13)	(11.49)	(56.58)	(2.30)	(1.32)	(16.09)	(0.13)	(11.96)	(100.00)
1984-85	795	81,226	5,70,129	—	16,434	1,55,318	1,146	91,365	9,16,333
	(0.08)	(8.86)	(62.22)		(1.79)	(16.95)	(0.13)	(9.97)	(100.00)
6. Himachal Pradesh									
1982-83	—	—	1,53,000	—	—	48,989	11	12,235	2,14,235
			(71.42)			(22.87)		(5.71)	(100.00)
1983-84	—	—	2,00,000	—	—	55,740	—	9,516	2,65,256
			(75.40)			(21.01)		(3.59)	(100.00)
1984-85	—	—	2,22,250	—	—	50,126	—	40,268	3,20,664
			(69.31)			(18.13)		(12.56)	(100.00)

(Contd.)

TABLE 4.5 *Contd.*

1	2	3	4	5	6	7	8	9	10
7. Jammu & Kashmir									
1982-83	—	15,790	3,29,050	—	500	38,354	—	9,790	3,93,484
		(4.01)	(83.62)		(0.13)	(9.75)		(2.49)	(100.00)
1983-84	—	—	1,46,000	—	—	19,154	—	—	1,65,154
			(88.40)			(11.60)			(100.00)
1984-85	—	6,000	2,34,250	—	—	21,819	—	12,967	2,75,036
		(2.18)	(85.17)			(7.93)		(4.72)	(100.00)
8. Karnataka									
1982-83	—	43,926	12,78,921	2,700	28,718	316,182	15,258	78,068	17,63,773
		(2.49)	(72.51)	(0.15)	(1.63)	(17.93)	(0.87)	(4.42)	(100.00)
1983-84	433	17,219	13,65,235	—	24,309	403,307	53,310	755,891	26,19,704
	(0.02)	(0.66)	(52.11)		(0.93)	(15.39)	(2.03)	(28.86)	(100.00)
1984-85	2,488	—	14,86,476	—	18,755	256,554	151,601	159,615	20,75,389
	(0.12)		(71.63)		(0.90)	(12.36)	(7.30)	(7.69)	(100.00)
9. Kerala									
1982-83	—	2,552	4,17,177	—	—	5,15,357	—	1,07,312	10,42,398
		(0.24)	(40.02)			(49.45)		(10.29)	(100.00)
1983-84	—	22,292	6,29,660	219	4,690	4,90,245	—	73,086	12,20,692
		(1.82)	(51.58)	(0.03)	(0.38)	(40.20)		(5.99)	(100.00)
1984-85	—	4,669	5,02,090	—	7,346	3,41,073	60	2,38,783	10,94,021
		(0.42)	(45.89)		(0.67)	(31.18)	(0.01)	(21.83)	(100.00)

(Contd.)

TABLE 4.5 *Contd.*

1	2	3	4	5	6	7	8	9	10
10. Manipur									
1982-83	—	—	1,06,000 (86.59)	—	—	16,414 (13.41)	—	—	1,22,414 (100.00)
1983-84	—	—	54,000 (76.56)	—	—	16,533 (23.44)	—	—	70,533 (100.00)
1984-85	—	3,500 (4.00)	54,000 (61.74)	—	—	29,961 (34.26)	—	—	87,461 (100.00)
11. Orissa									
1982-83	—	10,818 (2.13)	3,07,621 (60.54)	508 (0.10)	2,329 (0.46)	1,70,858 (33.65)	3,151 (0.62)	12,392 (2.45)	5,07,677 (100.00)
1983-84	616 (0.29)	7,373 (3.26)	1,54,568 (68.34)	—	4,170 (1.84)	52,795 (23.34)	60 (0.02)	6,590 (2.91)	2,26,169 (100.00)
1984-85	—	—	1,04,790 (62.79)	—	8,000 (4.79)	50,471 (30.24)	990 (0.59)	2,650 (1.59)	1,66,901 (100.00)
12. Punjab									
1982-83	400 (0.02)	31,280 (1.51)	14,92,859 (72.14)	—	—	4,97,049 (24.02)	800 (0.03)	47,085 (2.28)	20,69,473 (100.00)
1983-84	—	44,136 (2.61)	13,23,210 (78.09)	—	—	2,83,079 (16.70)	2,050 (0.12)	40,008 (2.48)	16,94,483 (100.00)
1984-85	350 (0.02)	11,055 (0.55)	16,89,189 (83.45)	—	—	2,68,994 (13.29)	800 (0.04)	53,756 (2.65)	20,24,144 (100.00)

(Contd.)

TABLE 4.5 *Contd.*

1	2	3	4	5	6	7	8	9	10
13. Rajasthan									
1982-83	—	49,500	7,47,320	—	20,940	2,44,029	—	16,342	10,78,131
		(4.60)	(69.32)		(1.94)	(22.63)		(1.51)	9100.00)
1983-84	—	87,977	9,66,384	—	18,190	3,04,235	—	32,737	14,10,127
		(6.24)	(68.53)		(1.29)	(21.62)		(2.32)	(100.00)
1984-85	—	—	—	—	—	—	—	—	—
14. Tamil Nadu									
1982-83	43,550	54,090	5,56,755	—	77,650	6,40,048	7,720	58,703	14,39,416
	(3.03)	(3.82)	(38.58)		(5.31)	(44.47)	(0.54)	(4.00)	(100.00)
1983-84	28,810	87,115	4,66,730	—	29,025	6,00,369	64,684	2,92,474	14,78,702
	(1.96)	(5.89)	(31.56)		(1.96)	(40.60)	(4.35)	(13.69)	(100.00)
1984-85	19,200	12,906	6,50,002	—	45,786	7,22,292	45,166	34,236	14,65,742
	(1.17)	(7.84)	(39.50)		(2.78)	(43.89)	(2.74)	(2.08)	(100.00)
15. Uttar Pradesh									
1982-83	1,197	7,45,821	10,17,877	2,297	28,767	6,78,372	9,786	79,083	25,57,200
	(0.09)	(29.18)	(39.81)	(0.08)	(0.39)	(26.52)	(0.38)	(3.09)	(100.00)
1983-84	29,989	59,235	11,39,538	1,681	10,950	9,66,699	10,258	52,634	22,71,484
	(1.32)	(2.61)	(50.18)	(0.07)	(0.48)	(42.56)	(0.46)	(2.32)	(100.00)
1984-85	31,578	22,046	7,25,064	882	6,625	2,12,688	10,958	15,568	10,26,409
	(3.07)	(2.25)	(70.64)	(0.08)	(0.65)	(20.72)	(1.07)	(1.52)	(100.00)
16. West Bengal									
1982-83	6,375	29,048	11,48,163	—	6,902	58,989	110	53,020	13,02,607
	(0.48)	(2.28)	(88.13)		(0.52)	(4.52)	(neg)	(4.07)	(100.00)
1983-84	200	18,113	11,83,716	—	1,490	84,558	330	61,739	13,29,246
	(0.01)	(1.42)	(86.49)		(0.59)	(6.62)	(0.02)	(4.85)	(100.00)
1984-85	400	14,763	8,06,813	—	—	58,546	450	49,958	9,30,931
	(0.04)	(1.59)	(86.67)			(6.28)	(0.05)	(5.37)	(100.00)

Source: University Grants Commission

Note: Figures in parenthesis are proportion of Income in terms of percentages.

of income (21.79 per cent) was in the case of Orissa State and the lowest (0.07 per cent) in the case of Uttar Pradesh Universities. The other sources of non-recurring income were available to the universities in almost all the States, except that of Haryana, Himachal Pradesh, Manipur and Rajasthan. The highest percentage of 53.75 was in the case of Karnataka State Universities followed by Punjab (44.77 per cent) and the lowest was 0.32 per cent in the case of Uttar Pradesh (Table 4.6).

TABLE 4.6: Non-recurring Income (Plan and Non-plan) of State General Universities (1982-83 to 1984-85)

(Amount in '00 rupees)

Sr. No.	University Institution/ State and year	Sources of Non-Recurring Income					
		Central Govern-ment	University Grants Commission	State Govern-ment	Local Boards	Other Sources	Total
1	2	3	4	5	6	7	8
1.	Andhra Pradesh						
	1982-83	—	86,160	44,540	—	20,921	1,51,621
			(56.83)	(29.37)		(13.80)	(100.00)
	1983-84	—	2,09,072	35,652	9,000	35,636	2,89,360
			(72.26)	(12.32)	(3.11)	(12.31)	(100.00)
	1984-85	9,688	69,873	61,226	9,500	3,218	1,51,505
		(6.35)	(45.82)	(40.15)	(6.23)	(1.45)	(100.00)
2.	Assam						
	1982-83	24,349	36,540	14,644	—	1,538	77,071
		(31.60)	(47.41)	(19.00)		(1.99)	(100.00)
	1983-84	22,097	7,219	11,500	—	723	41,539
		(53.20)	(17.38)	(27.68)		(1.74)	(100.00)
	1984-85	—	—	—	—	—	—
3.	Bihar						
	1982-83	6,645	71,697	84,506	—	1,650	1,62,598
		(2.86)	(44.09)	(51.97)		(1.08)	(100.00)
	1983-84	10,365	55,665	1,11,290	—	22,721	2,00,041
		(5.1)	(29.83)	(55.63)		(11.36)	(100.00)
	1984-85	—	1,425	7,146	—	—	8,571
			(16.63)	(83.37)			(100.00)
4.	Gujarat						
	1982-83	4,528	35,623	89,281	—	1,527	1,30,959
		(3.46)	(27.20)	(68.17)		(1.17)	(100.00)
	1983-84	1,729	1,08,868	66,206	—	11,162	1,87,965
		(0.92)	(57.92)	(35.22)		(5.94)	(100.00)

(Contd.)

1	2	3	4	5	6	7	8
	1984-85	3,453	62,750	48,818	—	2,312	1,17,333
		(2.94)	(53.48)	(41.61)		(1.97)	(100.00)
5.	Haryana						
	1982-83	—	—	5,000	—	—	5,000
				(100.00)			(100.00)
	1983-84	—	—	5,000	—	—	5,000
				(100.00)			(100.00)
	1984-85	—	—	34,900	—	—	34,900
				(100.00)			(100.00)
6.	Himachal Pradesh						
	1982-83	13,747	15,387	13,313	–	–·	42,447
		(32.39)	(36.25)	(31.36)			(100.00)
	1983-84	15,463	36,700	3,659	—	—	55,822
		(27.70)	(65.75)	(6.55)			(100.00)
	1984-85	24,701	8,900	3,284	—	—	36,885
		(66.97)	(24.13)	(8.90)			(100.00)
7.	Jammu & Kashmir						
	1982-83	—	6,009	85,675	—	—	91,684
			(6.55)	(93.45)			(100.00)
	1983-84	—	24,925	48,634	—	—	73,559
			(33.88)	(66.12)			(100.00)
	1984-85	1,500	3,296	—	—	113	4,909
		(30.56)	(67.14)			(2.30)	(100.00)
8.	Karnataka						
	1982-83	3,884	6,500	81,270	—	1,06,540	1,98,194
		(1.96)	(3.28)	(41.01)		(53.75)	(100.00)
	1983-84	6,942	98,606	1,03,779	—	72,093	2,81,500
		(2.47)	(35.03)	(36.88)		(25.62)	(100.00)
	1984-85	891	29,102	83,615	—	12,561	1,26,169
		(0.71)	(23.06)	(66.27)		(9.96)	(100.00)
9.	Kerala						
	1982-83	4,837	40,472	36,960	—	1,011	82,280
		(5.81)	(48.60)	(44.38)		(1.21)	(100.00)
	1983-84	34,189	94,817	16,926	—	5,073	1,51,005
		(22.64)	(62.79)	(11.21)		(3.36)	(100.00)
	1984-85	20,901	57,006	9,527	—	1,101	88,535
		(23.61)	(64.39)	(10.76)		(1.24)	(100.00)
10.	Madhya Pradesh						
	1982-83	12,795	20,910	9,588	—	—	43,293
		(29.55)	(48.30)	(22.15)			(100.00)
	1983-84	955	2,01,197	23,340	—	6,481	2,31,973
		(0.41)	(86.74)	(10.06)		(2.79)	(100.00)
	1984-85	10,288	20,037	22,674	—	8,336	61,335
		(16.77)	(32.67)	(36.97)		(13.59)	(100.00)

(Contd.)

1	2	3	4	5	6	7	8
11.	Maharashtra						
	1982-83	50,584	3,40,539	93,080	—	17,961	5,02,164
		(10.07)	(67.81)	(18.54)		(3.58)	(100.00)
	1983-84	1,63,00	6,85,863	1,31,119	6,002	20,692	8,59,976
		(16.19)	(68.14)	(13.02)	(0.60)	(2.05)	(100.00)
	1984-85	87,435	4,43,085	1,14,601	31,189	35,089	7,11,383
		(12.29)	(62.28)	(16.12)	(4.38)	(4.93)	(100.00)
12.	Manipur						
	1982-83	—	—	—	—	—	—
	1983-84	—	50,000	54,990	—	—	1,04,990
			(47.62)	(52.37)			(100.00)
	1984-85	—	29,950	57,750	—	—	87,700
			(34.15)	(65.85)			(100.00)
13.	Orissa						
	1982-83	1,917	43,426	28,472	—	4,874	78,689
		(2.44)	(55.19)	(36.18)		(6.19)	(100.00)
	1983-84	514	57,828	11,426	—	12,827	82,595
		(0.62)	(70.02)	(13.83)		(15.53)	(100.00)
	1984-85	—	5,180	10,000	4,230	—	19,410
			(26.69)	(51.52)	(21.79)		(100.00)
14.	Punjab						
	1982-83	7,004	58,007	15,244	—	65,087	1,45,392
		(4.82)	(39.90)	(10.52)		(44.77)	(100.00)
	1983-84	17,270	2,14,130	27,879	7,356	53,176	3,19,811
		(5.00)	(66.95)	(8.72)	(2.30)	(16.63)	(100.00)
	1984-85	12,600	1,01,054	51,424	—	30,851	1,95,939
		(6.43)	(51.57)	(26.25)		(15.75)	(100.00)
15.	Rajasthan						
	1982-83	10,000	25,240	39,630	—	—	74,870
		(13.36)	(33.71)	(52.93)			(100.00)
	1983-84	13,550	40,410	46,110	—	—	1,20,070
		(11.29)	(50.31)	(38.40)			(100.00)
	1984-85	—	—	—	—	—	—
16.	Tamil Nadu						
	1982-83	1,08,250	24,420	3,53,050	—	11,950	4,97,670
		(21.75)	(4.91)	(70.94)		(2.40)	(100.00)
	1983-84	61,870	3,56,620	1,16,500	—	80,630	6,15,620
		(10.05)	(57.93)	(18.92)		(13.10)	(100.00)
	1984-85	51,020	1,51,720	3,31,570	—	1,77,317	7,11,627
		(7.17)	(21.32)	(46.59)		(24.92)	(100.00)
17.	Uttar Pradesh						
	1982-83	88,028	96,749	1,21,138	4,198	12,483	3,12,596
		(28.16)	(30.96)	(38.75)	(1.34)	(3.99)	(100.00)
	1983-84	92,753	2,33,198	1,30,404	299	1,496	4,58,150
		(20.25)	(50.89)	(28.47)	(0.07)	(0.32)	(100.00)

(Contd.)

1	2	3	4	5	6	7	8
	1984-85	97,540 (18.98)	3,07,497 (59.86)	1,04,091 (20.26)	—	4,603 (0.90)	5,13,731 (100.00)
18	West Bengal						
	1982-83	200 (0.41)	38,636 (79.57)	7,172 (14.77)	—	2,550 (5.25)	47,558 (100.00)
	1983-84	7,000 (2.14)	2,61,436 (79.96)	55,132 (16.86)	—	3,390 (1.04)	3,26,958 (100.00)
	1984-85	43,400 (35.66)	46,559 (18.26)	31,750 (26.08)	—	—	11,21,709 (100.00)

Source: University Grants Commission
Note: Figures in parenthesis are proportion of Income in terms of percentages.

From the analysis of recurring and non-recurring income of Central Universities, Deemed Universities and State General Universities, it can be inferred that in respect of Central Universities, both for recurring and non-recurring, the main source of income is the University Grants Commission. The income from fees is negligible. In the case of Deemed Universities, the main sources of recurring finances are the University Grants Commission, income from fees and State Governments, whereas for non-recurring finances, the University Grants Commission and Central Government are the sources of income. The State General Universities are receiving recurring income mainly from State Governments. The other main source of recurring income is fees. Non-recurring income is mainly from the University Grants Commission, State Governments and Central Government in the same order of proportional share. The contribution from the 'Local Boards', 'Endowments' and 'Other Sources' is not significant except in the case of universities in the State of Karnataka. It can be inferred that University Institutions in India are mainly dependent on Central Government/the University Grants Commission and State Governments for funds. The income from fees is not substantial and grants from 'Local Boards', 'Endowments', and 'Other Sources' are decreasing. This system of financing is shrinking, the resources of University Institutions and almost all the State General Universities are facing a financial crisis, which is adversely affecting their growth and future development. This is mainly due to the fact that Governments due to financial constraints cannot meet in full the requirements of the University Institutions. The University Institutions have to give serious thought for augmenting their financial resources by changing fee structure, undertaking consultancy services, tapping other sources like 'Local Boards' and 'Endowments', and commercialising utility services like the Press, Computers, Guest Houses and University Farms. Besides, the disparity in funding of Central Universities and other types of universities has to be dispensed with in the interest of equity and justice. The resource position of University Institutions can be improved in case the funds are decided upon and earmarked by the Finance Commission, Planning Commission and accordingly provided under the head, "Grants-in-Aid" in the Budget of the Central/State Governments.

Grants-in-Aid

Article 282 of the Constitution of India (1972)[2] provides that the Union or State may make any grant for any public purposes, notwithstanding that the purpose is not one with respect to which Parliament or the Legislature of the State, as the case may be, may make laws. The Grants-in-Aid are final payments in the nature of donations or subscriptions to the grantee (1981).[3] Grants-in-Aid are the contributions made by Central or State Governments and other authorised funding agencies to an organisation to run their activities, as financial assistance to existing programmes, in order to improve them and to start new programmes for further development and growth. The grants-in-aid are mainly dependent upon some economic indicators like State Net Domestic Product, its revenue, income and enrolments in the universities. State Governments grants to the University Institutions are in the form of (i) Matching Share of development grants given by the University Grants Commission, (ii) Plan Grants for development and (iii) Grants for committed expenditure under Non-Plan. The Grants to the University Institutions are governed by either of the systems, namely, (i) deficit grants, (ii) block grants. Block grants may be statutory, *ad hoc* or based on past expenditure with or without an allowance for normal increase. Under the system of deficit grants, maintenance grant is worked out on the basis of estimated approved expenditure minus the estimated approved income subject to adjustment in subsequent years on the basis of actual income and actual expenditure as revealed by the audited accounts. Under the system of deficit grant it becomes difficult to adjust cuts, if any, imposed by the Government subsequent to its determination. The approval of the Government is required for creation and filling up of new and vacant posts. The block grant is based on criteria for fixation and frequency of its revision. The system of block grant which is comparatively flexible, is preferable to deficit grants and gives more autonomy to the University Institutions.

The grants-in-aid to the University Institutions are provided by the Union or State Governments on receipt of a written request indicating the purpose for which it is required. The release/payment of grants-in-aid is regulated with certain rules promulgated by the Union or State Governments called, Rules regulating payments of grants-in-aid.

The grants-in-aid play a predominant role in the management of university finances and as such an attempt has been made to study the different parameters relating to it viz., reflection of grants-in-aid in the Government Budget, periodicity for release of grants, procedure of payment of grants; nature of grants; adequacy of grants; and measures adopted to overcome the difficulties due to untimely release of grants; grants-in-aid rules and criteria for fixation of grants-in-aid. The findings of the study, based on reported facts and opinions expressed by Vice-Chancellors/Directors and Finance Officers/Comptrollers/ Registrars are discussed as given hereinafter.

Reflection of Grants-in-Aid in Government Budget

In case of all the sampled Institutions of National Importance and most of the State General Universities and State Agricultural Universities, grants-in-aid is reflected in the Government budget under a major head of 'Grant-in-Aid Department', indicating a minor head of grants to University Institutions (Table 4.7). Grants-in-aid is depicted under one head of account in respect of all Grants-in-Aid Departments and released by the Central Agency in the case of all Institutions of National Importance and more than sixty per cent of the State General Universities, whereas such a practice exists in a number of Central and State Agricultural Universities. In case of most of Agricultural Universities, the grant-in-aid is reflected in the Government budget under different heads of accounts of departments and released subsequently.

TABLE 4.7: Reflection of Grants in Government Budget

(Percentage responses)

Sr. No.	Particulars/Description	Central Univer-sities	Deemed Univer-sities	Institutions of National Importance	State General Univer-sities	State Agricul-tural Univer-sities
1	2	3	4	5	6	7
Finance Officers/Comptrollers/ Registrars						
1.	Grant reflected in Government Budget					
1.1	Major head of grants-in-aid Department without indicating minor head of grants to the University Institution	33.33	0.00	0.00	44.00	30.77
1.2	Major head of grants-in-aid Department indicating minor head of grant to University Institution	33.33	0.00	100.00	68.00	84.62
2.	Grants-in-aid shown in the Government Budget to University Institution under					
2.1	One Head of account in respect of grants-in-aid department and released by one agency	33.33	0.00	100.00	64.00	23.08
2.2	Different head of account of grants-in-aid Departments and released by various grants-in-aid Departments	0.00	33.33	0.50	20.00	69.23

It can be inferred that there is no uniformity with regard to reflection of grants in the Government budget and its release by one agency or various agencies. The non-reflection of grants meant for the University Institutions under a minor head of the major head of account of the concerned Government Departments may entail the risk of not releasing the desired quantum of grants to the University Institutions for want of a specific amount under the minor head as grants-in-aid in the University Institutions. The Government may in such cases reappropriate the grant for other purposes. Once the grant is provided under a minor head as 'Grants-in-aid to the University Institutions', the same cannot be reduced or reappropriated by the Government to the disadvantages of the University Institutions. The release of grants by one agency is not free from the risk of time lag in release of grants.

It is suggested that the grants-in-aid to the University institutions be reflected as a minor head under a major head of account of the Department concerned, with the caption, "Grants-in-Aid to the University Institution (name)". The grants-in-aid should be released by various departments without seeking sanction of the Finance Department of the Government, once these have been provided in the budget and voted by the State Legislature.

Periodicity for Release of Grants

The Vice-Chancellors of the Deemed Universities were not in favour of full release of grants in the beginning of the year, whereas they fully supported the release of half-yearly grants (Table 4.8). Most of the Vice-Chancellors of Central Universities, State General Universities and State Agricultural Universities favoured the release of full grant in the beginning of the year. The quarterly release of grant (in the beginning of each quarter) has been favoured by some of the Vice-Chancellors of State General Universities. Most of the Vice-Chancellors of Deemed Universities, State General Universities and State Agricultural Universities have stated that the uncooperative attitude of funding agencies is the main reason for delay in release of grants. Some of the Vice-Chancellors of Central Universities, State General Universities and State Agricultural Universities have also reported that there is a defective system of release which results in delays.

The untimely release of grants may entail delay to the University Institutions in further payment of personal claims, salaries and payments to suppliers, and may also result in the taking of loans from the banks or availing of over-draft facilities or of even resorting to the mortgaging of the property of the University Institutions. Due to resource availability with the Government, it may not be possible for them to release the grants-in-aid on a half-yearly basis. As such, it is suggested that quarterly grants, in the beginning of the quarter, should be released to the University Institutions.

TABLE 4.8: Periodicity for Release of Grants

(Percentage responses)

Sr. No.	Particulars/Description	Central Universities	Deemed Universities	State General Universities	State Agricultural Universities
1	2	3	4	5	6
Vice-Chancellors/Directors					
1.	Grants should be released				
1.1	Full in beginning of the year	50.00	0.00	56.25	44.44
1.2	Half yearly (1st installment in beginning and 2nd before 3 months of closure of financial year)	50.00	100.00	25.00	55.55
1.3	Quarterly (in the beginning of each quarter)	0.00	0.00	37.50	11.11
2.	Delay in release of grants is due to				
2.1	Defective system of release	50.00	0.00	68.75	44.44
2.2	Uncooperative attitude of funding agencies	0.00	100.00	62.50	66.66

The Funding Agencies/Governments should issue sanction letters for the whole year in the beginning of the financial year, specifying therein the month and date on which the quarterly grant is to be paid to the University Institutions. The grants for every quarter should be released to the University Institutions automatically as per time schedule given in the sanction letter.

Existing Procedure for the Payment of Grants

The existing procedure of payment of grants in respect of surveyed University Institutions was obtained from the Finance Officers/Comptrollers/Registrars (Table 4.9).

TABLE 4.9: Procedure for the Release of Grants-in-Aid

(Percentage responses)

		University Institutions				
Sr. No.	Particulars/ Description	Central Universities	Deemed Universities	Institutions of National Importance	State General Universities	State Agricultural Universities
1	2	3	4	5	6	7
Finance Officers/ Comptrollers/Registrars						
1.	Grants-in-aid through	—	—	—	—	—
1.1	Bank draft	66.66	33.33	100.00	48.00	69.33
1.2	Treasury	0.00	0.00	0.00	64.00	46.15

All the Surveyed Institutions of National Importance, nearly two thirds of sampled central Universities and State Agricultural Universities are paid grants through Bank drafts. Nearly fifty per cent of the State General universities and one-third of the Deemed Universities are also receiving grants through Bank draft. Most of the State General Universities and some of the State Agricultural Universities have reported that they are getting grants through the Treasury.

The payment of grants through the Treasury involves the procedure of first getting the grant bill countersigned from the funding agency, getting authorisation from the Treasury and thereafter presenting it to the bank for crediting it to the university account. All this results in delay and as such grants should be paid through bank draft.

Nature of Grants

The grants paid to University Institutions are either lapsable or non-lapsable with the close of the financial year. The Finance Officers/Comptrollers/Registrars of the sampled University Institutions were requested to comment on the existing position (Table 4.10).

TABLE 4.10: Nature of Grants (Existing)

(Percentage responses)

		University Institutions				
Sr. No.	Particulars/ Description	Central Universities	Deemed Universities	Institutions of National Importance	State General Universities	State Agricultural Universities
1	2	3	4	5	6	7
	Finance Officers/ Comptrollers/Registrars					
1.	Grants lapsable with the close of financial year in respect of					
1.1	Central Government	0.00	33.33	50.00	32.00	46.15
1.2	State Government	0.00	0.00	0.00	44.00	30.77
1.3	University Grants Commission	66.66	33.33	0.00	16.00	30.77
1.4	Indian Council of Agricultural Research	0.00	0.00	0.00	8.00	23.08
1.5	Local Bodies	0.00	0.00	0.00	0.00	7.69
2.	Capital Grants	0.00	33.33	0.00	16.00	7.69

In half of the cases of Institutions of National Importance and State Agricultural Universities, it has been reported that the grants of Central Government are lapsable with the close of the financial year, whereas in few of the State General Universities and State Agricultural Universities, the State Government grants has been reported to lapse. The University Grants Commission grant has been reported to be lapsable by two thirds of the Central Universities and nearly one-third of the Deemed Universities and State Agricultural Universities. The capital grants has been shown to be lapsable by one-third of the sampled. Deemed Universities and less than seventeen per cent by the State General and State Agricultural Universities.

The Vice-Chancellors/Directors of the Surveyed Universities were requested to express their opinion whether the grants should be lapsable or non-lapsable with the close of the financial year

(Table 4.11).

TABLE 4.11: Nature of Grants (Proposed)

(Percentage responses)

		University Institutions				
Sr. No.	Particulars/ Description	Central Universities	Deemed Universities	Institutions of National Importance	State General Universities	State Agricultural Universities
1	2	3	4	5	6	7
Vice-Chancellors/ Directors						
1.1	Grants should be lapsable	50.00	0.00	—	18.75	0.00
1.2	Non-lapsable	100.00	100.00	—	81.25	100.00
1.3	Revenue grants lapsable	100.00	100.00	—	31.25	11.11
1.4	Capital grants non-lapsable	100.00	0.00	—	62.50	77.77

It is evident that all the Vice-Chancellors of Central Universities, Deemed Universities and State Agricultural Universities and most of the Vice-Chancellors of State General Universities are in favour of non-lapsable grants to the University Institutions. The Vice-Chancellors of Central Universities and Deemed Universities were of the view that revenue grants should be lapsable with the close of the financial year whereas such a step is not favourable to some State General and State Agricultural Universities. All the Vice-Chancellors of Central Universities and most of them in the case of State General Universities and State Agricultural Universities are of the view that capital grants should be non-lapsable.

The last instalment of grants is released to most of the University Institutions at the fag and of the year and it cannot be utilised properly within such a short span of time. Even if capital grants are released during the beginning of the financial year time is needed for its utilisation due to complexity in procedure for the execution and completion of construction works. It has also been observed that in most of the University Institutions the unspent balance held at the close of the financial year is adjusted/deducted from the next year's grants.

All this results in the reduction of the amount of effective grants to the University Institutions thus affecting the various activities of the University Institutions adversely. Therefore, it is suggested that the revenue grants should lapse after one year from the date of sanction/payment. Capital grants should not lapse with the close of the financial year and be allowed to be expended even beyond the plan period in case the situation so warrants.

Types of Grants

The opinion of the Vice-Chancellors/Directors of Surveyed University Institutions on the types of grants, they would prefer, for the University Institutions was also obtained (Table 4.12).

TABLE 4.12: Types of Grants (Proposed)

(Percentage responses)

		University Institutions			
Sr. No.	Particulars/Description	Central Universities	Deemed Universities	State General Universities	State Agricultural Universities
1	2	3	4	5	6
Vice-Chancellors/Directors					
1.	Type of grants desired				
1.1	Block Grants	100.00	0.00	68.75	88.88
1.2	Specific Grants	100.00	100.00	31.25	22.22
1.3	Matching Grants	0.0	0.00	25.00	11.00
1.4	Deficit Grants	50.00	0.00	37.50	33.33

All the Vice-Chancellors of the sampled Central Universities favoured block grants and specific grants to the University. However, they were not in favour of matching grants and only fifty per cent of them also favoured deficit grants to the University Institutions. The Vice-Chancellors of the Deemed Universities were only in favour of specific grants. Most of the Vice-Chancellors of State General Universities and State Agricultural Universities favoured the payment of block grants to University Institutions, whereas some of them also favoured the concept of specific, matching and deficit grants to

University Institutions. The deficit grant has demerits namely, lack of universally agreeable criteria for the determination of deficit and direct interference of the funding agencies thus affecting the autonomy of the University Institutions. Matching grants delay the execution of the various activities particularly the developmental activities as the matching share by the State Governments to lift the University Grants Commission Development Assistance is either not provided at all or provided at a very late stage. The system of block grants as well as specific grants is recommended to the University Institutions in India.

Adequacy of Grants and Measures Adopted to Overcome Difficulties due to Untimely Release of Grants

The position so reported by the Vice-Chancellors/Directors and Finance Officers/Comptrollers/Registrars on the issues of adequacy of grants and measures taken to overcome difficulties due to untimely release of grants are given hereinafter (Table 4.13).

TABLE 4.13: Adequacy of Grants and Measures Adopted to Overcome Difficulty owing to Untimely Release and Inadequacy of Grants

(Percentage responses)

Sr. No.	Particulars/Description	Central Universities	Deemed Universities	Institutions of National Importance	State General Universities	State Agricultural Universities
1	2	3	4	5	6	7
I.	*Vice-Chancellors/Directors*					
1.	Block/maintenance grant adequate	50.00	0.00	N.A.	6.25	33.33
2.	Management of affairs due to delay in release of grant was by					
2.1	Borrowing funds from nationalised banks	0.00	0.00	N.A.	43.75	0.00
2.2	Mortgaging property of University Institutions	0.00	0.00	N.A.	6.25	0.00
2.3	Deferring/postponing contingent/other payments	0.00	100.00	N.A.	75.00	22.22
2.4	Delaying salary of staff	0.00	0.00	N.A.	18.75	0.00

(Contd.)

TABLE 4.13 *(Contd.)*

1	2	3	4	5	6	7
II.	*Finance Officers/ Comptrollers Registrars*					
1.	Grant released during last 5 years was adequate in respect of					
1.1	Central Government	0.00	33.33	50.00	24.00	53.85
1.2	State Government	0.00	0.00	0.00	24.00	53.85
1.3	University Grants Commission	66.66	33.33	0.00	32.00	23.08
1.4	Indian Council of Agricultural Research	33.33	0.00	0.00	36.00	38.46
1.5	State Government Grant Commission/Committee	0.00	0.00	0.00	12.00	0.00
1.6	State bodies	0.00	0.00	0.00	8.00	2.69
2.	Management of affairs due to delay in release of grant was done by					
2.1	Borrowing funds from nationalised banks	33.33	33.33	0.00	40.00	7.69
2.2	Mortgaging property of the University Institution	0.00	0.00	0.00	12.00	7.69
2.3	Deferring/Postponing the contingent payments	66.66	33.33	0.00	64.00	46.15
2.4	Delaying salary of staff	33.33	0.00	0.00	12.00	15.38
2.5	Borrowing funds from CPF/ GPF fund of the employees	33.33	33.33	0.00	8.00	23.08

It can be seen from the above table that half of the Vice-Chancellors of Central Universities are of the opinion that the block/maintenance grant is adequate, whereas one-third who responded in the case of State Agricultural Universities, have also reported in the affirmative. All the Vice-Chancellors of Deemed Universities have reported inadequacy of grants whereas a few of the Vice-Chancellors of State General Universities (6.25 per cent) have reported adequacy of funds. It is only less than half of the Vice-Chancellors of State General Universities who have reported that they resorted to borrowing funds from the nationalised banks, when grants were not released in time, and very few resorted to mortgaging of the university property. All the

Vice-Chancellors of Deemed Universities and three fourths of Vice-Chancellors of State General Universities postponed the payments of 'Contingency and other Payments' on account of delay. The payment of salary has been also delayed in such exigencies by some of the State General Universities.

The adequacy of Central Government grants has been reported by nearly half the Finance Officers/Comptrollers/Registrars of the Institutions of National Importance and State Agricultural Universities, whereas State Government grants have been reported to be adequate in case of most of State Agricultural Universities. Two-thirds of the Finance Officers/Comptrollers/Registrars of Central Universities and nearly one-third of the Deemed Universities and State General Universities have reported adequacy of grants from the University Grants Commission during the past five years. The grants from the Indian Council of Agricultural Research have also been reported to be adequate in the case of about one-third of Central Universities, State General and Agricultural Universities. In certain State General Universities, Central Universities and Deemed Universities, it has been reported by the Finance Officers/Comptrollers/Registrars that they resorted to borrowing funds from nationalised banks. Nearly two thirds of the Finance Officers/Comptrollers/Registrars of Central Universities, State General Universities have reported that they have to postpone the Contingency payments on account of untimely release of grants, whereas such a response has been reported in the case of forty six per cent and thirty per cent of State Agricultural Universities and Deemed Universities, respectively. Delay in payment of salaries has been also reported in some of the Central Universities, few of the State General and Agricultural Universities. Borrowing of funds from CPF/GPF have also been reported by one third of the Finance Officers/Comptrollers/Registrars of Central Universities, Deemed Universities and few State General and Agricultural Universities.

From the above description it can be inferred that the financial position of University Institutions is not sound and this affects the execution of existing programmes as well as the future growth of the University Institutions. It is, therefore, recommended that grants-in-aid to University Institutions should be periodically fixed after taking into account the existing programmes and new schemes/projects. The period for fixation of grants should coincide with the duration of the period covered by the recommendations of the Finance Commission and the Planning Commission to the Government of India.

Grants-in-Aid Rules

The grants-in-aid rules are formulated and promulgated by the Central and State Governments, University Grants Commission, Indian Council of Agricultural Research and other autonomous bodies which are funding agencies. It has been observed that in a very few cases, the Union or the Sate Government has formulated and promulgated separate grants-in-aid rules. Well defined and clearly spelt-out grants-in-aid rules by the funding agencies help in judicious and speedier utilisation of available funds without misappropriation and misutilisation, issuance of grants utilisation certificates by the statutory auditors and submission to the funding agencies for timely release of grants. The examination of existing grants-in-aid rules of some of the State Governments, Central Government and University Grants Commission reveals the following salient points:

The Kerala Government Notification (1978)[4] on grants-in-aid rules provides for (i) block grant and plan schemes grant. The block grant is released on a monthly basis whereas grant for plan scheme is released on a quarterly basis. Provisions exist for making adjustments on the basis of actual expenditure for the whole year at the time of releasing the grant for the subsequent year. In the rules the Government has been vested with powers to withhold, postpone or defer the payment of any of the grants without assigning any reason.

The West Bengal Government has formulated grants-in-aid rules (1981)[5] for release of grants to universities for development schemes. According to which grants are to be released in three instalments on the recommendations of the Chief Engineer. The first instalment (50 per cent) is released on receipt of drawings and estimates. The second instalment (40 per cent) on receipt of vetted progress report (Construction Board Directorate) alongwith statement of funds as received from the University Grants Commission. The third instalment (10 per cent) is released after the receipt of a utilisation certificate and statement of expenditure, vetted by the Construction Board Directorate. Thereafter, the grants utilisation certificate along with the completion report, vetted by the Construction Board Directorate is required to be submitted to the State Government.

The Uttar Pradesh Government (1986)[6] has stipulated the condition that the grant is to be spent only on items so approved by the Government and its utilisation, even temporarily, on items not approved by the Government is not permitted.

The Government of Rajasthan rules for release of grants-in-aid (1983)[7] provides for (i) utilisation of grants for maintenance only, (ii) work-load to university teachers, (iii) change of service conditions of employees, (iv) creation of new posts with the prior approval of Government, (v) non-utilisation of 'non-plan' saving for other purposes and counting it for next year, as grant for dearness allowance increases, (vi) acceptance of schemes/projects involving matching grants of the State Government and devolving financial liability on the university after their completion with the prior approval of the State Government, (vii) prior approval of the Government on decisions, reducing the income of the university, (viii) financial benefits to university employees not to exceed similar benefits to State Government employees and (ix) release of grants once in a quarter on the production of certificate from the Registrar that none of the conditions of grant-in-aid have been violated.

The Government of Tamil Nadu Order (1987)[8] on grants-in-aid rules stipulates the conditions that the retired personnel are to be appointed in the university in accordance with Government policy. Separate accounts for each type of grant are to be maintained. The recruitment in the university services is to be done through the Employment Exchange. The report on recruitment has to be furnished to the State Government within a month of the close of financial year, failing which Government shall stop forthwith the release of further grants.

The grants-in-aid rules so formulated and promulgated by the Government of Jammu and Kashmir provide for the following conditions: Grants to be paid for expenditure already incurred and amount to be sanctioned to the expenditure likely to be expended during the year and grants to be released in three equal instalments payable w.e.f. April every year. The area of a building constructed which exceeds the minimum requirement, when rented out, shall share the rent with the Government. The grant is to be utilised within one year from the date of issue of sanction and the unspent balance thereafter shall be surrendered to the Government or adjusted against the next year's grant.

The conditions stipulated by the Haryana Government (1985)[9] for release of grants are: that the instruction as contained in P.F.R. (Rule 8.14) Vol. I., shall be followed, expenditure shall not exceed the budget provisions; the university shall agree with the Government in the objections raised by the Public Accounts Committee and recurring expenditure shall not be included in respect of vacant/new posts, new schemes and new works carried out in the Plan.

The Government of Maharashtra (1981)[10] has stipulated the following conditions in the grants-in-aid rules: annual increase of six per cent over the previous year grants, grants for establishment expenditure on teaching/non-teaching staff excluding medical allowance, overtime allowance and expenditure on employees engaged on daily wages/consolidated salary. The expenditure on non-salary items has to be managed out of the university income from tuition fees, examination fees, consultancy charges, etc. The grants should be released in three instalments – the first instalment be released in the months of December-January on the basis of six-monthly revised estimates of salary grants.

The State Government of Gujarat has formulated and promulgated grants-in-aid rules (1976)[11] for payment of grants to Gujarat Agricultural University. The salient points provided in the grants-in-aid rules are: grants to be released quarterly on receipt of progress of expenditure in the previous quarter, new schemes out of State grants to be initiated only with the prior approval of Government, expenditure on items of new services; creation of new posts and large scale expansion on approved items with the prior approval of Government and refund of unspent balance at the close of the financial year to the Government failing which interest would be charged from the University.

The Government of Himachal Pradesh (1980)[12] has formulated and promulgated grants-in-aid rules for the release of grants to agricultural universities. The salient features are namely: – the grants can be utilised within one year from the date of its payment and the unspent balance can be spent after the period of one year with the approval of Government, the grant should be utilised for the purpose for which it is sanctioned, the grant is to be released quarterly; the first three quarters of grant to be released on the basis of an unaudited utilisation certificate and the last quarter, after the receipt of audited grants utilisation certificate.

The University Grants Commission (1986)[13] has stipulated the conditions for release of grants to Central Universities – that assets acquired out of the grant will not be disposed of without the prior permission of the Commission and grants shall not be utilised for the purpose other than that for which the grants was sanctioned and the university shall fully implement the official language policy of the Union Government.

The Government of India for release of grants to University Institutions through its Ministry (1986)[14] stipulates the conditions that a performance-cum-achievement report should be enclosed with audited statement of accounts. The Government of India's policy for reservation in appointment should be followed, diversion of grants is not permitted and the sanctioned schemes cannot be transferred to other institutions for implementation; the grants could be refunded in case of misutilisation; unspent balance should be refunded to the Government and the Government at its discretion, may adjust the unspent amount of the previous year in the grants approved for the next year and sufficient number of copies of audited annual accounts alongwith audited report, both in Hindi and English should be made available to the Government.

The Vice-Chancellor/Director and Finance Officer/Comptroller/Registrar has expressed their opinion on various issues concerning grants-in-aid rules (Table 4.14). All the Vice-Chancellors of Deemed Universities are in favour of rigid grants-in-aid rules whereas Vice-Chancellors of sampled Central Universities do no subscribe to this point of view at all. Some of the Vice-Chancellors of State Agricultural Universities and a few of the State General Universities are also in favour of rigid grants-in-aid rules. The Vice-Chancellors of Deemed Universities are satisfied with the existing grants-in-aid rules whereas none of the Vice-Chancellors of sampled Central Universities, one-fourth of State General Universities and about half of the State Agricultural Universities are satisfied with it. The Vice-Chancellors of Deemed Universities are of the opinion that grants-in-aid rules stand in the way of release of grants, whereas such an opinion has not been expressed by Vice-Chancellors of Central Universities and some of the State General Universities and State Agricultural Universities. Most of the Vice-Chancellors of State Agricultural Universities, Central Universities and some of the State General Universities are of the opinion that grants-in-aid rules help in the timely release of grants. Most of the Vice-Chancellors have expressed the view for change of existing grants-in-aid formula.

TABLE 4.14: Grants-in-Aid Rules

(Percentage responses)

Sr. No.	Particulars/Description	Central Univer-sities	Deemed Univer-sities	Institutions of National Importance	State General Univer-sities	State Agricul-tural Univer-sities
1	2	3	4	5	6	7
I.	*Vice-Chancellors/Directors*					
1.	Rigid grants-in-aid rules for release of grants-in-aid	0.00	100.00	N.A.	18.75	44.44
2.	Satisfaction with existing grants-in-aid rules	0.00	100.00	N.A.	25.00	44.44
3.	Grants-in-aid rules					
3.1	Help in timely release of grants	50.00	0.00	N.A.	37.50	77.77
3.2	Stand in the way of release of grants	0.00	100.00	N.A.	43.77	22.22
4.	Grants-in-aid formula needs to be changed	50.00	100.00	N.A.	68.75	66.66
II.	*Finance Officers/ Comptrollers/Registrars*					
1.	Uniform grants-in-aid rules for all University Institutions	0.00	0.00	0.00	56.00	61.54
2.	Separate grants-in-aid rules formulated by funding agencies	33.33	33.33	50.00	52.00	69.33
3.	Grants-in-aid rules as contained in General Financial Rules of the Government are followed	0.00	33.33	0.00	44.00	38.46

Most of the Finance Officers/Comptrollers/Registrars of State General Universities and State Agricultural Universities are of the view that there should be uniform grants-in-aid rules for all University Institutions and each funding agency should formulate its own grants-in-aid rules. About one third of the Vice-Chancellors of Deemed

Universities, State General Universities and State Agricultural Universities have expressed views in favour of grants-in-aid rules as contained in General Financial Rules.

In can be inferred from the above description that there is no uniformity in the grants-in-aid rules so formulated by the Central Government, State Governments and the University Grants Commission, despite the fact that the General Financial Rules and State Financial Rules (published books) provide for standard grants-in-aid rules.

Provision in the grants-in-aid rules conditions like teaching loads for the teachers, creation of posts with the approval of the Government, service conditions for university staff with the approval of Government, non-acceptance/implementation of new schemes without approval of the Government, sanction of grants to meet the expenditure already incurred etc. is an attempt to have an effective control of the management of university finances. This erodes the function and financial autonomy of University Institutions in India. There is no denying the fact that Government and other funding agencies have to satisfy themselves that the funds released by them have been utilised for the purpose for which they have been sanctioned. This can be assured by making necessary provisions in the grants-in-aid rules without affecting the autonomy of University Institutions. The uniformity in grants-in-aid rules of the Central Government, State Governments, the University Grant Commission and the Indian Council of Agricultural Research will go a long way in the improvement of the existing financial management system of University Institutions. The recommendations so made in Model Grants-in-Aid Rules as given hereinafter will provide guidelines and a sound base for the formulation of grant-in-aid rules to the Governments and other funding agencies. These recommendations will also meet the requirements of funding agencies for ensuring utilisation of funds for the purpose for which they are sanctioned and honour the autonomous character of University Institutions.

Model Grants-in-Aid Rules

The salient items/points to be incorporated in the grants-in-aid rules are:

(1) The grants shall be utilised for the maintenance, development and

promotion of facilities for education under various activities of the University Institutions. The maintenance grants shall be utilised for expenditure on staff (teaching and non-teaching); equipments; land; buildings and such other purposes as jointly decided by the funding agencies and University Institutions from time to time.

(2) The grants shall be sanctioned and released by the Government on receipt of written requests from the University Institutions indicating the purpose for which it is required.

(3) The unaudited utilisation certificate shall be furnished for the preceding year on the prescribed proforma by the 15th of April and audited utilisation certificate by 31st December of the next year to the Grants-in-Aid Agencies.

(4) The first three quarterly grants shall be released on the receipt of an unaudited utilisation certificate and last quarterly grant on receipt of an audited utilisation certificate.

(5) The accounts of the university shall be open for test check by the Comptroller and Auditor-General of India.

(6) The audited annual accounts of the university showing the funds received and expenditure there against with a certificate from the statutory auditors that these accounts are properly drawn up so as to exhibit a true and fair picture of the state of affairs of the university shall be submitted by the University Institutions to the Government.

(7) It shall be open to the Government/funding agency to cause physical verification and other enquiries as it may consider necessary to satisfy itself in regard to the expenditure incurred and/or its reasonableness.

(8) In case of misutilisation of funds/grants, it shall be open to the Government to recover the grants from the University Institutions and stop further payments.

(9) Details of the permanent and semi-permanent assets acquired wholly and mainly out of Government grants shall be maintained in a Register in a prescribed proforma. Details of such assets shall be sent annually to the Government.

(10) The assets acquired out of Government grants shall not be disposed of or encumbered or utilised for the purpose other than those for which grants have been sanctioned without the prior approval of the Government.

(11) The diversion of grants-in-aid and entrusting of execution of

schemes from other institutions, though for the utilisation on the same or similar objects amounts to misutilisation of grants and shall not be permitted.

(12) A quarterly progress report of expenditure for the preceding quarter shall be submitted to the Government for the release of the next quarter grant. The expenditure in no case shall exceed the budget provision.

(13) The University Institutions shall assist the Government in the disposal of objections raised by the Public Accounts Committee.

Criteria for Fixation of Grants-in-Aid

The Central Government and the State Governments determine the grants-in-aid to University Institutions in India. The system of adhocism and discrimination exist for determination of grants to most University Institutions in India and the quantum of grants is fixed sub-motto or by scrutinising the proposals of the University Institutions as contained in the budget. The grants to some of the University Institutions are cut due to the tapering system and are decreased due to the matching grants system. It has been observed that in a very few cases, the Union or the State Governments has formulated and promulgated the formula for determining the criteria for fixation of grants-in-aid. To give a strong financial base to University Institutions and to free them from uncertainty regarding funds and to plan judicious and timely utilisation of grants it is highly desirable that the funding agencies should formulate and promulgate criteria/formulae for fixation of grants-in-aid.

An attempt has been made to analyse the existing criteria/formulae of some of the Sampled University Institutions, identify the shortcomings therein and suggest model criteria/formulae for fixation of grants-in-aid to University Institutions in India. The examination of the existing criteria/formulae for determination of grants by some of the State Governments to the University Institutions reveals the following salient features.

The State Government of Kerala has not evolved any formula for determination of grants to the University Institutions. The Government has issued guidelines through notification (1976)[15] for payment of grants to University Institutions. Accordingly, the Government provides block grant and grant to fund plan schemes. Provisions for block grants to the University Institutions is made in the State

Government Budget (subject to availability of funds with the Government) after considering the finances of the University Institutions as verified by the Government auditors by scrutinising the budget estimates of the preceding year. Provision as grants for plan schemes may be made in the State Budget on the basis of estimates furnished by the University and the allocation determined as a result of discussions with the Planning Commission of the Government of India. Besides this the State Governments may provide specific grants to University Institutions.

The West Bengal Government (1979 and 1981)[16, 17] provides grants to University Institutions, the quantum of which is determined on the basis of the budget of the University Institutions. No formula exists for fixation of grants.

The Government of Tamil Nadu has formulated criteria/formulae (1987)[18] for fixation of grants to the University Institutions by determining the base year, net deficit with reference to normal income and expenditure of the University, the revision of pay scales (both teachers and non-teachers) and the block grant is fixed after allowing the per cent increase over the deficit. In addition to block grants so fixed additional expenditure on additional instalments of dearness allowance is also allowed. After adopting the above guidelines, the block grant is being calculated as under:

	Rs. in lakh
Total Income	
Part-I (Non-Plan)	X
Part-II (Plan)	
Grants in respect of transferred/taken over schemes	Y
Total	X + Y
Less income to be deducted	Z
Net income generated by the University	(X+Y) - Z
Total Expenditure	
Part-I (Non-Plan)	H
Part-II (Committed schemes)	

Less capital expenditure and interest on over-draft I
Net expenditure (H - I)
The deficit thus works out to: (H-I) - [(X+Y) - Z]
Block grant works out to: (H-I) + (H-I) - [(X+Y) - Z]
+ 10% of (H-I) + (H-I) - [(X+Y) -Z]

The Government of Karnataka has evolved a separate criteria/Formulae for determination of grants-in-aid (1983 & 1985)[19, 20] for Agricultural Universities and State General Universities. The criteria adopted for fixation of grants-in-aid to Agriculture Universities takes into account net expenditure for the base year as arrived at by deducting the average receipt for five years from the audited expenditure, five per cent growth for each succeeding year is added to the net expenditure, the expenditure for the posts approved by the Government during the year of grant and 3.5 per cent of book value of buildings is also added for fixation of grants.

The formula works out as under:

1. Total expenditure for the base year = X
2. Less average of receipts for the previous five years = Y
3. Net expenditure for the base year = X-Y
4. Plus 5 per cent growth rate for each succeeding year = 105 × (X-Y)
5. Plus salaries on posts approved by the Government and filled up during the year of grant = Z
6. Total block grant for the year = $\frac{105}{100} \times (X-Y) + Z$
7. Book value of buildings = Bd.
8. Add 3.5 per cent of building for maintenance = $\frac{3.5 \text{ Bd.}}{100}$
9. Total block grant for the year = $\frac{105}{100} \times [(X-Y) + Z] + \frac{3.5}{100}$ Bd

The criteria was evolved by the Karnataka Government for fixation of grants to State General Universities for the period 1983-84 to 1988-89 after inviting suggestions of the Vice-Chancellors and taking into consideration the sixty first report of the Estimate Committee (Seventh Lok Sabha) University Funds (1984).[21] The salient features of the criteria are: the expenditure incurred for the year 1982-83 on settled channels, was taken as the base year.

The expenditure on 'settled channels' includes salaries of staff, travelling allowance, office expenditure, pension and leave salary contribution, CPF contribution, fellowships, scholarships, audit charges, equipments costing upto rupees five thousand, examination expenditure, cost of medical allowance, library, printing press expenditure and committed expenditure on posts sanctioned by the University Grants Commission during the plan period. From the gross expenditure so arrived at, the net domestic receipt is deducted for calculation of block grants. Growth rate of 10 per cent per annum, expenditure on maintenance of buildings at the rate of State PWD, an amount of rupees five lakhs for minor works and replacement of equipment and furniture are added to the net expenditure for arriving at the quantum of grant. A special provision of rupees ten lakh has been provided for replacement of obsolete and broken equipment. The expenditure on dearness allowance to staff salaries is not added to the expenditure and separately reimbursed to the university against separate claim. The development expenditure of the universities is met out of development grants for buildings, purchase of equipment and furniture, staff filled on recommendations of the University Grants Commission, continued development scheme of plan period, new development schemes and establishment of new courses of studies. The block grant is refixed at the interval of five years. The expenditure on items not covered under block grants is reimbursed to the university after examining the justification put forth.

The Government of Maharashtra Resolution (1980)[23] on fixation of grants to general universities provides for meeting the establishment expenditure on teaching and non-teaching staff. The establishment expenditure includes salary proper, allowances such as dearness allowance, house rent allowance, leave travel concession, compensatory local allowance, encashment of leave, university's contribution to the contributory provident fund at $8^1/_3$ per cent, but excludes allowances such as cash, medical allowance, overtime expenditure and on employees on daily wages/consolidated salary. The establishment expenditure on self-supporting schemes such as hostels, printing presses, computer centre, management institutions/courses and such other services as identified by the Director of Higher Education or financed by other outside agencies is excluded from the scope of compiling establishment expenditure admissible for the grant. The University is to give an undertaking that it is regulating and managing the expenditure on non-salary items from within its own income from tuition fees, examination fees, consultancy charges, etc.

The State Government of Gujarat through a resolution (1976)[23] has evolved criteria for determination of grants to its Agricultural Universities. According to the said criteria the annual estimates on account of standing charges and new items of expenditure (including 'works' expenditure) as furnished by the university after having been scrutinised by the Government is included in the budget estimates of the Government as lump sum grants-in-aid to the university. The scrutiny of the State Government is restricted to the proposal of the University for staffing pattern and pay-scales proposed by the university with the intention of ensuring that the scales of pay are not more liberal than prescribed by the State Government. No provision on account of any individual works will be admitted in the University budget unless plans and estimates have been approved administratively. The State Government shall not stand committed to bear any additional burden caused by the starting of new schemes without approval of Government and un-approved items of expenditure by the university. Net admitted expenditure on account of standing charges and development expenditure that is total expenditure minus receipt subject to the ceiling of expenditure on the annual plan shall be the basis of determining the quantum of grant-in-aid payable to the university in any financial year.

The Government of Gujarat through a letter (1971)[24] has laid down the criteria for fixation of block maintenance grant and additional block grant for a triennium period (1985-86 onward) for general Universities in the State. While fixing the block grant, the expenditure on repayment of loan and interest, interest on over-draft, schemes not approved by the Government, furniture, equipment, special repair of buildings, scholarships and stipends exceeding fifteen per cent of the total income of tuition fees is not admitted by the Government.

As per these norms the State Government pays during triennium additional block grants amounting to $3^1/_2$ per cent of the wage bill of the preceding year on cumulative basis during last year of triennium. Increase on account of enhanced rates of allowances sanctioned by the Government from time to time during the currency of the triennium the entire expenditure on the approved development schemes of the University Grants Commission and filling up of essentially needed posts as approved bv the Government during the triennium is also provided for.

The Government of Andhra Pradesh (1979)[25] has fixed the block grant to the universities in the State from the period 1978-79 to 1983-84 on the basis of anticipated gross expenditure minus anticipated income of the university at the estimated rates of rupees five lakh per annum. The block grant provision was also made for normal increase in salaries and contingencies at the rate of about 2.9 per cent and 1.9 per cent per annum respectively.

The opinion of Finance Officers/Comptrollers/Registrars on various pertinent issues concerning the fixation of grants-in-aid, was obtained from the University Institutions and is given in Table 4.15.

The Finance Officers/Comptrollers/Registrars of all sampled Central Universities, most of the Agricultural Universities, about half of State General Universities and one third of Deemed Universities are of the view that the grants to University Institutions be assessed on the basis of past year's expenditure with annual percentage increase and the requirements of existing and new programmes should be taken into account. Some of the Vice-Chancellors of State Agricultural Universities and State General Universities also desired that grants-in-aid be fixed on a deficit basis. It has also been reported by all the Institutions of National Importance, by most of the State General Universities and State Agricultural Universities, that the grants-in-aid be fixed on the basis of proposals submitted by them as also endorsed by one third Central Universities and Deemed Universities.

A coordination committee exists for discussion of the requirement of the universities only in the case of some of the State General Universities, and few of the State Agricultural Universities. Discrimination in fixation of grants has also been reported in case of some State General and few State Agricultural Universities. Release of more grants to newly established universities has been reported by some of the State General Universities and few of State Agricultural Universities and Central Universities.

TABLE 4.15: Fixation of Grants-in-Aid

(Percentage responses)

Sr. No.	Particulars/Description	Central Univer-sities	Deemed Univer-sities	Institutions of National Importance	State General Univer-sities	State Agricul-tural Univer-sities
1	2	3	4	5	6	7
	Finance Officers/Comptrollers/ Registrars					
1.	Criteria recommended for the assessment of grants-in-aid					
1.1	Past years grant with increase of certain percentage	0.00	0.00	0.00	16.00	38.46
1.2	Past years' expenditure with increase of certain percentage	100.00	33.33	0.00	44.00	69.33
1.3	Increase in the enrolment of students	0.00	0.00	0.00	8.00	30.77
1.4	On the basis of existing and new programmes	100.00	0.00	0.00	56.00	76.92
1.5	On deficit basis	0.00	0.00	0.00	32.00	38.46
2.	Grant fixed by the Government after getting proposals from the University Institution	33.33	33.33	100.00	84.00	84.62
3.	University Institution associated while finalising quantum of grant	33.00	0.00	100.00	56.00	69.33
4.	Coordination Committee exists to discuss and improve the requirement of University Institution	0.00	0.00	0.00	64.00	38.46
5.	Discrimination by Government while fixing grant	0.00	0.00	0.00	40.00	23.08
6.	Government releases more grant to newly established University Institutions	33.33	0.00	0.00	56.00	38.46

It can be inferred from the above analysis of fixation of grants-in-aid to University Institutions that there is no uniformity in criteria for fixation of grants and the following glaring shortcomings have been observed:

1. The identification and fixing of items of expenditure that is 'settled channels' varies from university to university.
2. The projection of income at the estimated rates during the currency of a block period of the grant is hypothetical and its deduction from the expenditure while fixing grants stand in the way of generating incentive for obtaining more income by the University Institutions.
3. The anticipated expenditure taken into account at the time of fixing the grants is also not realistic.
4. Deduction from total expenditure on account of interest on over-draft and repayment of loans and interest thereon at the time of fixation of grants is not desirable since over-draft and loan facilities are normally resorted to in case of inadequacy of grants and untimely release of grants.
5. Allowing of expenditure to the extent of fifteen per cent of the total income of tuition fee for scholarships, stipends etc. to the students is against the national policy for upliftment of poor sections of the society and encouragement of talent for higher education.
6. Periodicity of block grants and normal rise over the yearly grant is not uniform, rather adhocism prevails.
7. Disallowing of expenditure for special repairs to buildings while fixing the grants adversely affects their maintenance.
8. Adoption of different criteria for fixation of grants by some of the State Governments for the State General and State Agricultural Universities, is irrational.

No Central/State Nodel Agency exists in the country which could advise the Union or State Governments and other funding agencies on various issues concerning funding of University Institutions in India. The University Grants Commission and the Indian Council of Agricultural Research are also not in a position to contribute much due to the fact that their advice is not mandatory on State Governments since education is a State subject though on concurrent list. The efforts of the Government of some States like Madhya Pradesh for channelising grants to the University Institutions through the State University Committee has not been of much help to the University Institutions for improving their financial positions/status. It is, therefore, desirable to suggest guidelines for determination of uniform criteria for fixation of grants to University Institutions in India.

Model Criteria for Fixation of Grants-in-Aid

The criteria suggested is:

1. The fixation of block grant for maintenance (non-plan) should coincide with the duration of the period covered by the recommendations of the Finance Commission of the Government of India and development assistance (Plan) should coincide with the Five Year Plans, based on the recommendations of the Planning Commission to the Government of India. This is desirable because the quantum of grants to State Governments under Non-plan and plan is determined by the Finance Commission and Planning Commission to the Government of India in terms of guidelines 5(iv) (a) of the Finance Commission and instructions of the Central Government. The quantum of grants under Non-plan and plan should be determined after discussing the proposals/requirement of the University Institutions at the Government/University Grants Commission level thereafter with these two national bodies.
2. The expenditure for determining the grants should be taken for the year preceding the base year.
3. The requirement of the University Institutions under Non-Plan should be based on the items of expenditure, viz., (i) Salaries including Travelling Allowance, (ii) Filling up of the posts essentially required during the period for which the grant is to be fixed; (iii) Revision of pay-scales of university staff (inclusive of arrears and normal increase) during the currency of the period for fixation of grants; (iv) Transfer of plan scheme to non-plan; (v) Contingent expenditure like laboratory equipment, chemicals, wages etc.; (vi) Maintenance of buildings, roads, water, electricity, etc.; (vii) Scholarships and stipends to students; (viii) Replacement of obsolete or broken equipments; (x) Retiring benefits to employees i.e., pension, gratuity, contributory provident fund, leave encashment, ex-gratia grants, etc.
4. The domestic income of the University Institutions should not be deducted from the total expenditure while fixing grants-in-aid so as to provide incentive to University Institutions to generate more

income and to help in improving their financial position.

5. The amount of grants so fixed should be provided to the University Institutions as block grants and not deficit grants.
6. Annual growth of ten per cent to meet expenditure on account of grant of annual increments, rise in wages of labour, general rise in prices index should be allowed.
7. The interest on overdraft, repayment of loans etc. should not be deducted from the total expenditure at the time of fixation of grants-in-aid as in the case of most of the universities, these facilities are availed of with the prior approval of the Government as per provision of the Act and Statutes of the University concerned.
8. The plan grants should include the requirement of the university for raising infrastructures and other physical facilities, starting of new schemes, programmes of teaching, research etc., and matching grants for claiming development assistance from the University Grants Commission, the Indian Council of Agricultural Research and other funding agencies, based on the future development programmes of the University Institutions.

REFERENCES

1. University Grants Commission, Letter No. F.20-1/79 (OH) (State) (Misc.), 1987.
2. Comptroller and Auditor General of India. Account Code Vol. I, Article 34(b), 1972, p.78.
3. P. Muthuswamy. *Introduction to Indian Government Accounts and Audit*, Swamy Publications, 1981.
4. Government of Kerala. Higher Education (B) Department Notification No. 5035/B 2/78-2/H-Edn., 1978.
5. Government of West Bengal. Education Department (University Education Branch), Letter No. 252 (7)-Edn., (U), 1981.
6. Government of Uttar Pradesh. Letter No. 2464/15-86-46(14)/75, 1986.
7. Government of Rajasthan. Education (GR-VI) Department, Letter No. F. 13(5) Edn./VI/83, 1983.
8. Government of Tamil Nadu. Agriculture (AU-1), Department Order No. G.O. MS No. 878 & 1380, 1987.
9. Government of Haryana. Education and Agriculture Department. Letter No. 42/18/86-Edn. 196, 1987 and Memo No. 1439 – Agr.-II (I)-85, 1985.
10. Government of Maharashtra. Education and Employment Department, Resolution No. NISG-1180/174980(5555) UNI-I, 1981.
11. Government of Gujarat. Agriculture Forest and Cooperation Department, Resolution No. GAU-1372/11/E, 1976.
12. Government of Himachal Pradesh. Department of Agriculture, Notification No. Agr. A(3)-1/80, 1980.

13. University Grants Commission. Letter No. F.21-4/86 (NP-I), 1986.
14. Government of India, Ministry of Planning, Department of Statistics. Letter No. O-13012/186-Coord., 1986.
15. Government of Kerala, Department of Higher Education. Notification No. 5035/B 2/78-2/Edn., 1976.
16. The Calcutta University Act, 1979. Section 46(1).
17. The Rabindra Bharti Act, 1981. Section 41(1).
18. Government of Tamil Nadu, Education (HI) Department. Letter No. G.O.Ms. No. 575, 1987.
19. Government of Karnataka, Department of Agriculture and Animal Husbandry. Letter No. AAH 73 AKM 82, 1983.
20. Government of Karnataka, Department of Education. Letter No. E D. 2111 IE (A) (B & A) 84, 1985.
21. Government of India, Ministry of Education and Culture, Department of Education No. F.I. 12/84 Sch 2, 1984.
22. Government of Maharashtra. Education and Employment Department. Resolution No. USG -1 (80)/174980 (5555) UNI - I, 1980.
23. Government of Gujarat, Department of Agriculture, Forest and Cooperation. Resolution No. GAU-1372-11-E, 1976.
24. Government of Gujarat, Education Department. Letter No. USG/1170/110389 Kh., 1971.
25. Government of Andhra Pradesh, Education (C) Department. G.O.Ms. No. 32 D Edn., 1979.

5

PATTERN OF EXPENDITURE AND FINANCIAL HEALTH OF UNIVERSITY INSTITUTION IN INDIA

THE AVAILABLE funds at the disposal of an organisation like University Institution are to be utilised on various activities for the achievement of objectives/goals set for it. The available funds are classified into two broadly accepted categories of recurring and non-recurring income and are accordingly expended on various activities so falling under each category. The recurring income of the University Institution is by tradition expended on various items for the maintenance of existing activities viz. salaries of teaching and non-teaching staff, grants to colleges, apparatus, chemicals and consumable stores, furniture, library and other miscellaneous items like scholarships, stipends, sports and conduct of examinations. The non-recurring income of the University Institution is expended for raising various infrastructure of permanent nature like library (books, journals and other related expenditure), buildings (both academic, and non-academic), equipment and other items (including expenditure on maintenance of buildings etc). University Institutions are established mainly for the cause of education and as such the priority of expenditure should be on teaching inputs, cost of students welfare activities, cost of examinations, cost of supporting services and cost of construction of various infrastructures. The ingenuity of University Institutions lies in the optimal pattern of expenditure on its different activities keeping in view the priority. The growth, development and peace in University Institutions depends mainly upon its financial health which can be approximately known on the basis of surplus or deficit over income and expenditure.

The effectiveness and efficiency of management of university finances can be known to a great from its pattern of expenditure and its financial health. As such an attempt has been made to analyse the existing pattern of expenditure and financial health of University Institution in India. The normative pattern of expenditure both recurring and non-recurring has also been suggested for effective and efficient utilisation of available funds.

Pattern of Expenditure

The pattern of expenditure has been analysed separately for recurring and non-recurring items of expenditure in respect of Central Universities; Deemed Universities, and State General Universities. The findings given hereinafter are based on the data so obtained from the University Grants Commission for the three consecutive years i.e. 1982-83 to 1984-85.

Central Universities

The item-wise examination of recurring expenditure as given in Table 5.1 reveals that highest expenditure on salary of teaching staff has been reported in the case of Visva Bharti (33.3 per cent) and the lowest (15.0 per cent) in the University of Hyderabad. The model value in respect of this item of expenditure is about 23 per cent. The highest expenditure (40.9 per cent) on non-teaching staff has been reported in the case of Aligarh Muslim University, and the lowest (14.3 per cent) in the case of Jawaharlal Nehru University, whereas its model value is about 27 per cent. The expenditure on apparatus, chemicals and other consumable stores varies from 0.2 per cent to 15.9 per cent, the highest in the University of Hyderabad and the lowest in Banaras Hindu University. The highest expenditure (57.8 per cent) in the case of Visva Bharti and the lowest (27.8 per cent) in the University of Hyderabad has been reported on 'Miscellaneous Items', which is the highest amongst the items of expenditure. The expenditure on library varies from 0.3 to 14.0 per cent, the highest (14.0 per cent) in the case of the University of Hyderabad and the lowest (0.3 per cent) in the University of Delhi. Only in the case of two universities, viz. the University of Hyderabad and the North Eastern Hill University the expenditure on 'Library' has been reported to be more than the national recommendations of six per cent.

The position of non-recurring expenditure as given in Table 5.2 reveals that consistently highest expenditure is under the item 'Building', varying from 9.46 per cent to 84.68 per cent in respect of

TABLE 5.1: Recurring Expenditure (Plan and Non-Plan) of Central Universities (1982-85)

(Amount in 00's Rupees)

University Institution and Year	Items							
	Salaries		Grants to Colleges	Apparatus, chemicals and consumable stores	Furniture	Library	Other Misc. items scholarships, stipends, sports, conduct of exams. etc	Total
	Teaching staff	Non-Teaching staff						
1	2	3	4	5	6	7	8	9
University of Hyderabad								
1982-83	27,377 (15.9)	48,900 (28.4)	—	24,398 (14.2)	957 (0.6)	22,599 (13.1)	47,808 (27.8)	1,72,040 (100.0)
1983-84	30,654 (15.0)	56,776 (27.7)	—	32,673 (15.9)	871 (0.4)	26,445 (12.9)	57,616 (28.1)	2,05,035 (100.0)
1984-85	37,572 (15.6)	65,882 (27.4)	—	33,873 (14.1)	1,790 (0.8)	33,672 (14.0)	67,467 (28.1)	2,40,256 (100.0)
North Eastern Hill University								
1982-83	45,601 (19.3)	67,624 (28.7)	—	-	5,905 (2.5)	22,145 (9.4)	94,533 (40.1)	2,35,808 (100.0)
1983-84	45,780 (16.2)	81,267 (28.7)	—	-	8,696 (3.1)	30,857 (10.9)	1,16,633 (41.1)	2,83,233 (100.0)
1984-85	87,897 (24.7)	79,119 (22.2)	1,000 (0.2)	-	6,023 (1.7)	27,518 (7.7)	1,54,470 (43.51)	3,56,027 (100.0)

(Contd.)

TABLE 5.1 *Contd.*

1	2	3	4	5	6	7	8	9
Aligarh Muslim University								
1982-83	2,66,371	4,72,561	—	7,582	4,913	26,650	3,78,158	11,56,235
	(23.0)	(40.9)		(0.7)	(0.4)	(2.3)	(32.7)	(100.0)
1983-84	3,00,185	5,24,865	—	41,245	11,202	32,780	4,64,720	13,74,977
	(21.8)	(38.2)		(3.0)	(0.8)	(2.4)	(33.8)	(100.0)
1984-85	3,44,778	6,45,631	—	23,525	7,302	35,762	5,72,582	16,29,530
	(21.1)	(39.6)		(1.5)	(0.5)	(2.2)	(35.1)	(100.0)
Banaras Hindu University								
1982-83	3,72,415	5,26,288	—	11,345	4,616	26,123	10,06,903	19,47,690
	(19.1)	(27.0)		(0.6)	(0.2)	(1.3)	(51.8)	(100.0)
1983-84	4,10,884	5,96,029	—	3,342	4,857	28,689	11,65,091	22,08.892
	(18.6)	(27.0)		(0.2)	(0.2)	(1.3)	(52.7)	(100.0)
1984-85	4,82,380	6,31,738	—	24,800	4,607	30,767	14,25,478	25,99,770
	(18.6)	(24.3)		(1.0)	(0.1)	(1.1)	(54.9)	(100.0)
Visva Bharti								
1982-83	80,500	84,139	—	14,753		7,023	2,55,019	4,41,434
	(18.2)	(19.1)		(3.3)		(1.6)	(57.8)	(100.0)
1983-84	1,14,809	1,13,736	—	8,149	961	8,171	2,14,349	4,60,175
	(24.9)	(24.7)		(1.8)	(0.2)	(1.8)	(46.6)	(100.0)
1984-85	1,31,281	1,07,418	—	3,631	2,948	13,460	2,15,692	5,14,430
	(33.3)	(20.9)		(0.7)	(0.6)	(2.6)	(41.9)	(100.0)

(Contd.)

TABLE 5.1 *Contd.*

1	2	3	4	5	6	7	8	9
University of Delhi								
1982-83	1,92,075	2,76,352	—	9,885	5,894	—	2,95,227	7,79,443
	(24.6)	(35.4)		(1.3)	(0.2)		(37.9)	(100.0)
1983-84	2,14,739	3,30,902	—	10,645	6,064	5,372	3,57,452	9,25,174
	(23.2)	(35.8)		(1.2)	(0.06)	(0.6)	(38.6)	(100.0)
1984-85	2,40,452	3,88,221	—	11,680	8,566	3,630	4,31,957	10,84,496
	(22.11)	(35.8)		(1.1)	(0.8)	(0.3)	(39.9)	(100.0)
Jawaharlal Nehru University								
1982-83	1,03,644	96,387	—	13,695	—	5,376	2,02,296	4,21,398
	(24.6)	(22.91)		(3.2)		(1.3)	(48.0)	(100.0)
1983-84	1,12,516	75,292	—	13,306	3,737	25,189	2,95,718	5,25,758
	(21.4)	(14.3)		(2.52)	(0.7)	(4.8)	(56.3)	(100.0)
1984-85	1,32,369	1,25,241	—	16,660	—	8,233	2,58,523	5,41,026
	(24.5)	(23.1)		(3.1)		(1.5)	(47.8)	(100.0)

Source: University Grants Commission.

Note: Figures in parenthesis are proportion of Income in terms of percentages.

TABLE 5.2: Non Recurring Expenditure (Plan and Non-Plan) of Central Universities (1982-85)

(Amount in 00's Rupees)

University Institution and year	Items				
	Library	Building	Equipments	Other items	Total
1	2	3	4	5	6
University of Hyderabad					
1982-83	2,867	22,560	4,415	10,920	40,762
	(7.03)	(55.35)	(10.83)	(26.79)	(100.0)
1983-84	260	43,602	20,445	5,799	70,106
	(0.37)	(62.19)	(29.17)	(8.27)	(100.0)
1984-85	887	87,154	71,967	9,459	1,69,467
	(0.52)	(51.43)	(42.47)	(5.58)	(100.0)
North Eastern Hill University					
1982-83	—	21,103	18,962	16,091	56,156
		(37.58)	(33.77)	(28.65)	(100.0)
1983-84	—	1,18,019	19,463	1,885	1,39,367
		(84.68)	(13.97)	(1.35)	(100.0)
1984-85	13,089	2,00,827	60,869	71,618	3,46,403
	(3.78)	(57.97)	(17.57)	(20.68)	(100.0)
Aligarh Muslim University					
1982-83	7,846	66,492	33,909	2,815	1,11,062
	(7.06)	(57.86)	(30.55)	(2.53)	(100.0)
1983-84	10,281	1,19,584	63,794	2,371	1,96,030
	(5.24)	(61.00)	(32.55)	(1.21)	(100.0)
1984-85	22,292	1,24,562	1,85,780	870	3,33,504
	(6.68)	(37.34)	(55.72)	(0.26)	(100.0)
Banaras Hindu University					
1982-83	11,065	60,145	26,014	94,177	1,91,401
	(5.78)	(31.42)	(13.58)	(49.22)	(100.0)
1983-84	3,908	94,804	81,383	1,40,526	3,20,621
	(1.22)	(29.59)	(25.37)	(43.82)	(100.0)
1984-85	9,789	49,568	1,17,091	2,29,328	4,05,776
	(2.41)	(12.21)	(28.85)	(56.53)	(100.0)
Visva Bharti					
1982-83	3,980	4,030	—	2,60,449	2,68,459
	(1.48)	(1.50)		(97.02)	(100.0)
1983-84	6,245	10,891	967	48,798	66,901
	(9.33)	(16.28)	(1.45)	(72.94)	(100.0)

(Contd.)

TABLE 5.2 Contd.

1	2	3	4	5	6
1984-85	17,159	19,101	24,464	1,41,177	2,01,901
	(8.49)	(9.46)	(12.12)	(69.93)	(100.0)
University of Delhi					
1982-83	61,864	47,825	32,246	—	1,41,935
	(43.58)	(33.69)	(22.73)		(100.0)
1983-84	68,961	63,177	25,374	18,420	1,75,932
	(39.20)	(35.91)	(14.42)	(10.47)	(100.0)
1984-85	1,15,804	68,083	1,39,727	—	3,23,614
	(35.78)	(21.04)	(43.18)		(100.0)
Jawaharlal Nehru University					
1982-83	17,329	30,148	6,892	1,930	56,299
	(30.78)	(53.55)	(12.24)	(3.43)	(100.0)
1983-84	17,832	39,621	17,379	2,359	77,191
	(23.10)	(51.34)	(22.51)	(3.05)	(100.0)
1984-85	45,713	69,098	85,522	4,787	2,05,120
	(22.30)	(33.68)	(41.69)	(2.33)	(100.0)

Source: University Grants Commission.
Note: Figures in parenthesis are proportion of Income in terms of percentages.

all universities excepting Visva Bharti in whose case the highest expenditure is under 'Other Items', which varies from 69.93 to 97.02 per cent. The expenditure on library (including books, journals and other library equipments) was the highest (43.58 per cent) in the case of the University of Delhi and the lowest in the University of Hyderabad (0.37 per cent). The University of Delhi and Jawaharlal Nehru University are spending more than 20 per cent on library whereas in the case of the rest of the universities the expenditure on this item is less than 9 per cent. The highest expenditure (55.72 per cent) on the item 'Equipments' was in the case of Aligarh Muslim University, and the lowest (1.45 per cent) in Visva Bharati. Except for Visva Bharti, the highest expenditure (56.53 per cent) on 'Other Items' was in the case of Banaras Hindu University and the lowest (0.26 per cent) in the case of Aligarh Muslim University.

Demand Universities

It can be seen from Table 5.3 that amongst the items of recurring expenditure, the highest expenditure has been reported on 'Other

TABLE 5.3: Recurring Expenditure (Plan and Non-Plan) of Deemed Universities (1982-83 to 1984-85)

(Amount in 00's Rupees)

University Institution and State and Year	Items							
	Salaries		Grants to Colleges	Apparatus, chemicals and consumable stores	Furniture	Library	Other Misc. items scholarships, stipends, sports, conduct of exams. etc	Total
	Teaching staff	Non-Teaching staff						
1	2	3	4	5	6	7	8	9
Andhra Pradesh								
1982-83	29,963	25,475	6,314	1,478	223	454	23,139	87,046
	(34.42)	(29.27)	(7.25)	(1.70)	(0.26)	(0.52)	(26.58)	(100.00)
1983-84	36,278	31,301	7,157	2,064	172	399	26,449	103,820
	(34.94)	30.15)	(6.89)	(1.99)	(0.17)	(0.38)	(25.48)	(100.00)
1984-85	39,268	35,455	7,554	2,448	1,527	645	27,,859	114,756
	(34.22)	(30.90)	(6.58)	(2.13)	(1.33)	(0.56)	(24.28)	(100.00)
Bihar								
1982-83	12,660	26,800	—	—	—	3,930	120,670	164,060
	(7.72)	(16.34)				(2.40)	(73.54)	(100.00)
1983-84	15,020	27,170	—	—	—	3,700	140,000	185,890
	(8.08)	(14.62)				(1.99)	(75.31)	(100.00)
1984-85	36,530	67,000	—	—	—	4,460	108,980	216,970
	(16.84)	(30.88)				(2.05)	(50.23)	(100.00)

(Contd.)

TABLE 5.3 *Contd.*

1	2	3	4	5	6	7	8	9
Gujarat								
1982-83	17,407	12,460	—	—	137	75	17,958	48,037
	(36.24)	(25.94)			(0.29)	(0.16)	(37.37)	(100.00)
1983-84	18,865	16,028	—	26	—	73	29,913	64,705
	(28.88)	(24.77)		(0.01)		(0.11)	(46.23)	(100.00)
1984-85	22,016	18,922	—	95	—	71	45,119	86,223
	(25.53)	(21.95)		(0.11)		(0.08)	(52.33)	(100.00)
Karnataka								
1982-83	—	—	—	—	—	—	—	—
1983-84	359,130	—	100	48,640	4,340	52,650	207,270	672,130
	(53.43)		(0.01)	(7.24)	(0.65)	(7.83)	(30.84)	(100.00)
1984-85	454,398	—	—	133,778	1,639	50,603	182,499	822,917
	(55.22)			(16.26)	(0.20)	(6.15)	(22.17)	(100.00)
Maharashtra								
1982-83	15,843	10,968	—	—	2,390	1,842	12,570	43,613
	(36.33)	(25.15)			(5.48)	(4.22)	(28.82)	(100.00)
1983-84	18,271	12,880	—	—	2,668	1,892	15,451	51,162
	(35.72)	(25.17)			(5.21)	(3.70)	(30.20)	(100.00)
1984-85	14,988	21,836	—	—	3,978	3,179	18,979	62,960
	(23.81)	(34.68)			(6.32)	(5.05)	(30.14)	(100.00)
Rajasthan								
1982-83	—	—	—	—	—	—	—	—
1983-84	109,062	7,774	53	21,878	24	7,458	42,925	189,174
	(57.65)	(4.12)	(0.03)	(11.56)	(0.01)	(3.94)	(22.69)	(100.00)
1984-85	112,697	14,275	234	27,448	30	3,739	88,107	246,430
	(45.72)	(5.78)	(0.08)	(11.14)	(0.01)	(1.52)	(35.75)	(100.00)

(Contd.)

TABLE 5.3 *Contd.*

1	2	3	4	5	6	7	8	9
Tamil Nadu								
1982-83	12,591	8,168	—	481	335	435	16,997	39,007
	(32.28)	(20.94)		(1.23)	(0.86)	(1.12)	(43.57)	(100.00)
1983-84	14,640	11,258	—	1,241	707	1,168	20,416	49,430
	(29.62)	(22.78)		(2.51)	(1.43)	(2.36)	(41.30)	(100.00)
1984-85	26,118	14,321	—	4,459	2,076	1,012	23,004	70,990
	(36.79)	(20.17)		(6.28)	(2.92)	(1.42)	(32.42)	(100.00)
Uttar Pradesh								
1982-83	38,272	14,090	—	1,389	672	960	11,577	66,960
	(57.16)	(21.04)		(2.07)	(1.00)	(1.43)	(17.30)	(100.00)
1983-84	40,410	21,884	—	1,372	516	928	15,442	80,552
	(50.17)	(27.17)		(1.70)	(0.64)	(1.15)	(19.17)	(100.00)
1984-85	47,326	30,215	—	1,801	1,00	1,340	15,980	97,665
	(46.48)	(30.94)		(1.84)	(1.03)	(1.37)	(16.36)	(100.00)
Delhi								
1982-83	70,516	27,223	—	1,423	359	6,894	58,034	164,450
	(42.88)	(16.56)		(0.86)	(0.22)	(4.19)	(35.29)	(100.00)
1983-84	75,900	41,980	230	1,160	2,390	8,720	73,350	203,730
	(37.26)	(20.61)	(0.11)	(0.57)	(1.17)	(4.28)	(36.00)	(100.00)
1984-85	87,599	47,633	—	2,551	1,010	11,194	74,917	222,904
	(38.95)	(21.18)		(1.13)	(0.45)	(4.98)	(33.31)	(100.00)

Source: University Grants Commission

Note: Figures in parenthesis are proportion of income in terms of percentages.

Miscellaneous Items', the highest (75.31 per cent) being in the case of institutions in Bihar State and the lowest (16.36 per cent) being in respect of institutions in the State of Uttar Pradesh. The expenditure on teaching staff was the highest (57.65 per cent) in the case of institutions in the State of Rajasthan and the lowest (7.72 per cent) in respect of institutions located in the State of Bihar, whereas in the case of non-teaching staff the highest (34.68 per cent) and, lowest expenditure (14.62 per cent) has been reported in the case of institutions located in the States of Maharashtra and Bihar, respectively, The expenditure on teaching staff has been reported to be less than 20 per cent in the case of institutions in the State of Bihar, whereas it has been reported to be less than 25 per cent on non-teaching staff in respect of all institutions except those located in the States of Uttar Pradesh, Maharashtra and Andhra pradesh. The expenditure under the items, "Apparatus, Chemicals and other Consumable Stores", is reported to be the highest (16.26 per cent) in the case of institutions located in the State of Karnataka and the lowest (0.57 per cent) in the case of institutions of Delhi. The recurring expenditure under the item 'Library' was the highest (7.83 per cent) in the case of institutions in the State of Karnataka and the lowest (0.38 per cent) in respect of institutions located in the State of Andhra Pradesh. It is pertinent to point out that expenditure on the items, 'Apparatus, Chemicals and other Consumable Stores' and 'Library' is negligible in respect of institutions in Gujarat State.

It is revealed from Table 5.4 that non-recurring expenditure on the items, 'Buildings' is the first in order of priority. The highest expenditure (84.89 per cent) on this item has been reported in the case of institutions in Delhi, whereas in the case of institutions located in the State of Andhra Pradesh, it is the lowest (3.68 per cent). Under the item 'Library' the highest expenditure (41.98 per cent) has been reported in the case of institutions located in Maharashtra State and the lowest (0.85 per cent) in the case of institutions located in Karnataka State. The expenditure on 'Equipment' was the highest (72.39 per cent) in the case of institutions in the State of Bihar and the lowest (2.93 per cent) for institutions located in the State of Tamil Nadu. With one or two exceptions, the expenditure on this item was more than 20 per cent. The expenditure on 'Other Items', has been reported to be the highest (50.29 per cent) in the case of institutions located in the State of Maharashtra whereas it was negligible in the case of Rajasthan for all the two years.

TABLE 5.4: Non Recurring Expenditure (Plan and Non-Plan) of Deemed Universities (1982-83 to 1984-85)

(Amount in 00's Rupees)

University Institution/ State and year	Items				Total
	Library	Buildings	Equipments	Other items	
1	2	3	4	5	6
Andhra Pradesh					
1982-83	6,075	1,540	21,694	10,356	39,665
	(15.32)	(3.88)	(54.69)	(26.11)	(100.00)
1983-84	6,484	30,766	17,105	1,765	56,123
	(11.55)	(54.82)	(30.48)	(3.15)	(100.00)
1984-85	7,133	19,951	20,642	8,303	56,029
	(12.73)	(35.61)	(36.84)	(14.82)	(100.00)
Bihar					
1982-83	2,250	12,500	2,310	650	17,710
	(12.70)	(70.58)	(13.05)	(3.67)	(100.00)
1983-84	3,330	—	13,080	3,680	20,090
	(16.58)		(65.10)	(18.32)	(100.00)
1984-85	3,660	2,810	22,290	2,030	30,790
	(11.89)	(9.13)	(72.39)	(6.59)	(100.00)
Gujarat					
1982-83	5,456	5,377	4,838	—	15,671
	(34.82)	(34.31)	(30.87)		(100.00)
1983-84	6,246	3,351	6,272	363	16,232
	(38.48)	(20.64)	(38.64)	(2.24)	(100.00)
1984-85	8,499	23,333	21,380	—	53,212
	(15.97)	(24.04)	(50.73)	(21.57)	(100.00)
Karnataka					
1982-83	2,900	85,760	—	47,710	136,370
	(2.13)	(62.89)		(34.98)	(100.00)
1983-84	2,430	169,220	62,130	51,150	284,930
	(0.85)	(59.39)	(21.81)	(17.95)	(100.00)
1984-85	17,751	116,642	246,086	104,660	485,139
	(3.66)	(24.04)	(50.73)	(21.57)	(100.00)
Maharashtra					
1982-83	1,486	767	1,212	3,506	6,971
	(21.32)	(11.00)	(17.39)	(50.29)	(100.00)
1983-84	1,888	—	1,297	1,312	4,497
	(41.98)		(28.84)	(29.18)	(100.00)
1984-85	2,961	4,382	5,335	3,607	16,285
	(18.18)	(26.91)	(32.76)	(22.15)	(100.00)

(Contd.)

1	2	3	4	5	6
Rajasthan					
1982-83	2,220	2,784	3,121	—	8,105
	(27.14)	(34.35)	(38.51)		(100.00)
1983-84	5,300	5,433	3,885	215	14,833
	(35.73)	(36.63)	(26.19)	(1.45)	(100.00)
1984-85	10,625	14,723	29,620	584	55,552
	(19.12)	(26.20)	(53.33)	(1.05)	(100.00)
Tamil Nadu					
1982-83	1,546	8,981	840	—	11,367
	(13.60)	(79.01)	(7.39)		(100.00)
1983-84	984	11,910	496	3,494	16,884
1984-85	2,599	7,564	2,629	2,908	15,700
	(16.55)	(48.18)	(16.75)	(18.52)	(100.00)
Uttar Pradesh					
1982-83	2,304	1,215	6,294	2,707	12,520
	(18.40)	(9.71)	(50.24)	(21.62)	(100.00)
1983-84	4,958	12,599	7,416	2,914	27,887
	(17.78)	(45.18)	(26.59)	(10.45)	(100.00)
1984-85	6,871	27,026	13,935	8,078	55,910
	(12.29)	(48.34)	(24.92)	(14.45)	(100.00)
Delhi					
1982-83	3,983	83,124	4,600	6,201	97,917
	(4.07)	(84.89)	(4.71)	(6.23)	(100.00)
1983-84	3,330	12,260	11,130	2,440	29,160
	(11.42)	(42.04)	(38.17)	(8.37)	(100.00)
1984-85	4,839	75,529	19,237	18,891	118,496
	(4.88)	(63.74)	(16.24)	(15.94)	(100.00)

State General Universities

The percentage recurring expenditure on the salary of non-teaching staff ranged from 5.93 per cent in the universities in Bihar State to 47.65 per cent in the universities of Jammu and Kashmir State (Table 5.5). On the other hand, the proportionate expenditure on the salary of teaching staff in the Universities of Bihar, Karnataka, Manipur, Punjab and Rajasthan States ranged from 28.68 per cent (Karnataka State Universities) to 36.47 per cent (Rajasthan State Universities). The alarming figure of expenditure (81.44 per cent) on teaching staff in case of universities in Bihar State is due to the fact that all the affiliated colleges in the said State were converted into Constituent Colleges and grants/funds are released to them by the universities. On the next item of expenditure in order of priority viz. 'Miscellaneous

TABLE 5.5: Recurring Expenditure (Plan and Non-Plan) of State General Universities (1982-83 to 1984-85)

(Amount in 00's Rupees)

University Institution/ States and Year	Items							
	Salaries		Grants to Colleges	Apparatus, chemicals and consumable stores	Furniture	Library	Other Misc. items scholarships, stipends, sports, conduct of exams. etc	Total
	Teaching staff	Non-Teaching staff						
1	2	3	4	5	6	7	8	9
1. Andhra Pradesh								
1982-83	6,39,081	8,03,155	2,10,397	86,869	5,442	30,720	5,61,304	23,56,969
	(27.11)	(34.07)	(8.98)	(3.68)	(0.23)	(2.15)	(23.81)	(100.00)
1983-84	8,45,564	9,31,015	2,53,921	87,602	13,652	58,572	6,55,400	24,35,016
	(24.61)	(38.23)	(10.43)	(3.59)	(0.56)	(2.40)	(26.91)	(100.00)
1984-85	2,72,487	3,73,820	2,23,207	18,294	7,893	23,513	3,24,429	12,43,643
	(21.91)	(30.06)	(17.95)	(1.47)	(1.83)	(1.89)	(26.89)	(100.00)
2. Assam								
1982-83	88,504	93,822	85	1,683	58	9,703	1,54,171	348,026
	(25.43)	(26.96)	(0.02)	(0.48)	(0.12)	(2.78)	(44.80)	(100.00)
1983-84	99,752	1,24,505	618	3,150	211	10,925	1,49,672	3,84,832
	(24.88)	(32.35)	(0.16)	(0.82)	(0.05)	(2.84)	(38.89)	(100.00)
1984-85	—	—	—	—	—	—	—	—

(Contd.)

TABLE 5.5 *Contd.*

1	2	3	4	5	6	7	8	9
3. Bihar								
1982-83	9,56,333	3,82,687	6,52,091	82,330	3,007	19,598	3,80,116	20,76,242
	(46.06)	(18.43)	(31.41)	(3.96)	(0.14)	(0.94)	(18.31)	(100.00)
1983-84	13,36,020	4,85,176	17,67,306	1,39,992	4,637	25,299	4,58,554	42,11,914
	((31.72)	(11.52)	(41.96)	(3.20)	(0.11)	(0.60)	(10.89)	(100.00)
1984-85	10,13,153	73,831	36,599	6,427	6,686	—	1,07,535	12,44,031
	(81.44)	(5.93)	(2.94)	(0.52)	(0.54)	—	(8.62)	(100.00)
4. Gujarat								
1982-83	10,36,153	2,10,978	30	26,173	2,525	25,883	3,18,936	7,07,648
	(14.64)	(29.81)	(0.004)	(3.70)	(0.36)	(3.66)	(45.07)	(100.00)
1983-84	1,38,388	2,70,030	50	16,423	3,634	32,914	3,85,144	8,57,883
	(16.13)	(31.48)	(0.005)	(1.91)	(0.42)	(3.84)	(44.89)	(100.00)
1984-85	1,63,392	3,04,804	46	32,000	4,460	46,235	4,31,560	9,82,497
	(16.63)	(31.02)	(0.004)	(3.25)	(0.45)	(4.78)	(48.92)	(100.00)
5. Haryana								
1982-83	1,54,361	2,17,789	—	5,409	21	21,248	2,57,388	6,56,216
	(23.52)	(33.18)		(0.82)	(0.003)	(3.24)	(39.22)	(100.00)
1983-84	1,68,935	2,42,429	—	4,425	68	22,437	2,69,920	7,08,204
	(23.85)	(34.23)		(0.62)	(0.009)	(0.17)	(31.11)	(100.0)
1984-85	1,80,594	2,54,666	—	10,475	184	26,640	2,96,926	7,69,485
	(23.47)	(33.09)		(1.36)	(0.02)	(3.46)	(38.58)	(100.00)

(Contd.)

TABLE 5.5 *Contd.*

1	2	3	4	5	6	7	8	9
6. Himachal Pradesh								
1982-83	53,255	71,680	—	2,055	2,802	7,505	1,03,925	2,41,225
	(22.06)	(29.71)		(0.85)	(1.16)	(3.11)	(43.08)	(100.00)
1983-84	58,347	1,06,828	—	1,915	3,212	394	91,501	2,62,177
	(22.25)	(40.74)		(0.73)	(1.22)	(0.15)	(34.90)	(100.00)
1984-85	63,311	1,24,062	—	2,189	3,840	437	1,12,185	3,06,024
	(20.69)	(40.54)		(0.28)	(0.25)	(0.14)	(36.65)	(100.00)
7. Jammu & Kashmir								
1982-83	1,12,827	1,06,745	—	5,735	957	22,689	64,585	3,13,538
	(35.98)	(34.04)		(1.83)	(0.31)	(7.24)	(20.60)	(100.00)
1983-84	34,395	57,118	—	2,550	727	8,073	22,266	1,25,129
	(27.49)	(47.65)		(2.04)	(0,58)	(6.45)	(17.79)	(100.00)
1984-85	44,350	70,617		2,044	10	302	98,226	2,15,560
	(20.57)	(33.22)		(0.95)	(0.01)	(0.14)	(45.56)	(100.00)
8. Karnataka								
1982-83	5,20,554	3,05,317	1,750	59,155	20,538	49,747	7,17,810	16,70,871
	(31.15)	(18.27)	(0.10)	(3.53)	(1.23)	(2.74)	(42.96)	(100.00)
1983-84	6,08,618	3,71,899	100	45,191	16,517	56,753	6,93,712	17,97,790
	(33.85)	(20.69)	(0.005)	(2.51)	(0.92)	(3.16)	(38.59)	(100.00)
1984-85	4,76,069	4,19,650	1,445	22,523	12,454	48,770	66,78,857	16,59,768
	(28.68)	(25.28)	(0.08)	(1.36)	(0.75)	(0.94)	(40.90)	(100.00)

(Contd.)

TABLE 5.5 *Contd.*

1	2	3	4	5	6	7	8	9
9. Kerala								
1982-83	1,33,604	2,96,507	525	11,120	4,896	34,252	5,53,938	10,34,552
	(12.91)	(28.65)	(0.05)	(1.07)	(0.47)	(3.31)	(53.53)	(100.00)
1983-84	1,64,467	2,81,489	270	8,155	3,341	43,762	7,56,701	12,58,185
	(13.07)	(22.37)	(0.02)	(0.65)	(0.27)	(3.48)	(60.14)	(100.00)
1984-85	1,29,469	3,66,158	465	17,171	1,252	47,760	4,88,000	10,50,275
	(12.33)	(34.86)	(0.04)	(1.63)	(0.12)	(4.55)	(46.46)	(100.00)
10. Madhya Pradesh								
1982-83	1,51,645	2,63,589	471	10,102	3,303	21,200	406,986	8,57,290
	(17.68)	(30.74)	(0.05)	(1.18)	(0.38)	(2.47)	(47.47)	(100.00)
1983-84	1,71,469	2,75,717	322	26,033	1,625	15,759	3,79,790	8,61,565
	(19.89)	(32.00)	(0.04)	(3.03)	(0.19)	(1.83)	(44.08)	(100.00)
1984-85	1,85,392	2,97,823	—	23,740	6,498	11,838	3,41,553	8,66,844
	(21.39)	(34.35)		(2.74)	(0.75)	(1.37)	(39.40)	(100.00)
11. Maharashtra								
1982-83	4,07,835	7,11,982	68,539	39,391	1,06,229	46,186	8,03,711	22,35,873
	(18.24)	(31.84)	(3.06)	(1.76)	(4.75)	(2.06)	(35.95)	(100.00)
1983-84	4,85,172	8,24,519	84,558	1,30,193	1,20,313	61,479	8,02,969	25,18,263
	(19.27)	(32.74)	(3.36)	(5.53)	(4.78)	(2.44)	(31.89)	(100.00)
1984-85	4,54,621	8,28,979	1,47,614	83,272	1,54,883	50,509	8,67,983	25,83,287
	(17.60)	(32.09)	(5.71)	(3.22)	(5.99)	(1.95)	(33.60)	(100.00)

(Contd.)

TABLE 5.5 *Contd.*

1	2	3	4	5	6	7	8	9
12. Manipur								
1982-83	16,510	20,643	—	1,679	1,893	5,397	9,517	55,635
	(29.68)	(37.10)		(3.02)	(3.40)	(9.70)	(17.10)	(100.00)
1983-84	21,080	14,053	—	2,444	1,940	465	32,372	72,354
	(29.13)	(19.42)		(3.38)	(2.68)	(0.64)	(44.74)	(100.00)
1984-85	41,6686	28,329	—	3,324	1,201	1,075	44,966	1,20,581
	(34.30)	(23.60)		(2.77)	(1.00)	(0.90)	(37.45)	(100.00)
13. Orissa								
1982-83	1,11,488	1,50,546	18,493	5,449	3,228	9,405	1,76,963	4,75,572
	(23.44)	(31.65)	(3.88)	(1.14)	(0.67)	(1.97)	(37.21)	(100.00)
1983-84	46,343	99,217	20,674	2,633	1,503	3,302	98,442	2,72,094
	(17.03)	(36.46)	(7.60)	(0.97)	(0.55)	(1.21)	(36.18)	(100.00)
14. Punjab								
1982-83	4,86,548	3,90,839	41,060	44,670	7,360	71,799	5,41,173	15,84,149
	(30.71)	(24.67)	(2.59)	(2.82)	(0.46)	(4.53)	(34.16)	(100.00)
1983-84	5,50,630	4,27,154	45,287	28,260	9,456	82,983	6,04,266	17,48,074
	(31.50)	(24.44)	(2.59)	(1.62)	(0.54)	(4.75)	(34.57)	(100.00)
1984-85	6,34,260	5,00,072	49,142	52,761	19,525	1,00,478	6,80,547	19,86,785
	(31.92)	(25.17)	(2.47)	(2.66)	(0.98)	(5.06)	(34.25)	(100.00)

(Contd.)

1	2	3	4	5	6	7	8	9
15. Rajasthan								
1982-83	3,71,746	2,55,277	—	8,130	725	23,622	3,59,698	10,19,178
	(36.47)	(25.04)		(0.89)	(0.07)	(2.32)	(35.29)	(100.00)
1983-84	4,10,179	2,91,835	—	9,816	118	31,292	4,90,208	12,33,442
	(33.25)	(23.66)		(0.80)	(0.009)	(2.54)	(39.74)	(100.00)
1984-85	—	—	—	—	—	—	—	—
16. Tamil Nadu								
1982-83	3,53,475	3,65,780	—	7,14,002	9,268	59,916	6,84,847	15,44,688
	(22.88)	(23.68)		(4.62)	(0.60)	(3.88)	(44.34)	(100.00)
1983-84	4,42,197	3,96,641	—	78,513	7,870	31,660	6,75,049	16,06,930
	(25.96)	(24.38)		(4.89)	(0.49)	(1.97)	(42.01)	(100.00)
1984-85	3,42,337	3,78,896	3,570	97,886	8,143	59,425	6,15,435	15,05,782
	(22.73)	(25.16)	(0.23)	(6.50)	(.054)	(3.94)	(40.87)	(100.00)
7. Uttar Pradesh								
1982-83	6,40,113	6,40,113	748	1,14,874	28,149	34,761	6,65,126	20,87,783
	(28.94)	(30.66)	(0.04)	(5.50)	(1.35)	(1.66)	(31.86)	(100.00)
1983-84	6,32,789	7,65,599	340	1,14,988	13,117	50,858	7,41,497	23,19,180
	(27.29)	(33.01)	(0.01)	(4.96)	(0.57)	(2.19)	(31.97)	(100.00)
1984-85	7,24,159	6,99,522	363	1,38,322	16,272	58,971	5,66,192	9,36,262
	(33.27)	(32.14)	(0.02)	(6.35)	(0.75)	(2.71)	(26.01)	(100.00)
18. West Bengal								
1982-83	4,15,158	4,60,971	29,333	26,322	7,567	19,895	2,57,432	12,16,678
	(34.12)	(37.89)	(2.41)	(2.16)	(0.62)	(1.64)	(21.16)	(100.00)
1983-84	4,69,524	5,21,080	35,160	24,658	6,851	18,806	3,13,993	13,90,072
	(33.78)	(37.48)	(2.53)	(1.77)	(0.49)	(1.35)	(22.59)	(100.00)
1984-85	3,07,737	3,50,015	35,163	7,898	1,534	10,844	2,23,071	9,36,262
	(32.87)	(37.38)	(3.76)	(0.84)	(0.16)	(1.16)	(23.83)	(100.00)

Source: University Grants Commission

Note: Figures in Parenthesis are proportion of income in terms of percentages

Items', the highest expenditure (60.14 per cent) in the universities of Karnataka State and the lowest expenditure (8.62 per cent) in the universities of Bihar State have been reported. The expenditure on the items 'Grants to Colleges' has been reported only in the case of universities in the States of Andhra Pradesh, Bihar, Maharashtra, Orissa, Punjab and West Bengal. Expenditure on this item ranged from 2.53 per cent (West Bengal State Universities) to 41.96 per cent (Bihar State Universities). Non-significant expenditure on the item, 'Apparatus, Chemicals and other Consumable Stores' has been reported, which ranged from 0.48 per cent (Assam State Universities) to 6.50 per cent (Tamil Nadu State Universities). The expenditure on the item, 'Library' in the majority of the universities ranged from 1.16 per cent (West Bengal State Universities) to 6.45 per cent (Jammu and Kashmir State Universities). The expenditure on this item has been reported to be less than 1 per cent in the case of universities in the State of Bihar, Himachal Pradesh and Manipur. Most of the universities have incurred less than 1 per cent expenditure on the item, 'Furniture', exception being in the case of Maharashtra State Universities, where expenditure of about 5 per cent has been reported on this item.

Further the major portion of the non-recurring funds of State General Universities has been expended on 'Buildings' (Table 5.6). The highest expenditure (100.00 per cent) on this account is for the universities in the State of Manipur and the lowest (8.83 per cent) in the State Universities of Orissa. Universities in the States of Bihar and Jammu and Kashmir are consistently spending considerable amounts on the items of 'Buildings' ranging from 64.76 to 94.50 per cent. In the State Universities of Karnataka, Kerala, Manipur and Uttar Pradesh, a consistent expenditure of more than 45 per cent on this item has been reported whereas expenditure of less than 25 per cent has been reported in the case of universities in the States of Assam and Orissa. The non-recurring expenditure on 'Library' has been reported to be the highest (43.32 per cent) in the universities in the State of Haryana and the lowest (0.85 per cent) in the case of universities in the State of Karnataka. The State Universities in West Bengal are incurring expenditure consistently on this item ranging from 21.51 per cent to 32.80 per cent for all the three years. The universities in the States of Himachal Pradesh, Orissa and Rajasthan have expended more than 20 per cent on this item for two years out of three years. Universities in the States of Jammu and Kashmir and Karnataka have been reported to be spending the least ranging from 0.85 per cent to 5.26 per cent on this item. On the item, 'Equipments', the highest (58.43 per cent) and the lowest expenditure (0.70 per cent) has been reported in the case of universities in the States of Orissa and Bihar State Universities, respectively. Consistent expenditure ranging from 20 to 33.45 per cent on this item has been reported in the case of universities in the States of Andhra Pradesh and Madhya Pradesh. The universities in the States of Assam and Bihar have spent less than 3 per cent on this item for two years. The expenditure on 'Other Items', is reported to be the highest (68.09 per cent) in the case of universities in the State of Assam and the lowest (0.47 per cent) in the case of universities in Rajasthan. The universities in the States of Karnataka, Kerala, Orissa and Tamil Nadu have spent more than 20 per cent under this item for two years. Consistently low expenditure i.e., less than 3 per cent has been reported on this item in the case of universities in the State of Bihar. It has been further revealed that non-recurring expenditure for one of the three years under study has been reported to be less than 4.05 per cent in universities in the States of Jammu and Kashmir and Rajasthan.

TABLE 5.6: Non Recurring Expenditure (Plan and Non-Plan) of State General Universities (1982-83 to 1984-85)

(Amount in 00's Rupees)

Sr. No.	University Institutions, State and year	Items				Total
		Library	Buildings	Equipments	Other items	
1	2	3	4	5	6	7
1.	Andhra Pradesh					
	1982-83	13,091	65,494	41,703	37,303	1,57,591
		(8.31)	(41.56)	(26.46)	(23.67)	(100.00)
	1983-84	34,113	1,14,989	63,262	96,814	3,09,178
		(11.03)	(37.19)	(20.46)	(31.32)	(100.00)
	1984-85	50,457	64,076	56,487	50,714	2,21,784
		(22.76)	(28.89)	(25.48)	(22.87)	(100.00)
2.	Assam					
	1982-83	11,988	27,588	2,738	90,296	1,32,610
		(9.04)	(20.80)	(2.07)	(68.09)	(100.00)
	1983-84	9,408	21,435	1,844	30,541	63,328
		(14.85)	(33.86)	(2.93)	(48.25)	(100.00)
	1984-85	—	—	—	—	—
3.	Bihar					
	1982-83	11,122	46,646	1,196	564	59,528
		(18.68)	(78.36)	(2.01)	(0.95)	(100.00)

(Contd.)

TABLE 5.6 *Contd.*

1	2	3	4	5	6	7
	1983-84	43,897	1,87,793	1,666	3,640	2,36,996
		(18.52)	(79.24)	(0.70)	(1.54)	(100.00)
	1984-85	19,749	61,013	10,790	2,666	94,207
		(20.96)	(64.76)	(11.46)	(2.82)	(100.00)
4.	Gujarat					
	1982-83	19,243	97,988	11,908	27,302	1,51,441
		(12.71)	(64.70)	(7.86)	(18.03)	(100.00)
	1983-84	23,880	76,661	13,388	21,382	1,35,511
		(17.62)	(56.57)	(10.03)	(15.78)	(100.00)
	1984-85	53,038	59,410	20,784	27,008	1,60,240
		(33.10)	(37.07)	(12.97)	(16.86)	(100.00)
5.	Haryana					
	1982-83	18,841	4,551	4,480	15,616	43,488
		(43.32)	(10.46)	(10.31)	(35.91)	(100.00)
	1983-84	32,426	1,26,212	11,442	9,523	1,79,603
		(18.05)	(70.27)	(6.37)	(5.31)	(100.00)
	1984-85	20,705	1,97,819	8,100	15,392	2,42,016
		(8.55)	(81.74)	(3.35)	(6.36)	(100.00)
6.	Himachal Pradesh					
	1982-83	8,401	22,968	3,855	15,826	51,050
		(16.46)	(44.99)	(7.55)	(31.00)	(100.00)
	1983-84	13,214	13,193	1,801	5,567	33,775
		(39.13)	(39.06)	(5.33)	(16.48)	(100.00)
	1984-85	18,513	26,605	11,461	—	50,579
		(36.60)	(40.74)	(22.66)		(100.00)
7.	Jammu & Kashmir					
	1982-83	—	99,129	5,772	—	1,04,901
			(94.50)	(5.50)		(100.00)
	1983-84	3,791	64,055	1,807	2,360	72,013
		(5.26)	(88.95)	(2.51)	(3.28)	(100.00)
	1984-85	3,011	58,192	12,020	3,089	76,312
		(3.95)	(76.25)	(15.75)	(4.05)	(100.00)
8.	Karnataka					
	1982-83	2,043	1,29,770	13,432	95,371	2,40,616
		(0.85)	(53.93)	(5.58)	(39.64)	(100.00)
	1983-84	66,521	2,08,641	12,973	1,40,629	4,28,764
		(15.51)	(48.66)	(3.03)	(32.30)	(100.00)
	1984-85	8,627	2,89,698	61,315	53,343	4,12,882
		(2.09)	(70.16)	(14.85)	(12.90)	(100.00)
9.	Kerala					
	1982-83	7,815	74,042	15,498	23,982	1,21,337
		(6.44)	(61.02)	(12.78)	(19.76)	(100.00)
	1983-84	8,783	1,05,326	26,051	64,566	2,04,726
		(4.29)	(51.44)	(12.73)	(31.54)	(100.00)
	1984-85	12,199	77,387	29,060	46,984	1,65,630
		(7.36)	(46.72)	(17.55)	(28.37)	(100.00)

(*Contd.*)

TABLE 5.6 *Contd.*

1	2	3	4	5	6	7
10.	Madhya Pradesh					
	1982-83	9,643	14,777	16,571	8,542	49,533
		(19.47)	(29.83)	(33.45)	(17.25)	(100.00)
	1983-84	16,038	56,775	23,285	12,672	1,08,770
		(14.74)	(52.20)	(21.41)	(11.65)	(100.00)
	1984-85	35,825	68,454	53,337	7,373	1,64,989
		(21.71)	(41.49)	(32.33)	(4.47)	(100.00)
11.	Maharashtra					
	1982-83	58,866	4,55,183	45,670	37,116	5,96,835
		(9.86)	(76.27)	(7.65)	(6.32)	(100.00)
	1983-84	86,175	5,02,677	63,793	1,45,247	7,97,892
		(10.80)	(63.00)	(7.99)	(18.21)	(100.00)
	1984-85	1,27,598	5,51,756	3,10,576	2,23,304	12,13,234
		(10.52)	(45.48)	(25.60)	(18.40)	(100.00)
12.	Manipur					
	1982-83	—	63,131	—	—	63,131
			(100.00)			(100.00)
	1983-84	5,492	46,437	22,306	—	74,235
		(7.40)	(62.55)	(30.05)		(100.00)
	1984-85	22,784	53,609	21,853	—	98,246
		(23.19)	(54.57)	(22.24)		(100.00)
13.	Orissa					
	1982-83	7,101	30,680	8,710	39,845	86,336
		(8.22)	(35.54)	(10.09)	(46.15)	(100.00)
	1983-84	9,190	10,100	8,884	14,540	42,714
		(21.52)	(23.64)	(20.80)	(34.04)	(100.00)
	1984-85	9,680	2,680	17,740	260	30,360
		(31.88)	(8.83)	(58.43)	(0.86)	(100.00)
14.	Punjab					
	1982-83	9,393	58,322	15,631	15,331	98,677
		(8.52)	(59.10)	(15.84)	(15.54)	(100.00)
	1983-84	7,563	90,024	13,800	19,070	1,30,457
		(5.80)	(69.00)	(10.58)	(14.62)	(100.00)
	1984-85	18,081	1,28,000	1,25,577	34,055	3,05,712
		(5.91)	(41.87)	(41.08)	(11.14)	(100.00)
15.	Rajasthan					
	1982-83	14,520	44,410	3,040	290	62,260
		(23.32)	(71.33)	(4.88)	(0.47)	(100.00)
	1983-84	24,460	35,760	4,950	1,210	66,380
		(36.85)	(53.87)	(7.46)	(1.82)	(100.00)
	1984-85	—	—	—	—	—
16.	Tamil Nadu					
	1982-83	30,162	1,95,274	56,851	1,16,387	3,98,674
		(3.78)	(24.49)	(7.13)	(14.60)	(100.00)
	1983-84	31,319	2,87,746	87,917	1,04,051	5,11,032
		(6.13)	(56.31)	(17.20)	(20.36)	(100.00)

(*Contd.*)

TABLE 5.6 *Contd.*

1	2	3	4	5	6	7
	1984-85	36,128	2,77,463	1,46,158	1,34,441	5,94,190
		(6.08)	(46.70)	(24.60)	(22.62)	(100.00)
17.	Uttar Pradesh					
	1982-83	33,957	2,06,777	75,469	26,287	3,42,490
		(9.92)	(60.37)	(22.03)	(7.68)	(100.00)
	* 1983-84	76,748	2,96,348	80,594	21,895	4,75,585
		(16.14)	(62.31)	(16.95)	(4.60)	(100.00)
	1984-85	36,831	2,10,697	1,64,899	17,593	4,30,020
		(8.56)	(48.99)	(38.36)	(4.09)	(100.00)
18.	West Bengal					
	1982-83	28,832	52,480	7,726	3,817	92,855
		(31.05)	(56.52)	(8.32)	(4.11)	(100.00)
	1983-84	32,275	73,088	34,973	10,061	1,50,497
		(21.51)	(48.56)	(23.24)	(6.69)	(100.00)
	1984-85	40,320	43,968	30,314	8,314	1,22,916
		(32.80)	(35.77)	(24.67)	(6.76)	(100.00)

Source: University Grants Commission.
Note: Figures in parenthesis are proportion of Income in terms of expenditure

Normative Pattern of Expenditure

A comparison of average pattern of recurring expenditure has been drawn in respect of Central Universities, Deemed Universities and State General Universities (Table 5.7). Variation exists in the item-wise pattern of expenditure, within three types of University Institutions. The average expenditure on staff (both teaching and non-teaching) has been reported to be fifty per cent or more in the case of all the three types of Universities. The expenditure on teaching staff has been reported to be the highest (ranging from 30.61 per cent to 35.45 per cent) in the case of State General Universities and Deemed Universities, which is reported to be the lowest in the case of Central Universities (21 per cent against 30 per cent on non-teaching staff). The expenditure on the item, 'Apparatus, Chemicals and Consumable Stores' is highest (8.17 per cent) in the case of Deemed Universities and lowest (1.97 per cent) in the case of Central Universities. The expenditure on this item is less than four per cent (3.71 per cent) in the case of State General Universities. The low expenditure on this item has an adverse effect on the teaching, research and extension activities of the University Institutions in India. The expenditure under the item, 'Library' is less than 5 per cent in the case of all the three types of

TABLE 5.7: Pattern of Recurring Expenditure (1982-85)

(Amount in 00's Rupees)

Sr. No.	Type of the University Institution	Items of Expenditure							Total
		Teaching staff	Non-Teaching staff	Grants to Colleges	Apparatus, chemicals and consumable stores	Furniture	Library	Other Misc. items scholarships, stipends, sports, conduct of exams.	
1	2	3	4	5	6	7	8	9	10
1.	General Universities	1,79,728 (20.77)	2,56,875 (29.68)	1,000 (0.12)	16,955 (1.97)	4,995 (0.58)	21,023 (2.44)	3,84,652 (44.44)	8,65,227 (100.00)
2.	Deemed Universities	69,031 (35.45)	35,919 (18.45)	3,092 (1.59)	15,909 (8.17)	1,299 (0.67)	8,070 (4.14)	61,370 (31.53)	1,94,690 (100.00)
3.	State General Universities	4,15,796 (30.61)	3,39,334 (24.98)	1,06,757 (7.86)	50,225 (3.71)	13,232 (0.98)	30,334 (2.24)	4,02,281 (29.62)	13,57,959 (100.00)

Note: Figures in parenthesis are proportion of expenditure in terms of percentage.

University Institutions. Keeping in view the utility of library service this expenditure is much on the lower side. It is also interesting to observe that expenditure on 'Other Miscellaneous Items' (Scholarships, Stipends, Sports and Conduct of Examination etc.) is the highest (44.44 per cent) in the case of Central Universities and the lowest (29.62 per cent) in the case of State General Universities, which should be otherwise keeping in view the affiliating character of most of the State General Universities. The expenditure on this item is seemingly on the higher side in the case of Central Universities.

The comparison of item-wise non-recurring expenditure in respect of three types of universities reveals that variation exists in respect of average expenditure among the three types of University Institutions (Table 5.8). All the three types of University Institutions are spending more than thirty three per cent of resources on the item, 'Buildings'. The variation in expenditure on this item is from 33.12 to 53.12 per cent. The variation of percentage of non-recurring expenditure on the item 'Equipment' ranges from 16.86 per cent in respect of State General Universities to 31.07 per cent in the case of Deemed Universities. The non-recurring expenditure on the item, 'Library' is the highest (11.76 per cent) in the case of Central Universities and the lowest (6.98 per cent) in the case of Deemed Universities. The expenditure on 'Other Items' varies from 18.28 per cent to 28.62 per cent among the three types of University Institutions.

TABLE 5.8: Pattern of Non-Recurring Expenditure (1982-85)

(Amount in 00's rupees)

Sr. No.	Type of University Institution	Items of expenditure				Total
		Library	Buildings	Equipments	Other items	
1	2	3	4	5	6	7
1.	Central Universities	23,009 (11.76)	64,781 (33.12)	51,833 (26.50)	55,988 (28.62)	1,95,611 (100.00)
2.	Deemed Universities	4,745 (6.98)	29,582 (43.54)	21,111 (31.07)	12,501 (18.41)	67,939 (100.00)
3.	State General Universities	25,740 (11.74)	1,16,463 (53.12)	36,974 (16.86)	40,055 (18.28)	2,19,232 (100.00)

Note: Figures in parenthesis are proportion of expenditure in terms of percentages.

The pattern of expenditure as emerged, both recurring and

non-recurring in respect of three types of universities, as discussed above, does not conform to the objectives of a University Institution, that is maintenance and improvement of standards of higher education in the country. Some of the shortcomings of the existing pattern of expenditure are given as under:

1. There is no uniformity in the pattern of expenditure in different types of University Institutions. The Central Universities are spending the highest proportion of recurring income on 'Other Miscellaneous Items', whereas the Deemed Universities and State General Universities are spending on payment of salary of teaching staff. The expenditure on payment of salary to non-teaching staff is more than that of teaching staff in the case of Central Universities.
2. The highest priority for recurring expenditure is for the payment of salaries of teaching and non-teaching staff, and 'Other Miscellaneous Items', (conduct of examination, scholarships, stipends, sports, etc.) whereas the items like 'Apparatus, Chemicals, and consumable Stores', and 'Library', are not give due priority.
3. The major share of non-recurring income is spent on 'Buildings' and 'Other Miscellaneous Items', and low priority is given for items of expenditure like 'Equipments' and 'Library' (purchase of books, journals and equipments).

The existing pattern of expenditure is not meeting in full the requirements of the University Institutions for the maintenance and improvement of standards of higher education but is creating a bottleneck for the speedier all round development of such institutions in the country. This has also created imbalances in the financial management of University Institutions. All this is happening due to the fact that the University Grants Commission, the Indian Council of Agricultural Research and other bodies, responsible for the coordination and maintenance of standards of higher education have not formulated and promulgated any norms for the utilisation of available funds, both recurring and non-recurring on various items of expenditure. Moreover, their advice on such matters is not mandatory on University Institutions due to the fact that education is a state subject through on the concurrent list.

For the effective and efficient utilisation of available limited financial resources, both recurring and non-recurring, it is desirable that a normative pattern of expenditure be suggested to University Institutions. The following suggestions/recommendations emanating as a result of discussion with the Vice-Chancellors/Directors and Professors and Heads, during the course of the study are made for working out a Normative Pattern of expenditure for University Institutions in India:

1. The expenditure on the salary of teaching staff should get priority over the expenditure on the salary of the non-teaching staff. At least 35 per cent of recurring expenditure should be incurred on the salary of teaching staff and expenditure on the salary of non-teaching staff should not exceed 18 per cent of recurring expenditure.
2. The expenditure on 'Library', 'Apparatus, Chemicals and Consumable Stores', should get due priority. At least 10 per cent of the recurring expenditure should be spent on 'Library' and a minimum of 6 per cent on 'Apparatus, Chemicals and other Consumable Stores'.
3. The expenditure on 'Other Miscellaneous Items', (scholarships, stipends, sports, conduct of examination etc.) should not exceed 30 per cent of the total recurring expenditure. The expenditure on conduct of examination should match the income so realised on this account from the students.
4. The expenditure on 'Furniture' items should get the last priority and should not exceed 0.5 per cent of the total recurring expenditure.
5. The expenditure under non-recurring items should be incurred as under:

   (a) For the newly established University Institutions where infrastructures are to be raised, the first priority should go to 'Buildings', followed by 'Equipment', and 'Library'. Atleast 20 per cent of the non-recurring income should be earmarked for the purchase of equipments and library items (books, journals and other library equipments) so that they could be raised simultaneously.

   (b) For the University Institutions which have good insfrastructures in terms of 'Buildings' etc. the barest minimum buildings should be added and more funds should be provided for equipping the library and laboratories. The proportion of expenditure between these two items should be in the ratio of 60 and 40.

(c) The expenditure on 'Other Items (Maintenance etc.)' should not exceed, in any case, 20 per cent of the total non-recurring expenditure.

Financial Health

University Finance is a matter of grave concern and constant criticism. The major problem faced by every University Institution in India is that on the one hand costs are rising at a rapid rate while on the other hand the growth rate of income is almost steady. The financial constraints in management of University Institutions are not being felt in India only but also in several other countries of the world. It is, therefore, desirable to know the financial health in all types of University Institutions in India to ascertain their financial status, which plays a predominant role in efficient and effective management of University Institutions. The major indicator of financial health of University Institutions has been taken as proportionate, surplus or deficit of recurring, non-recurring and total (both recurring and non-recurring) income and expenditure. The financial health of Central Universities, Deemed Universities and State General Universities has been examined on the basis of available data of income and expenditure as obtained from the University Grants Commission (1987).[1] The findings of the said analysis are given hereinafter:

Central Universities

It can be seen that in the case of Universities of Hyderabad, Aligarh Muslim University, Visva Bharti and University of Delhi, there has been surplus finance (recurring) in all the three years. The surplus finances ranged from 0.99 per cent (Visva Bharti) to 105.30 per cent (University of Delhi). The Banaras Hindu University was in deficit finance (recurring) only for one year, the Jawaharlal Nehru University for two years and North Eastern Hill University for all the three years (Table 5.9).

TABLE 5.9: Range of Surplus/Deficit Finances (Recurring) of the Central Universities (1982-83 to 1984-85)

(Percentage)

Sr. No.	Name of the University Institution	Range of surplus or deficit			
		Surplus in all the three year (+)	Deficit in only one year (-)	Deficit in two years (-)	Deficit in three years (-)
1	2	3	4	5	6
1.	University of Hyderabad	2.17 - 3.46	—	—	—
2.	Aligarh Muslim University	4.11 - 5.34	—	—	—
3.	Visva Bharti	0.99 - 6.57	—	—	—
4.	University of Delhi	11.13 - 105.38	—	—	—
5.	Banaras Hindu University	—	1.45	—	—
6.	Jawaharlal Nehru University	—	—	0.01 - 3.55	—
7.	North Eastern Hill University	—	—	—	6.89 - 17.25

It is revealed that there was no surplus finance (non-recurring) with any of the Central Universities in either of the years taken for the study. All the universities remained under deficit ranging from one to three years. The Banaras Hindu University was under deficit for all three years; the North Eastern Hill University, Aligarh Muslim University, the University of Delhi and the University of Hyderabad were under consistent deficit for two years whereas the Visva Bharti and Jawaharlal Nehru University were under deficit only for one year (Table 5.10).

As far the position of surplus/deficit in totality (both recurring and non-recurring) goes, it has been observed that the Aligarh Muslim University, the Banaras Hindu University and the Jawaharlal Nehru University were having surplus during all the three years. The remaining universities were under deficit either for one year or two years. The North Eastern Hill University and the University of Delhi were under deficit for two years, whereas the University of Hyderabad and Visva Bharti were under deficit only for one year (Table 5.11)

TABLE 5.10: Range of Surplus/Deficit Finances (Non-recurring) of the Central Universities (1982-83 to 1984-85)

(Percentage)

Sr. No.	Name of the University Institution	Range of surplus or deficit			
		Surplus in all the three year (+)	Deficit in only one year (-)	Deficit in two years (-)	Deficit in three years (-)
1	2	3	4	5	6
1.	Visva Bharti	—	123.96	—	—
2.	Jawaharlal Nehru University	—	24.94	—	—
3.	North Eastern Hill University	—	—	15.27 - 27.55	—
4.	Aligarh Muslim University	—	—	4.34 - 7.81	—
5.	University of Delhi	—	—	200.60 - 211.97	—
6.	University of Hyderabad	—	—	3.09 - 106.49	—
7.	Banaras Hindu University	—	—	—	2.41 - 9.18

TABLE 5.11: Range of Surplus/Deficit Finance (Total) of the Central Universities (1982-83 to 1984-85)

(Percentage)

Sr. No.	Name of the University Institution	Range of surplus or deficit			
		Surplus in all the three year (+)	Deficit in only one year (-)	Deficit in two years (-)	Deficit in three years (-)
1	2	3	4	5	6
1.	Aligarh Muslim University	2.28 - 10.24	—	—	—
2.	Banaras Hindu University	1.58 - 3.99	—	—	—
3.	Jawaharlal Nehr University	0.29 - 14.63	—	—	—
4.	University of Hyderabad	—	12.97	—	—
5.	Visva Bharti	—	15.96	—	—
6.	North Eastern Hill University	—	—	19.0 - 25.07	—
7.	University of Delhi	—	—	0.29 - 0.31	—

Deemed Universities

It can be observed that Deemed Universities located in Delhi were having surplus finance (recurring) in all the three years, whereas the institutions located in the States of Bihar and Karnataka were under deficit during all the three years. The Institutions in the States of Andhra Pradesh, Maharashtra, Rajasthan and Uttar Pradesh were under deficit consistently for two years, whereas the institutions in the States of Gujarat and Tamil Nadu were under deficit only for one year (Table 5.12).

TABLE 5.12: Range of Surplus/Deficit Finances (Recurring) of the Deemed Universities in various States of India (1982-83 to 1984-85)

(Percentage)

Sr. No.	Name of the University Institution State	Range of surplus or deficit			
		Surplus in all the three year (+)	Deficit in only one year (-)	Deficit in two years (-)	Deficit in three years (-)
1	2	3	4	5	6
1.	Delhi	6.19 - 11.18	—	—	—
2.	Gujarat	—	3.50	—	—
3.	Tamil Nadu	—	2.69	--	—
4.	Andhra Pradesh	—	--	-	—
5.	Maharashtra	—	—	8.19 - 16.93	—
6.	Rajasthan*	—	—	4.04 - 0.57	—
7.	Uttar Pradesh	—	—	1.70 - 4.71	—
8.	Bihar	—	—	0.72 - 7.56	0.53 - 6.01
9.	Karnataka	—	—	—	2.93 - 19.04

* Based on two years data.

The position of surplus/deficit finances (non-recurring) for Deemed Universities reveals that the institutions in the States of Karnataka and Maharashtra were having surplus finances during all the three years, whereas those located in the States of Bihar were under deficit for two years. The institutions in the States of Andhra Pradesh, Gujarat, Rajasthan, Tamil Nadu, Uttar Pradesh and Delhi were under deficit finances (non-recurring) only for one year (Table 5.13)

TABLE 5.13: Range of Surplus/Deficit Finances (Non-recurring) of the Deemed Universities in various States of India (1982-83 to 1984-85)

(Percentage)

Sl. No.	Name of the University Institution State	Range of surplus or deficit			
		Surplus in all the three years (+)	Deficit in only one year (-)	Deficit in two years (-)	Deficit in three years (-)
1	2	3	4	5	6
1.	Karnataka	1.99 - 48.35	—	—	—
2.	Maharashtra*	46.45 - 49.38	—	—	—
3.	Andhra Pradesh	—	0.61	—	—
4.	Gujarat	—	13.02	—	—
5.	Rajasthan	—	65.77	—	—
6.	Tamil Nadu	—	120.29	—	—
7.	Uttar Pradesh	—	22.18	—	—
8.	Delhi	—	0.08	—	—
9.	Bihar	—	—	26.50 - 90.89	—

* Based on two years data

It is revealed from the position as a whole (both recurring and non-recurring) that institutions located in the States of Andhra Pradesh, Maharashtra and Delhi were having surplus finances, consistently during all the three years. The institutions in the States of Bihar and Rajasthan were under deficit during two years, whereas institutions in the States of Gujarat, Karnataka, Uttar Pradesh and Tamil Nadu were deficit in only one year (Table 5.14).

State General Universities

It can be seen from Table 5.15 that the State General Universities in the States of Haryana, Karnataka, Rajasthan and Assam were having surplus finances (recurring) during all the three years, whereas universities in the States of Gujarat, Uttar Pradesh, Orissa and West Bengal were under deficit during all the three years. The universities in the States of Bihar, Himachal Pradesh, Jammu and Kashmir, Kerala and Punjab were under deficit only for one year.

TABLE 5.14: Range of Surplus/Deficit Finances (Total) of the Deemed Universities in various States of India (1982-83 to 1984-85)

(Percentage)

Sl. No.	Name of the University Institution State	Range of surplus or deficit			
		Surplus in all the three years (+)	Deficit in only one year (-)	Deficit in two years (-)	Deficit in three years (-)
1	2	3	4	5	6
1.	Andhra Pradesh	1.60 - 18.75	—	—	—
2.	Maharashtra	7.27 - 75.72	—	—	—
3.	Delhi	1.15 - 10.41	—	—	—
4.	Gujarat	—	6.94	—	—
5.	Karnataka	—	10.23	—	—
6.	Uttar Pradesh	—	12.46	—	—
7.	Tamil Nadu	—	10.77	—	—
8.	Bihar	—	—	2.58 - 12.21	—
9.	Rajasthan	—	—	0.46 - 4.64	—

TABLE 5.15: Range of Surplus/Deficit Finances (Recurring) of the State General Universities in various States of India (1982-83 to 1984-85)

(Percentage)

Sl. No.	Name of the State	Range of surplus or deficit			
		Surplus in all the three years (+)	Deficit in only one year (-)	Deficit in two years (-)	Deficit in three years (-)
1.	Haryana	3.20 - 16.03	—	—	—
2.	Karnataka	5.21 - 31.43	—	—	—
3.	Rajasthan*	5.47 - 12.52	—	—	—
4.	Assam*	1.71 - 10.55	—	—	—
5.	Bihar	—	16.66	—	—
6.	Himachal Pradesh	—	12.59	—	—
7.	Jammu & Kashmir	—	18.99	—	—
8.	Kerala	—	3.09	—	—
9.	Madhya Pradesh	—	—	—	—
10.	Punjab	—	3.16	—	—
11.	Andhra Pradesh	—	—	6.15 - 15.01	—
12.	Manipur	—	—	2.58 - 37.30	—
13.	Tamil Nadu	—	—	0.99 - 7.31	—
14.	Gujarat	—	—	—	1.55 - 10.01
15.	Uttar Pradesh	—	—	—	2.10 - 112.07
16.	Orissa	—	—	—	20.30 - 70.47
17.	West Bengal	—	—	—	0.57 - 288.95
18.	Maharashtra**	—	—	—	—

* Based on two years data

** Data for income were not available and hence surplus or ueficit could not be computed.

As far as the position of surplus/deficit finances (non-recurring) is concerned, it can be seen that universities in the States of Tamil Nadu and Rajasthan were in surplus for all the three years, whereas universities in the States of Andhra Pradesh, Haryana, Karnataka, Kerala and Orissa were under deficit consistently for all the three years. The universities in the States of Assam, Bihar, Gujarat, Madhya Pradesh, Jammu and Kashmir, Himachal Pradesh, Maharashtra, Uttar Pradesh and West Bengal were under deficit for two years, whereas deficit in the case of universities in the States of Manipur and Punjab, it was only for one year (Table 5.16).

TABLE 5.16: Range of Surplus/Deficit Finances (Non-recurring) of the State General Universities in various States of India (1982-83 to 1984-85)

(Percentage)

Sr. No.	Name of the State	Range of surplus or deficit			
		Surplus in all the three years (+)	Deficit in only one year (-)	Deficit in two years (-)	Deficit in three years (-)
1	2	3	4	5	6
1.	Tamil Nadu	16.50 - 19.89	—	—	—
2.	Rajasthan*	16.84 - 44.72	—	—	—
3.	Manipur	—	0.12	—	—
4.	Punjab	—	56.02	—	—
5.	Assam*	—	—	7.19 - 52.45	—
6.	Bihar	—	—	18.47 - 999.14	—
7.	Gujarat	—	—	15.64 - 36.57	—
8.	Himachal Pradesh	—	—	20.26 - 37.13	—
9.	Jammu & Kashmir	—	—	14.42 - 1454.53	—
10.	Madhya Pradesh	—	—	14.41 - 168.99	—
11.	Maharashtra	—	—	18.85 - 70.54	—
12.	Uttar Pradesh	—	—	3.81 - 9.56	—
13.	West Bengal	—	—	0.99 - 91.22	—
14.	Andhra Pradesh	—	—	—	3.94 - 741.52
15.	Haryana	—	—	—	593.45 - 3492.06
16.	Karnataka	—	—	—	24.40 - 227.24
17.	Kerala	—	—	—	35.58 - 87.08
17.	Orissa	—	—	—	9.71 - 1276.49

* Based on two years data

The position of surplus/deficit finance (total), both for recurring and non-recurring reveals that universities in the States of Karnataka and Rajasthan were having surplus in all the three years, whereas universities in the States of Gujarat, Kerala, Madhya Pradesh, Maharashtra, and Uttar Pradesh were under deficit consistently for three years. The universities in the States of Andhra Pradesh, Haryana, Himachal Pradesh, Jammu and Kashmir, Orissa, Tamil Nadu and West Bengal were in a deficitary position for two years, whereas universities in the States of Assam, Bihar, Manipur and Punjab were under deficit only for one year (Table 5.17).

TABLE 5.17: Range of Surplus/Deficit Finances (Total) of the State General Universities in various States of India (1982-83 to 1984-85)

(Percentage)

Sr. No.	Name of the State	Range of surplus or deficit			
		Surplus in all the three years (+)	Deficit in only one year (-)	Deficit in two years (-)	Deficit in three years (-)
1	2	3	4	5	6
1.	Karnataka	2.57 - 5.65	—	—	—
2.	Rajasthan*	6.21 - 15.06	—	—	—
3.	Assam*	—	11.47	—	—
4.	Bihar	—	16.76	—	—
5.	Manipur	—	24.64	—	—
6.	Punjab	—	93.26	—	—
7.	Andhra Pradesh	—	—	7.03 - 14.03	—
8.	Haryana	—	—	20.52 - 143.56	—
9.	Himachal Pradesh	—	—	0.67 - 13.87	—
10.	Jammu & Kashmir	—	—	4.26 - 10.11	—
11.	Orissa	—	—	1.95 - 68.92	—
12.	Tamil Nadu	—	—	0.32 - 1.91	—
13.	West Bengal	—	—	0.62 - 262.39	—
14.	Gujarat	—	—	—	2.65 - 3.75
15.	Kerala	—	—	—	2.82 - 100.13
16.	Madhya Pradesh	—	—	—	318.30 - 1994.62
17.	Maharashtra	—	—	—	229.42 - 464.10
18.	Uttar Pradesh	—	—	—	2.39 - 69.26

* Based on two years data

From the foregoing description it can be observed that on the whole, the financial health of only three out of seven Central

Universities was found to be sound. The financial health of Deemed Universities located in three out of nine States was also found to be satisfactory. Out of eighteen States, it is only in the case of two States wherein the financial health of State General Universities has been found to be satisfactory. It can thus be inferred that the financial health of most of the University Institutions in India is not good. All this is affecting the growth and development of such institutions and may affect indirectly by diversion of attention of university staff, students and this may also affect teaching and research environment of the university. Despite the fact that education being on the concurrent list, there is no central coordinating agency, which could assist/guide the Union or State Governments at national level in the determination of funds and laying down of fiscal policies. In order to improve the financial health of University Institutions, to give them a sound financial base and to improve the existing financial management system, it is recommended that a central coordinating agency at national level be constituted by the Government of India which may function through State financial agencies.

REFERENCE

1. University Grants Commission Letter No. F. 20-1/79(OH) (State) (Misc), 1987.

6

BUDGETING AND PLANNING SYSTEMS OF UNIVERSITY INSTITUTIONS IN INDIA

PLANNING REFERS to the definition of missions, goals and objectives, the identification and evaluation of alternatives and the choices among the alternatives. Budgeting refers to the process of translating the decisions programmed in the long range planning framed into the annual budget format, with more precise measures of inputs, price tags and outputs which are possible and necessary when looking only one year ahead.

The planning and budgeting are vitally important complementary activities linked with each other. Planning separated from budgeting tends to be a sterile exercise, budgeting separated from planning tends to be short-sighted and not well-informed. It is vitally important that their complementary activities are linked. They are effective tools in the management of finances of an organisation. The budget of an organisation is prepared to have effective utilisation of funds and for the accomplishment of the objectives as efficiently as possible. Planning is one of the vital functions of every manager and is the basis for every activity in an organisation. The budget of University Institution is an effective management tool for the (i) procurement of funds, (ii) allocation of funds, (iii) control of funds, (iv) policy and decision-making, (v) achievement of set goals and objectives, (vi) effective use of funds, and (vii) assessment of the financial health of a University Institution. Planning in a University Institution means the process whereby the educational institution establishes its long-run vision, goals and objectives, the identification and evaluation of alternatives and the choices among alternatives. Budgeting and Planning in the realm of university administration hardly require any emphasis. Budgeting and Planning play a vital role in the management of university finances. Through sound and effective techniques of budgeting and planning, most of the maladies in the management of university finances can be settled. It is, therefore, desirable to examine the existing budgeting and planning system of University Institutions in India and suggest the most appropriate system of budgeting and planning to be followed in such institutions. An attempt has been made to suggest budgeting and planning systems, which could be of effective use for the University Institutions as discussed hereinafter.

Budgeting System

In order to examine the budgeting system of an organisation, it is desirable to know the conceptual framework of a budget and various budgeting systems.

The budget of an organisation is a predetermined statement of management policy during a given period which provides a standard for comparison with the results achieved. The budget reflects the financial aspects in the working of an organisation whether it is within government or not. The significance of preparing a budget can be better understood if we analyse the nature of the decision upon which documents are based. The three dimensions of these decisions are (a) the economic dimension which involves using available resources in an effective and efficient way so that achievement of goals of the organisation is maximised, (b) the technical dimension which is based on knowledge of other inputs and outputs, (c) the political dimension related to the political aspects of resource allocations both between the public and private institutions and within public institutions for different kinds of inputs. Budget is a financial and quantitative statement prepared and approved for carrying out a variety of functions, viz. planning, evaluation, performance, coordinating activities, implementing plans, communicating, motivating and authorising action.

The Budgeting Systems are namely (i) Line Item Budgeting; (ii) Programme Budgeting; (iii) Performance Budgeting; (iv) Planning, Programming and Budgeting; and (v) Zero Base Budgeting.

In order to have better comprehension and utility of each budgeting system further details are discussed as hereunder.

In Line Item Budgets expenditure are first classified on the basis of the objectives on which they are incurred, that is pay of officers and ministerial staff, etc. Secondly, the expenditure is classified into Non-Plan and plan categories and development and non-development categories. The limitation of this system of budgeting is that it is not easy to identify and allocate all items of expenditure relating to a single programme.

The Programme Budgeting System involves the documentation of decision or resource requirement and outputs to be achieved, scheduled over the year involved in the planning period and the accompanying information and documentation system.

The Performance Budgeting is a technique which seeks to bring out what an organisation proposes to do, how much of it and at what cost and with what results. It presents an organisation's operations in terms of functions, programmes, activities and projects. It operates within the framework of clearly defined objectives which are sought to be achieved through successful implementation of these programmes and activities undertaken by the concerned department. The Performance Budgeting serves the purposes, namely (i) to present more clearly the purpose and fields in which the funds are sought and to bring out the programmes and accomplishments in financial and fiscal terms, (ii) to help better understanding and better review of the budget by legislature or the fund sanctioning authority, (iii) to improve the formation of the budget and to facilitate the process of decision-making at all levels, (iv) to enhance the accountability of management and at the same time to provide assistance and management of financial operations, (v) to perform more purposeful and effective audit. The limitations of performance budgeting are; (i) its restrictive value in respect of activities which are not measurable in any precise manner, as for example some research schemes, (ii) only quantitative and financial evaluation of programme and activities since qualitative evaluation is beyond its scope, and (iii) difficulty in achieving programmes and activities in organisational units.

In the Planning Programming Budgeting System the functions of planning, programming and budgeting are drawn together and inter-related. It provides an ongoing evaluation of the extent to which results are being achieved, with data feedback into the system for the purpose of auditing and refining operations. This system of budgeting helps the management to classify objectives and to make better decisions for the allocation of resources among different alternatives for attaining objectives. The limitations of this system of budgeting are, namely, (i) difficulty in fitting into the current budgeting schedule, (ii) lack of relevant data to link broad programmes and plans to budgeting decisions, (iii) viable alternatives difficult to be defined, (iv) quantification of results, (v) creating measurement techniques in education, (vi) long gestation period of educational outputs, (vii) providing even greater utilisation and less local control, and (viii) difficulty in incorporating into the system the lump sum cut in the budget by the funding agencies.

The Zero Base Budgeting is an operating, planning and budgeting process which requires each manager to justify his entire budget, from scratch (hence zero base), and this shifts the burden of proof to each manager to justify why he should spend money at all. The concept of Zero Base Budgeting requires that activities of the organisation should be viewed afresh and priorities among competing claims for allocation of funds settled on the basis of justifications developed by the use of evaluation techniques, like cost benefit analysis, cost effective analysis, etc. and on other desirable considerations. This requires that activities be identified by a systematic analysis and rank in order of merit. The methodology involves (i) identification of decision units, (ii) formation and development of decision practices, (iii) evaluating and ranking decision practices in order of priority, and (iv) preparation of budget by allocating resource activities or decision packages by utilising hierarchical funding cut off levels. The limitations of Zero Base Budgeting are; (i) much of paper work involved, (ii) short-period of a few months for review and analysis of requirements, (iii) availability of trained personnel, (iv) lack of sound information system based on cumbersome evaluation techniques, and (v) distinction between Plan and Non-Plan expenditure.

The slight differences on the emphasis of these budgeting systems are namely, Line Item Budgeting which emphasises finances accordingly and ensures legality in regulating expenditures. Performance Budgeting emphasises the evaluation part of the function of a budget. Thus it is essentially oriented to the past. Programme Budgeting emphasises the future orientation of the budget. The Planning Programming Budgeting System applies a system of anlaysis to the process of budgeting which is nothing but the process of decision-making in the field of finances. The Zero Base Budgeting System seeks to justify each proposal/activity/programme for funds in detail from scratch.

The budgeting system of University Institutions has mainly to be on the Government system since University Institutions have been and will continue to be dependent almost entirely on budgeting allocation of the Central and State Governments, especially the latter. The Government of India has taken various steps to improve the budgeting system of the Government and has stressed the need for application of Zero Base Budgeting in various departments of the Central and State Governments (1987).[1] It is necessary to examine whether the system being adopted by the Government can be exactly made applicable in the case of University Institutions, keeping in view the fact that aims and objectives of University Institution are altogether different from those of Government and other Corporations/Undertakings of the Government.

With this conceptual framework of the system of budgeting, as explained to various respondents, the primary data so collected has been analysed on the issues of formulation of the budget (existing practices) and system of budgeting recommended by various functionaries of University Institutions as given hereinafter.

Formulation of Budget

It is evident (Table 6.1) that all the Finance Officers/ Comptrollers/Registrars of Central Universities and Deemed Universities, most of the State General Universities and nearly half of the Institutions of National Importance and State Agricultural Universities are formulating their budgets on the lines suggested by the University Grants Commission. It has been reported that in the case of Central Universities, Deemed Universities and Institutions of National Importance, the budget is not prepared on the basis of available funds and expenditure thereto. The budget in all the Central Universities, State Agricultural Universities and Institutions of National Importance and most of the State General Universities, is prepared after getting the proposals from departments whereas it is so in the case of one-third of the surveyed Deemed Universities. With regard to preparation of the budget by the Finance Department of the University Institutions after taking into account past year's expenditure with anticipated increase it has been reported in the affirmative in all Central Universities, most of the State General Universities, nearly two thirds of State Agricultural Universities and Deemed Universities. It has been reported that in case of all Institutions of National Importance and most of State Agricultural Universities, the budget is formulated after the proposal has been scrutinised and the quantum of funds indicated by the Government. It has also been found that in the case of all surveyed Deemed Universities, and some of the State General Universities and

TABLE 6.1: Formulation of Budget

(Percentage responses)

Sl. No.	Particulars/Description	Central Universities	Deemed Universities	Institutions of National Importance	State General Universities	State Agricultural Universities
1	2	3	4	5	6	7
I.	*Finance Officers/Comptrollers/Registrars*					
1.	Budget prepared on the lines suggested by University Grants Commission	100.00	100.00	50.00	80.00	53.85
2.	Budget is based on —					
	2.1 Estimated income and expenditure	100.00	100.00	100.00	100.00	76.92
	2.2 Available funds and expenditure thereto	0.00	0.00	0.00	24.00	69.23
3.	Budget formulated					
	3.1 After getting proposals from departments	100.00	33.33	100.00	96.00	100.00
	3.2 After the Finance Wing takes into account past year's income and expenditure with anticipated increase	100.00	66.66	50.00	80.00	69.23
	3.3 After proposals are scrutinised and grants indicated by Government/Funding Agency	33.33	0.00	100.00	24.00	76.92
4.	Posts cleared by the Government before inclusion in budget	33.33	100.00	0.00	44.00	38.04
5.	Budget assessed by Government on the basis of budget submitted to it	66.66	66.66	100.00	64.00	92.31

Contd.

TABLE 6.1 *Contd.*

1	2	3	4	5	6	7
6.	New scheme/programme included after approval of the Government	0.00	66.66	50.00	32.00	30.77
7.	University associated for scrutiny and determination of grants-in-aid by Funding Agency	33.33	33.33	0.00	48.00	53.81
8.	Budget approved by					
	8.1 Government/Funding Agency	66.66	100.00	100.00	32.00	23.08
	8.2 University authorities	66.66	66.66	100.00	92.00	92.31
9.	Budget is scrutinised by a Committee of experts within the University	33.33	0.00	0.00	44.00	30.77
II.	*Professors and Heads of the Departments*					
1.	Budget formulated by					
	1.1 Inviting proposals from Departments	100.00	100.00	100.00	86.67	84.21
	1.2 Finance Wing of its own	33.33	0.00	33.33	35.00	34.21
2.	Allocation of budget to Department is made					
	2.1 As per proposal of the budget by the Department	100.00	100.00	100.00	46.67	42.11
	2.2 By the Finance Wing of its own	0.00	50.00	33.33	55.00	60.53

one third of the State Agricultural Universities and Central Universities posts are cleared by the Government before inclusion in the budget. It is interesting to note that the budget requirements of all Institutions of National Importance, most of the State Agricultural Universities and nearly two thirds of other types of universities are assessed by the funding agencies on the basis of the budget estimates of the University Institutions. It has been reported in the case of all Central Universities that they cannot include new schemes/programmes in the budget without the approval of the funding agency. Two third of the Deemed Universities, half of the Institutions of National Importance and nearly one third of the State General and State Agricultural Universities have reported that approval of the Government is required for inclusion of any new scheme/programme in the budget. Nearly half of State Agricultural and State General Universities are associated by the funding agencies for the scrutiny and determination of grants-in-aid by funding agency, whereas such a response is there in the case of one third of the Central Universities and Deemed Universities. The budgets of all the Deemed Universities and Institutions of National Importance and nearly two third of the Central Universities are also approved by the Government/Funding Agency, whereas such a practice exists in nearly one third of the State General Universities and in few of the Agricultural Universities.

There is no budget scrutinising committee in the case of Deemed Universities and Institutions of National Importance, where the same is in existence in some of the State General Universities, State Agricultural Universities and Central Universities. In all the sampled Central Universities, Deemed Universities, Institutions of National Importance and most of the State General Universities and State Agricultural Universities that the budget is formulated on the basis of proposals from the Professors and Heads of Departments. It is also prepared by the Finance Wing of its own, except in the case of Institutions of National Importance.

The allocation of the budget as per proposal of the Department is done in all the Central Universities, Deemed Universities and Institutions of National Importance, whereas such a response is there in case of nearly 45 per cent of the State General Universities and State Agricultural Universities. The allocation of budget by the Finance Department of the University of its own has also been reported in the case of majority of State Agricultural Universities and nearly one half of State General Universities and Deemed Universities.

From the foregoing analysis on various issues concerning 'Formulation of Budget' it can be inferred that there is no uniformity amongst different types of sampled universities, and this is affecting the financial management system of University Institutions. The shortcomings in the existing practices and remedial measures suggested for their rectification are discussed as given hereinafter.

The format of the University Grants Commission is mainly based on "Line Item Budgeting" and does not take into account the latest techniques of budgeting systems. For want of uniformity in the preparation of budgets of different University Institutions, one cannot visualise the over all financial management system of University Institutions in the country. Preparation of a budget by the Finance Wing of its own without getting proposals from the Heads of the Departments may entail the risk of omissions of certain important activities and is also against the principle of participative management. The preparation of a budget after scrutiny by the Government/Funding Agencies, clearance of posts by them and inclusion of new schemes/programmes with prior approval of the Government is against the autonomy of the University Institutions. The absence of involvement of University Institutions at the time of fixing grants-in-aid by the Government/funding agencies may result in omission of certain important schemes which the University Institutions may like to execute on priority and/or inclusion of schemes/items to which the University Institutions may like to give low priority, especially when the proposals of the University Institutions are not fully financed. The approval of the budget by the Government is against the autonomy of the University Institutions and results in late approval of the budget, thus, causing uncertainty in planning of the expenditure. The allocation of the budget to the departments by the Finance Wing itself without consulting the Heads of the Departments is against the principle of participative management.

It is, therefore, suggested that budget format of the University Grants Commission should be critically examined and a 'Model Format' be formulated after taking into account the modern techniques of budgeting. The budget of the University institutions should be prepared on the basis of estimated income and expenditure. The Heads of the Departments should be actively associated in the preparation of the budget. It should be prepared after getting their proposals and discussing the same, if need be, before the same are included or rejected. The budget should be prepared well in advance of the time schedule so fixed by the Government/Funding Agencies and should be sent to the Government for assessing the requirements of the University Institutions in consultation with them. The new schemes which have been approved by the authorities of the University Institutions should be included in the budget and there is no necessity to get the prior approval of the Government/Funding Agencies because such new schemes when incorporated in the budget shall be discussed at the time of discussion for determining the grants-in-aid to the University Institutions. The budget should be approved by the authorities of the University Institutions and only then it should be sent to the Government. The allocation of available funds to the departments should invariably be done after discussing the requirements with the Heads of the Departments so that their active participation is also ensured.

System of Budgeting

It can be observed (Table 6.2) that half of the Vice-Chancellors of Central Universities are in favour of the Zero Budgeting System. The Vice-Chancellors of Deemed Universities do not favour it at all, whereas very few Vice-Chancellors of other types of universities have expressed in favour of the Zero Base Budgeting. All Vice-Chancellors of surveyed Central Universities and Deemed Universities are in favour of the Planning Programming Budgeting System, whereas nearly forty per cent of the Vice-Chancellors of State General and Agricultural Universities favour this system of budgeting.

The Vice-Chancellor of Deemed Universities are not at all in favour of Performance Budgeting and Programme Budgeting, whereas such a response has been reported by half of the Vice-Chancellors of Central Universities. The majority of the Vice-Chancellors of the State General and State Agricultural Universities are in favour of Planning Programming Budgeting and Programme Budgeting System.

The Finance Officers/Comptrollers/Registrars of Central Universities are not in favour of the Zero Base Budgeting and Planning Programming Budgeting Systems, however, two thirds of them have expressed opinions in favour of performance Budgeting and Programme Budgeting Systems. The majority of Finance Officers/ Comptrollers/ Registrars of Deemed Universities are in favour of Planning Programming Budget System, whereas in the case of

TABLE 6.2: Recommended Systems of Budgeting

(Percentage responses)

Sl. No	Particulars/Description	Central Universities	Deemed Universities	Institutions of National Importance	State General Universities	State Agricultural Universities
1	2	3	4	5	6	7
I.	*Vice-Chancellors/Directors*					
1.	Budgeting System recommended					
1.1	Zero Base Budgeting	50.00	0.00	—	18.75	11.11
1.2	Planning Programming and Budgeting	100.00	100.00	—	43.75	44.44
1.3	Performance Budgeting	50.00	0.00	—	37.50	11.11
1.4	Programme Budgeting	50.00	0.00	—	37.50	44.44
II.	*Finance Officers/Comptrollers/Registrars*					
1.	Budgeting system recommended					
1.1	Zero Base Budgeting	0.00	33.33	50.00	20.00	23.08
1.2	Planning Programme and Budgeting	0.00	66.66	50.00	48.00	38.46
1.3	Performance Budgeting	66.66	0.00	0.00	36.00	23.08
1.4	Programme Budgeting	66.66	0.00	0.00	32.00	53.85
III.	*Professors and Heads of the Departments*					
1.	Zero Budgeting System recommended	33.30	100.00	66.61	50.00	52.63

Institutions of National Importance they are equally divided in favour of Planning Programming Budget and Zero Base Budgeting System. In the case of State General Universities the majority of them have expressed in favour of the Planning Programming Budgeting System, whereas the majority of them in case of State Agricultural Universities are in favour of the Programme Budgeting System. All Professors and Heads of the Departments of Deemed Universities two thirds of the Institutions of National Importance and one half of the State Agricultural and State General Universities have expressed opinions in favour of the Zero Base Budgeting System.

In can be said from the above analysis that there are divergent opinions of the Vice-Chancellors/Directors, Finance Officers/ Comptrollers/Registrars and Professors and Heads of the Departments on the issue of Budgeting System to be followed/adopted in University Institutions in India. After taking into account the merits and demerits of each budgeting system, the opinions expressed by the Vice-Chancellors/Directors, Finance Officers/Comptrollers/Registrars and Professors and Heads of Departments of various Department and distinct character of University Institutions in India, the Performance Budgeting System is recommended for adoption in the University Institutions in India. The Planning Programming Budgeting System can also be considered for adoption separately in respect of Commercial Units like Press, Guest Houses, Computer Centres, Dairy Farms, etc.

Planning Process

It is imperative on the part of the University Institutions to prepare both long-term and short-term plans, taking into consideration the environment and the circumstances under which they are operating. In an atmosphere of fund scarcity and in the light of existing constraints on resources mobilisations, the allocation and conservation of funds in an orderly manner needs the utmost attention. Like every other business enterprise, the University Institutions should also effectively plan for the mobilisation and utilisation of their resources. The primary data so collected on items of formulation of plans, participation in discussions on plans, representation on the planning board and timely communication of approved plan allocations, have been analysed and the position emerges as under:

It can be seen (Table 6.3) that Finance Officers/

Comptrollers/Registrars of all the Central Universities and Institutions of National Importance have stated that long-term plans and Five Year Plans are formulated in respect of their Universities whereas such responses have been reported to be more than two-thirds of the cases in respect of other types of universities. All the Institutions of National Importance and State Agricultural Universities are also formulating Annual Plans, whereas nearly one-third of Deemed Universities are doing so. Planning Committees exist in most of the Deemed Universities, State General Universities and half of the State Agricultural Universities. Outside experts are associated/represented on the Planning Committees in case of a few Deemed Universities, State General Universities and State Agricultural Universities.

It has been reported that the plan requirements of the University Institutions are discussed by the State Planning Board in case of most of the State Agricultural Universities and some of the State General Universities. The plan requirements are discussed in the Planning Commission, Government of India in respect of most of the State Agricultural Universities and some of the Deemed Universities and Institutions of National Importance whereas such participation is almost negligible in the case of State General Universities. It is only in very few State General Universities and State Agricultural Universities that Vice-Chancellors are members of the State Planning Board, whereas in the case of half of the sampled State Agricultural Universities it has been reported that the Vice-Chancellor is a special invitee to the State Planning Board. In the case of all Central and State Agricultural Universities, most of the State General Universities and Deemed Universities and half of the Institutions of National Importance, it has been reported that plans are approved by the Government/Funding Agencies and communicated to them. All the sampled State Agricultural Universities, half of the Institutions of National Importance and one-third of State General Universities and Deemed Universities have reported that plan allocations are indicated to them before the start of plan period. A time lag in plan communication has been reported by all the Central Universities, and most of the Deemed Universities and some of the State General Universities.

The non-formulation of long-term, five-year and annual plans by the University Institutions may stand in the way of their speedier growth and development which is also mainly dependent on plan funds. This is the reason in respect of most of the State General

TABLE 6.3: Planning Systems

(Percentage responses)

Sl. No.	Particulars/Description	Central Universities	Deemed Universities	Institutions of National Importance	State General Universities	State Agricultural Universities
1	2	3	4	5	6	7
Finance Officers/Comptrollers/Registrars						
1.	University Institution formulates					
1.1	Long-term plans	100.00	66.66	100.00	64.00	61.54
1.2	Five Year Plans	100.00	66..66	100.00	88.00	100.00
1.3	Annual Plans	66.66	32.33	100.00	80.00	100.00
2.	Planning Committee exists	33.33	66.66	0.00	60.00	53.85
3.	Planning Committee is represented by					
3.1	Only internal representatives	100.00	33.33	0.00	44.00	30.77
3.2	Outside experts are associated	0.00	33.33	0.00	20.00	23.08
4.	University Institutions are called for Plan discussions by					
4.1	State Planning Board	—	—	—	36.00	84.60
4.2	Planning Commission/Government of India	33.33	33.33	50.00	8.00	76.92
5.	*Vice-Chancellors/Director is*					
5.1	Member of the State Planning Board	0.00	0.00	0.00	16.00	7.69
5.2	Special invitee to State Planning Board	0.00	0.00	0.00	4.00	53.85
6.	Five Year Plans/Annual Plans approved and communicated to the University Institution	100.00	66.66	50.00	64.00	100.00
7.	Plan allocated and indicated before tne start of Plan period	0.00	33.33	50.00	32.00	100.00
8.	Time lag for communication	100.00	66.66	0.00	56.00	30.22

Universities that they are not getting the matching share for claiming financial assistance from the University Grants Commission. The non-existence of a Planning Committee in a University Institution may result in imbalanced planning since some of the activities may escape the notice of the unit responsible for preparation of the plan documents. The non-association of outside experts may deprive the University Institution of the expert opinion in formulation of plans. The non-participation of University Institution in the State Planning Boards and Planning Commissions of the Government of India at the time of discussing the Five Year Plans and Annual Plans may deprive the University Institution from presenting its requirement for future growth and development, as well as for providing a matching share in the case of State General Universities for lifting the central assistance from the University Grants Commission. The time lag in communication of the Plan allocations may stand in the way of timely planning and execution of various programmes/activities and planning of expenditure. The non-representation of the Vice-Chancellors/Directors on the Planning Board may deprive the Governments of expert opinion for the socio-economic development of the masses. The non-participation of the Vice-Chancellors/Directors or their representatives in the Planning Commission, Government of India, may result in lesser allotment of funds to the University Institutions.

It is, therefore, suggested that University Institutions should prepare long term, five-year and annual plans fully reflecting their requirements and submit the same to the Government so that their plan requirements could be assessed and funds provided. Each University Institution should constitute a Planning Committee under the Chairmanship of the Vice-Chancellors/Directors, consisting of fifteen members, both internal and outside experts to be nominated by the Vice-Chancellors/Directors for a period of three years. While nominating members to the said Committee, it should be ensured that all sections of University Institution are represented, may be by rotation and only those outside experts are nominated who are well conversant with educational planning. The Vice-Chancellors/Directors should be permanent invitees to the Planning Board, if not members and they or their representatives should be associated by the Government while discussing the plan requirements with the Planning Commission, Government of India. The sanction/allocation for the five year and annual plans should be communicated to the University

Institutions without any time lag so that they could plan their programmes and expenditure accordingly.

REFERENCE

1. Government of India, Ministry of Finance, Letter No.F.11(5)WSM/87, 1987

7

ACCOUNTING AND AUDITING SYSTEMS OF UNIVERSITY INSTITUTIONS IN INDIA

THE ACCOUNTS of an organisation give a functional classification of receipt and payments showing fund-wise position of income and function-wise classification of expenditure and help to analyse and interpret the financial data generated during the process of record keeping. The audit is also necessitated to exercise necessary control over the activities and the functions discharged by subordinate staff, which can also be achieved through the system of internal audit and internal check. As such where there is an accounting there must be auditing. These two should go together, then only can they make the financial exercise meaningful and beneficial to the organisation. The financial accounting and reporting is also a statutory requirement for an organisation. As such the accounts of an organisation are got audited from authorised agency/department so as to verify its correctness and fairness for their maintenance before they are finally accepted by the competent authority. The preparation of Annual Accounts and submission to the Government funding agency, duly audited, is a requirement of Act and Statutes for further release of grants-in-aid to the University Institutions. Thus, the accounting and auditing systems play a predominent role in the financial management of an organisation like a University Institution. An attempt has been made in this chapter to examine the existing accounting and auditing systems of University Institutions in India and to make recommendations/suggestions for the effective and efficient systems to be adopted/followed for effective management of University finances.

Accounting System

In order to examine the accounting system of an organisation, it is desirable to know the conceptual framework of accounting procedures/systems. The accounting procedures/systems, are namely,

(i) Receipt and Payment Account, (ii) Income and Expenditure Account, and (iii) Commercial Accounts with (a) Trading Account, (b) Profit and Loss Account, and (c) Balance Sheet.

The Receipt and Payment Account is the summary of actual cash receipts and payments extracted from the cash book covering a particular period. All receipts and payments during the period whether on account of capital or revenue should be included in the account. The account commences with the opening balance of cash and similarly closes with the balance of cash at the end of the period. It does not include any income or expense outstanding, and naturally fails to reveal the actual income and expenditure of the period it covers. Receipt and payment account need not be necessarily accompanied by a balance sheet.

The Income and Expenditure Account is a revenue account prepared by a non-trading concern and includes all income earned during a given period (whether actually received or not) and expenditure incurred for the purpose of earning such income (whether actually paid or not). The account does not commence with any balance and difference between the two sides would mean either excess of income over expenditure or *vice versa.* The Income and Expenditure Account must always be accompanied by its relative balance sheet.

The Commercial Account is that account which is maintained on a double entry system by non-government commercial concerns, dealing primarily with the utilisation of capital for the purpose of making profits and it is interested to see at intervals, how it stands in relation to its debtors and creditors, whether it is gaining or losing, what are the sources of its gain or loss, whether it is solvent or insolvent. For the preparation of Commercial Account the 'Trading Account' is first prepared and thereafter 'Profit and Loss Account' is prepared and the 'Balance Sheet' is finally drawn. The Trading Account contains in a summarised form all the transactions occurring during the period which has a direct relation to the goods dealt in by the business. After preparation of a 'Trading Account' and ascertainment of the gross profit, the next step is to prepare the 'Profit and Loss Account', to show the trader the net profit or loss resulting from a transaction during a certain period. The balance sheet (a statement) is prepared with a view to measure the exact financial position of the business on a certain fixed date. It reflects the true picture of financial health of an organisation.

With this conceptual framework of accounting systems/procedures as explained to various respondents, the primary data so collected has been analysed on the issues of formulation of accounts (existing practices) and system of accounting recommended by various functionaries of University Institutions as given hereinafter.

System of Accounting

It can be seen (Table 7.1) that all the Vice-Chancellor of Central Universities, three-fourths of State Universities and about half of the State Agricultural Universities have stated that the accounts are prepared as Receipt and Payment Accounts. All the Vice-Chancellors of Deemed Universities, about two-thirds of the State Agricultural Universities and one-half of the State General Universities have stated that accounts are prepared as Income and Expenditure Accounts. The Vice-Chancellors of all types of sampled universities have stated that the Commercial Accounting System is not being followed in the University Institutions. The Balance Sheet is prepared by all the surveyed Central Universities and Deemed Universities, whereas a similar practice is there in about one-third of the State General Universities and with very few of the State Agricultural Universities. It is further revealed from the Finance Officers/Comptrollers/Registrars of all the Central Universities, most of the State General and Agricultural Universities, half of the Institutions of National Importance and one-third of Deemed Universities that the accounts are prepared as Receipt and payment Account with classified abstracts. It is interesting to note that nearly two thirds of the Central Universities and Deemed Universities have also reported that they are preparing an Income and Expenditure Account.

It is revealed (Table 7.2) that the Finance Officers/ Comptrollers/Registrars of Institutions of National Importance are not in favour of the single entry system of maintaining accounts whereas the majority of them in the case of State General Universities, about half of the State Agricultural Universities have expressed in favour of this system. All the Institutions of National Importance, two-third of the Deemed Universities and nearly one-third of the State General and Agricultural Universities have expressed opinion in favour of the double entry system, whereas none of the Finance Officers/ Comptrollers/Registrars of Central Universities are in favour of this system. Preparation of a balance sheet has been recommended in the

TABLE 7.1: Present Accounting System

(Percentage responses)

Sl. No.	Particulars/Description	Central Universities	Deemed Universities	Institutions of National Importance	State General Universities	State Agricultural Universities
1	2	3	4	5	6	7
I.	*Vice-Chancellors/Directors*					
1.	Accounts prepared on the lines of					
1.1	Receipt and payment account	100.00	0.00	N.A.	75.00	55.56
1.2	Income and expenditure account	00.00	100.00	N.A.	50.00	66.66
1.3	Commercial accounts					
	1.3.1 Trading account	0.00	0.00	N.A.	0.00	0.00
	1.3.2 Profit and loss account	0.00	0.00	N.A.	0.00	0.00
	1.3.3 Balance sheet	100.00	100.00	N.A	31.25	11.11
II.	*Finance Officers/Comptrollers/Registrars*					
1.	System of accounting is					
1.1	Receipt and payment account with classified abstract	100.00	33.33	50.00	84.00	92.31
1.2	Income and expenditure account	66.66	66.66	50.00	24.00	38.46
1.3	Commercial account with balance sheet	0.00	66.66	0.00	12.00	0.00

TABLE 7.2: Recommended Accounting System

(Percentage responses)

Sl. No.	Particulars/Description	Central Universities	Deemed Universities	Institutions of National Importance	State General Universities	State Agricultural Universities
1	2	3	4	5	6	7
Finance Officers/Comptrollers/Registrars						
1.	System of Accounting recommended					
1.1	Single entry system	33.33	33.33	0.00	56.00	46.15
1.2	Double entry system	0.00	66.66	100.00	32.00	38.77
	1.2.1 Trading account	0.00	0.00	0.00	0.00	15.38
	1.2.2 Profit and loss account	0.00	0.00	0.00	0.00	0.00
	1.2.3 Balance sheet	100.00	100.00	0.00	24.00	38.46
2.	Receipt and payment account with classified abstract	100.00	33.00	0.00	48.00	84.62
3.	Income and expenditure account	33.33	66.66	—	42.00	53.85

case of all Central Universities and Deemed Universities, whereas such a response is about half and little in the case of State Agricultural Universities and State General Universities, respectively. All the Central Universities, most of the State Agricultural Universities and nearly half of the State General Universities have recommended the preparation of accounts as 'Receipt and Payment Account' with classified abstract, whereas two-third of Deemed Universities, are in favour of 'Income and Expenditure Account'.

From the foregoing description of the system of accounting, it can be inferred that there is no uniformity in the maintenance and preparation of accounts of University Institutions in India. Divergent recommendations emerged from Finance Officers/Comptrollers/ Registrars of various types of University Institutions, on the pertinent issues concerning maintenance and preparation of accounts.

The accounting system of University Institutions is of vital importance for knowing the state of affairs of such institutions. As such keeping in view the conceptual framework, shortcomings in the existing accounting system and recommendations thereon, remedial measures suggested for the proper upkeep of university accounts are discussed as given hereinafter.

The major source of funds to the University Institutions are from Central or State Governments and as such the accounting system should be on the lines of Government Accounts, which are maintained on the single entry system. The University Institutions being non-profit earning organisations as such commercial accounting system is not required for University Institution. In University accounting the transactions of income and expenditure are to be taken into account on accrual basis and no cognizance can be given to anticipatory income or expenditure as this shall inflate cash balances and give an erroneous picture of cash flow analysis. Moreover, the opening and closing balance of funds have to be reflected in the accounts of the University Institutions to watch the unspent balance and to reconcile the figures with the bank account. The balances sheet is not required for the University Account as a whole. As such an Income and Expenditure Accounting System is also not required for University Institutions. The University Institutions may be running commercial types of activities like the university press, revolving funds, and production and sales accounts of university publications. Although these activities are maintained almost entirely for the benefit of University Institutions, yet it is necessary that the financial results of these activities should be expressed in a normal commercial form so that the cost of their undertaking may be accurately known. A separate balance sheet for such activity can be prepared and kept on a proforma basis outside the general accounts of the University Institutions. These accounts will form a part of the Receipt and Payment Account after taking into account the income and expenditure in the main account.

It is, therefore, suggested that the accounts of University Institutions may be maintained on a single entry system and compiled as Receipt and Payment Accounts with classified abstracts. The Receipt and Payment Account should contain Annexures in respect of all items of income/receipt and corresponding items of expenditure. The Annexures of Income should give the details of the sanction letters of the funding agency and the amount sanctioned there against, grants-in-aid wise. Similarly, the income of the University Institutions should be scheme-wise and annexed in the main account. On the expenditure side, the Annexures should contain the classified expenditure scheme-wise/unit-wise indicating there against the items of expenditure duly classified, viz. salary, allowances, recurring contingency, non-recurring contingency, travelling allowance, scholarships, etc. The expenditure and income under capital (Works) should form a separate classification in the main account and work-wise details of the receipts and expenditure be attached as Annexures with the main account. Items of income and expenditure in respect of units being in the University Institutions on commercial lines and for which a revolving fund is also created, should also be reflected in the main account under the income and expenditure columns, for which a proper account is prepared and a balance sheet drawn and attached as Annexure outside the University Account. Similarly, Receipt and Payment Account for retirement benefits like C.P.F. Account/G.P.F. Account, Pension Fund Account, Students Fund Account and other Welfare Fund Accounts which are kept outside the General Fund Account of the University Institutions be abstracted as separate Annexures and attached with the main accounts. The accounts should indicate the opening balance, grants received, domestic receipt realised, the expenditure there against and the balance at the end in respect of each source of funding to depict a clear picture of financial position of the University Institutions at a glance.

Maintenance of Bank Account

Almost all the Finance Officers/Comptrollers/Registrars of Deemed

Universities, most of the State Agricultural Universities and nearly two-thirds of Central Universities have reported that the combined account for all grants has been maintained by their universities (Table 7.3). It has also been reported from all the Central Universities, most of the State Agricultural Universities, State General Universities and about two-thirds of the Deemed Universities that a consolidated account is prepared. With regard to maintenance of separate account for retiring benefits of employees, it has been reported by all the Institutions of National Importance that a separate account is maintained. It may be seen from the table that Central Universities and Deemed Universities are not maintaining separate accounts for retiring benefits. In most of the State General Universities and in all other types of University Institutions, the University Fund is kept under the current bank account. Most of the State General and Agricultural Universities, half of the Institutions of National Importance and one-third of the Central Universities and Deemed Universities are also having saving bank accounts. There is no separate Students Fund Account in the case of Institutions of National Importance, whereas in the case of two-thirds of the Central Universities, Deemed Universities and State Agricultural Universities separate Students Fund Account is maintained. It is interesting to note that about one-third of the Central Universities have reported that a Students Fund forms a part of the General Fund, whereas in Deemed Universities two-thirds of them have reported in the affirmative. The accounts are maintained and operated centrally by the Finance Wing in almost all types of University Institutions. However, in some of the State Agricultural Universities and a few of the State General Universities, separate accounts in the name of Drawing and Disbursing Officer are maintained whereas no such accounts are maintained by any of the Central Universities, Deemed Universities and Institutions of National Importance. Accounts are compiled centrally by the Finance Wing by most of the State Agricultural and General Universities, nearly two-thirds of the Central Universities and half of the Institutions of National Importance. However, nearly one-third of the State Agricultural Universities, Central Universities, and a few of State General Universities are also getting their accounts compiled from the respective drawing and disbursing officers.

TABLE 7.3: Maintenance of Bank Account (Existing System)

(Percentage responses)

Sl. No.	Particulars/Description	Central Universities	Deemed Universities	Institutions of National Importance	State General Universities	State Agricultural Universities
1	2	3	4	5	6	7
	Finance Officers/Comptrollers/Registrars					
1.	Bank Account is maintained					
1.1	Separately for each grant	33.33	33.33	0.00	48.00	7.69
1.2	Combined for all grants	66.66	100.00	0.00	56.00	76.90
2.	Accounts compiled/prepared					
2.1	Separately for each grant	66.66	0.00	0.00	44.00	23.08
2.2	Consolidated account	100.00	66.66	50.00	72.00	92.31
3.	Separate account outside Main Account for retiring benefits of employees	0.00	0.00	100.00	60.00	46.15
4.	Funds are kept under					
4.1	Savings Bank Account	33.33	33.33	50.00	76.00	69.02
4.2	Current Bank Account	100.00	100.00	100.00	84.00	100.00
5.	Students Fund is maintained					
5.1	Separately under distinct head/Bank Account	66.66	66.66	0.00	52.00	69.23
5.2	Forms a part of Main Fund Account	33.00	66.66	0.00	28.00	15.38
6.	University Institutions Accounts are maintained and operated					
6.1	Centrally by the Finance Wing	100.00	100.00	100.00	84.00	100.00
6.2	Separately by all Drawing and Disbursing Officer	0.00	0.00	0.00	24.00	46.15
7.	Accounts of the University Institution are compiled by					
7.1	Respective Drawing and Disbursing Officers	33.33	0.00	0.00	20.00	30.77
7.2	Combined by the Finance Wing	66.66	33.33	50.00	76.00	92.31

It can be observed (Table 7.4) that all the Vice-Chancellors of Central Universities, Deemed Universities, most of the State General Universities and two-thirds of the State Agricultural Universities are in favour of having one university account, in the name of Finance Officer/Comptroller/Registrar. About half of the Vice-Chancellors of Central Universities and a few of State Agricultural Universities (22.22 per cent) are also in favour of accounts in the name of drawing and disbursing officers. All the Vice-Chancellors of Deemed Universities have expressed the opinion that the accounts in the name of drawing and disbursing officers stand in the way of speedy compilation of accounts and issuance of grants utilization certificates and release of grants, whereas Vice-Chancellors of Central Universities are of the contrary opinion.

The multiplication of accounts in the University Institutions results complexities (i) delay in the compilation of accounts; (ii) risk of fraudulent drawals, (iii) delay in reconciliation of expenditure with bank account, (iv) loss of time and interest in the process of transfer of money from one account to another, (v) delay in timely submission of grant utilization certificates. Keeping all funds in the current account results in loss of interest and loss of additional income to the University Institutions. Keeping of money of its retiring employees and students funds in the main account results in financial constraints to be faced by the University Institutions at the time of discharge of these liabilities, especially when the financial position of University Institutions is not very sound. The compilation of accounts by various drawing and disbursing officers results in unnecessary wastage of time and energy of academic staff which could otherwise be utilized for other academic pursuits.

It is suggested that there should be one university account in the name of the Finance Officer/Comptroller to the centrally operated. The drawing and disbursing officers should only keep a separate account for imprest money sanctioned for them in case the imprest amount exceeds rupees two thousand. There should be no multiplicity of bank accounts in the University Institutions and only one general account should be maintained for all types of grants and the accounts should be prepared in a consolidated manner incorporating therein the position of balances in respect of each type of grant. A separate fund should be created for the retiring employees and kept in a separate bank account outside the general account. Similarly, the students fund should be kept outside the general account. The funds should be initially deposited in

TABLE 7.4: Recommended System of Operation of Accounts

(Percentage responses)

Sl. No.	Particulars/Description	Central Universities	Deemed Universities	State General Universities	State Agricultural Universities
1	2	3	4	5	6
Vice-Chancellors/Directors					
1.	There should be				
1.1	One University Institution Account in the name of Finance Officer/Comptroller/Registrar	100.00	100.00	93.75	66.66
1.2	Accounts in the name of all Drawing and Disbursing Officers	50.00	0.00	0.00	22.22
2.	Accounts in the name of all Drawing and Disbursing Officers				
2.1	Stand in the way of speedy compilation of accounts and issuance of Grants Utilisation Certificates	0.00	100.00	18.75	11.11
2.2	Timely release of grants	0.00	100.00	31.25	11.11

the current bank account and a minimum amount should be kept in the current account to meet day to day expenditure. The surplus amount should be kept in a saving bank account so as to earn interest and thereby augmenting additional resources to the University Institutions. The accounts should be compiled centrally by the Finance Wing and the drawing and disbursing officers should only maintain the books of income and expenditure for reconciliation of expenditure with central office.

Accounts Manual/Codes

It can be seen (Table 7.5) that about two-thirds of the State Agricultural Universities and Deemed Universities have prepared their Accounts Manual/Codes. Nearly half of Institutions of National Importance and one third of the Central Universities have also prepared Accounts Manual/Code. All the Central Universities, Institutions of National Importance, State Agricultural Universities, most of the State General Universities and two thirds of Deemed Universities are in favour of having Accounts Manual/Codes of the University Institutions. The accounts of works are maintained on state public works departments pattern in most of the State Agricultural Universities and State General Universities, whereas all the Central Universities, Institutions of National Importance, and most of the Deemed Universities are maintaining accounts of works on central public works department pattern. About half of the State Agricultural Universities and nearly one-third of the State General Universities and Deemed Universities have also developed/formulated their own procedures for the maintenance of university accounts.

It can be inferred from the foregoing description that in the majority of cases, the University Institutions have not formulated their Accounts Manual/Codes. The non-manualisation and codification of various financial rules, instructions and procedures on the various activities of the University Institutions may create confusion and even result in financial irregularities. It, is, therefore, suggested that all the University Institutions should prepare their own Accounts Manuals and the State Governments/Governments of India's Financial Rules should be followed only where the financial rules of the University Institutions are silent.

TABLE 7.5: Accounts Manual/Code

(Percentage responses)

Sl. No.	Particulars/Description	Central Universities	Deemed Universities	Institutions of National Importance	State General Universities	State Agricultural Universities
1	2	3	4	5	6	7
Finance Officers/Comptrollers/Registrars						
1.	University Institution has prepared Account Manual/Code	33.33	66.66	50.00	40.00	61.54
1.1	University is following State Government Financial Rules	0.00	0.00	0.00	76.00	84.62
1.2	University Institution is following Central Government Financial Rules	100.00	66.66	100.00	52.00	0.00
2.	There is necessity for Accounts Manual/Code	100.00	66.66	100.00	96.00	100.00
3.	Works Accounts are maintained on the procedure					
3.1	Developed/formulated by the University Institution	0.00	33.00	0.00	32.00	53.85
3.2	On State/Central Public Works Department pattern	100.00	66.66	100.00	64.00	76.09

Auditing System

The audit plays a vital role in the management of university finances. If reflects on the proper management of university finances and their utilization for the purpose for which they have been allotted and sanctioned. The audit also draws attention to financial irregularities, if any, and also gives a fair picture of the maintenance of accounts. It advises the University Institutions with regard to improvement of its financial management systems and judicious utilisation of funds.

Audit is of vital importance to an organisation because spending departments have a constant fear that audit has to be conducted and irregularities found, if any, are bound to create problems. Thus, the audit provides code of conduct for all institutions. This is a statutory requirement and also an essential condition for the further release of funds by the funding agencies.

In order to examine the auditing system of an organisation, it is important to know the conceptual frame-work of various prevalent auditing systems being followed for the conduct of the audit.

The prevalent auditing systems are: (i) Internal Audit, (ii) Concurrent Audit, (iii) Pre-Audit, and (iv) Post Audit.

The internal audit is introduced by an organisation of its own out of its own staff. Internal auditors check irregularities, help the various departments under the organisation in the proper upkeep of their accounts, assist and guide settlement of audit paras of external audit and minimisation of audit objections. This audit is in addition to the statutory audit.

The concurrent audit is conducted by an external agency independent of the organisation. Under this audit the organisation make the payment and immediately thereafter the vouchers alongwith relevant records are presented to the such auditors for applying necessary checks. The observations with regard to such payments, which are required to be met by the organisation are conveyed to them through audit memorandum for compliance. The limitations of this audit is that overpayments, if any, cannot be stopped because when the records are checked, the payment had already been made. At times it may happen that overpayments made may not be recovered from the payees outside the organisation.

The pre-audit is conducted on day to day basis by an independent agency. In this system of audit the bills duly passed by the concerned department of the organisation are presented to statutory auditors with relevant records for clearing the bills for release of the payments after exercising necessary checks. In this system no payment can be made without pre-audit. The actual payees receipts, audit of stores, income and booking of expenditure is however, checked by the same auditors on a post-audit basis. The shortcomings of this system are: (i) sometimes it cause delay in releasing payments and (ii) in case of difference of opinion between the auditors and authorities of the organisation the cases have to be referred to the Government for clarification, etc. which may cause undue irritation and inconvenience to the payees. Despite these shortcomings this system of audit prevents overpayments and reduces the chances of defalcations. It goes a long way for the proper maintenance of accounts, timely certification of annual accounts, issuance of audit reports and submission of audited grant utilisation certificates to the funding agencies.

The post-audit is conducted by statutory auditors at convenient intervals. Under this system test check of the accounts of the organisation is conducted by auditors in respect of those months as are confidentially intimated by the head office of the statutory auditors to the officer-in-charge of the audit party. The audit party conducts the detailed audit of selected months. However, they are authorised to conduct the detailed audit of other months in case of any apprehensions of grave irregularities, etc. The limitations of this audit are: (i) time lag in the conduct of regular audit, (ii) some major irregularities in respect of months not selected for detailed audit may escape the notice of the auditors, (ii) delay in the certification of annual accounts and issuance of audit report, (iv) delay in release of grants by funding agencies for want of timely submission of grant utilization certificates.

With this conceptual framework of the system of auditing, as explained to various respondents the primary data so collected has been analysed as given hereinafter.

System of Auditing in University Institutions

It can be seen (Table 7.6) that Finance Officers/Comptrollers/ Registrars of all the Central Universities, two thirds of the Deemed Universities and fifty per cent of Institutions of National Importance have reported that the system of post-audit with internal audit is in vogue in their institutions. Nearly half of the State Agricultural Universities and State General Universities have reported that the pre-audit system is being followed in their cases. The system of

TABLE 7.6: Existing Audit System

(Percentage responses)

Sl. No.	Particulars/Description	Central Universities	Deemed Universities	Institutions of National Importance	State General Universities	State Agricultural Universities
1	2	3	4	5	6	7
I.	*Finance Officers/Comptrollers/Registrars*					
1.	System of audit followed					
1.1	Pre-audit	66.66	33.33	50.00	44.00	53.85
1.2	Post-audit with internal audit	100.00	66.66	50.00	36.00	23.00
1.3	Post-audit without internal audit	0.00	33.33	0.00	16.00	23.00
1.4	Concurrent audit	0.00	0.00	0.00	16.00	15.38
II.	*Professors & Heads of the Departments*					
1.	Satisfied with the system of audit	66.66	0.00	0.00	31.67	28.95
2.	System of audit followed	66.66	100.00	0.00	25.00	34.21
2.1	Pre-audit				-	
2.2	Post-audit with internal audit	66.66	50.00	100.00	40.00	36.84
2.3	Post-audit without internal audit	33.33	50.00	—	10.00	15.79
2.4	Concurrent audit	33.33	0.00	0.00	8.33	21.05

concurrent audit has been reported to be followed in a few State General Universities and State Agricultural Universities. It is further evident from the table that Professors and Heads of Departments of two-thirds of the Central Universities, and nearly one-third of State Agricultural and General Universities are satisfied with the existing system of audit, whereas those of Deemed Universities and Institutions of National Importance are not at all satisfied with the existing auditing system. It is interesting to note that the informaiton as reported by Professors and Heads of the Departments on the existing system of auditing is quite at variance from that of Finance Officers/Comptrollers/Registrars which shows that they are not fully aware of the system of audit being followed in their Institutions.

It can be inferred (Table 7.7) that all the Vice-Chancellors of Central Universities, half of the State General Universities and State Agricultural Universities have recommended that the pre-audit system of auditing. All the Vice-Chancellors of Deemed Universities have expressed opinions in favour of concurrent audit. Half of the Vice-Chancellors of Central Universities and State Agricultural Universities and nearly one-third of the State General Universities have also reported in favour of post-audit with internal audit. In the case of most of the State General Universities, nearly half of the State Agricultural Universities and Institutions of National Importance and one-third of Deemed Universities, the Finance Officers/ Comptrollers/Registrars have recommended pre-audit system for University Institutions. Two thirds of them in respect of Central Universities are in favour of post-audit with internal audit whereas such a concurrence is also evitable from half of the State Agricultural Universities and Institutions of National Importance. Only a few of the Vice-Chancellors of the State Agricultural Universities and State General Universities are in favour of post audit without internal audit.

It can be inferred from the foregoing description that there is no uniformity in the auditing system being followed by University Institutions in India. Divergent recommendations have been made by Vice-Chancellors/Directors and Finance Officers/Comptrollers/ Registrars on the system of auditing which could meet the requirement of University Institutions. Effective and efficient auditing system for University Institutions need no emphasis for the management of University Finances. Keeping in view the merits and demerits of prevalent auditing systems, opinions expressed by Vice-Chancellors/ Directors and Finance Officers/Comptrollers/Registrars and the

TABLE 7.7: Recommended System of Audit

(Percentage responses)

Sl. No.	Particulars/Description	Central Universities	Deemed Universities	Institutions of National Importance	State General Universities	State Agricultural Universities
1	2	3	4	5	6	7
I.	*Vice-Chancellors/Directors*					
1.	Audit System recommended					
1.1	Pre-audit	100.00	0.00	N.A.	56.25	44.44
1.2	Concurrent audit	0.00	100.00	N.A.	12.50	22.22
1.3	Post audit with internal audit	50.00	0.00	N.A.	37.50	55.51
1.4	Post audit without internal audit	0.00	0.00	N.A.	12.50	11.11
II.	*Finance Officers/Comptrollers/Registrars*					
1.1	Pre-audit	0.00	33.33	50.00	76.92	53.85
1.2	Concurrent audit	33.00	33.33	0.00	28.00	23.07
1.3	Post-audit with internal audit	66.66	33.33	50.00	40.00	53.85
1.4	Post-audit without internal audit	0.00	33.33	50.00	4.00	0.00

peculiar character and specified requirement of University Institutions in India the pre-auditing system with strong Internal Inspection is recommended for University Institutions. The pre-audit should be supplemented with a Test Check audit of Comptroller and Auditor General of India in cases where the expenditure under the Government grant exceeds seventy-five per cent of the total expenditure.

Role of Audit

It is revealed (Table 7.8) that all the Finance Officers/Comptrollers/ Registrars of Deemed Universities, Institutions of National Importance, State General Universities and most of the State Agricultural Universities are of the opinion that audit provides an independent scrutiny of the veracity and fairness of accounts. It has been reported by all the Finance Officers/Comptrollers/ Registrars of Deemed Universities and Institutions of National Importance, that pre-audit acts as a guide and advisor in the current financial transactions, whereas such opinions also have been expressed by the majority of the Finance Officers/Comptrollers/Registrars of other types of University Institutions. It is only in the case of nearly two-thirds of State General Universities and nearly one-third of the State Agricultural Universities, Central Universities and Deemed Universities that it has been reported that pre-audit stands in the way of speedier execution of programmes.

It is, therefore, suggested that audit should help, guide and advise the University Institutions to correct financial transactions. This will go a long way in the improvement of financial management of such institutions.

Existing Audit Agencies and Issuance of Grants Utilisation Certificates

It can be seen (Table 7.9) that in all the Central Universities, Deemed Universities and Institutions of National Importance, audit is being conducted by the Comptroller and Auditor General to Government of India. In most of the State Agricultural Universities and State General Universities the Examiner, Local Funds Accounts of the State Government conducts audit of universities. Comptroller and Auditor General Government of India conducts a second audit (test check) in most of the State Agricultural Universities and in about half of the

TABLE 7.8: Role of Audit

(Percentage responses)

Sl. No.	Particulars/Description	Central Universities	Deemed Universities	Institutions of National Importance	State General Universities	State Agricultural Universities
1	2	3	4	5	6	7
I.	*Finance Officers/Comptrollers/Registrars*					
1.	Audit provides an independent scrutiny of the veracity and fairness of accounts	66.66	100.00	100.00	100.00	92.31
2.	Pre-audit					
2.1	Stands in the way of speedier execution of programmes	33.33	33.33	0.00	64.00	38.46
2.2	Acts as a guide and advisor in the correct financial transactions	66..66	100.00	100.00	64.00	69.23
2.3	Helps in the timely submission of grant utilisation certificates	33.33	0.00	50.00	72.00	26.92

TABLE 7.9: Existing Audit Agencies and Issuance of Grant Utilisation Certificates

(Percentage responses)

Sl. No.	Particulars/Description	Central Universities	Deemed Universities	Institutions of National Importance	State General Universities	State Agricultural Universities
1	2	3	4	5	6	7
	Finance Officers/Comptrollers/Registrars					
1.	Auditing agency is					
1.1	Accountant General	100.00	100.00	100.00	40.00	61.54
1.2	Examiner Local Fund Accounts	0.00	0.00	0.00	72.00	76.92
1.3	Director Audit and Accounts of State Government	0.00	0.00	0.00	16.00	7.69
1.4	Chartered Accountant	0.00	0.00	0.00	16.00	0.00
2.	There is second audit by Comptroller and Auditor General under CAG Act	0.00	66.00	0.00	40.00	76.92
3.	Grant Utilisation Certificates are issued by the					
3.1	State Government Statutory Auditors	33.33	0.00	50.00	36.00	69.23
3.2	Accountant General	66.66	100.00	50.00	16.00	30.77
4.	Audit Report alongwith audited accounts laid on the table of State Assembly/Parliament	66.66	33.33	100.00	36.00	84.61
5.	Serious audit paras included in the public accounts committee	33.33	33.33	50.00	48.00	84.61

State General Universities. It has been reported that in most of the State Agricultural Universities, and one-third of State General Universities the grant utilisation certificates are issued by the statutory auditors of the State Government. It has been reported that the Comptroller and Auditor General issues grants utilisation certificates in all the Deemed Universities, two-thirds of the Central Universities and half of the Institutions of National Importance. In the case of all the Institutions of National Importance, most of the State Agricultural Universities, Central Universities and one-third of State General Universities and Deemed Universities, audit reports and audited accounts are laid on the table of the State Assembly/Parliament. In most of the State Agricultural Universities, nearly half of the State General Universities and Institutions of National Importance, and one-third of the Central Universities and Deemed Universities serious audit paras are included in the report of Public Accounts Committee.

From the foregoing description it can be inferred that there is no uniform audit agency for the conduct of audit of University Institutions in India. A similar position exists in respect of issuance of grant utilisation certificates. The second audit by the Comptroller and Auditor General of India when the expenditure is less than 75 per cent of the total expenditure out of Government grants, undermines the role of other statutory auditor's agencies. Laying of the audit report and audited accounts by some of the University Institutions on the table of Parliament/Assembly is against the principle of autonomy as recommended by the Committee on 'Model Act'.

It is, therefore, suggested that the Examiner Local Fund Account/Director of audit and accounts should be the statutory auditor in respect of State General Universities and State Agricultural Universities, in view of the fact pre-audit system can only function through this agency. There should be no second audit (test check) by the Comptroller and Auditor General of India, in case the expenditure does not exceed 75 per cent of the total Government grants. The audit report and annual accounts should be sent to the Government for information only and not for laying at the table of Parliament/Assembly in the interest of autonomy of the University Institutions.

8

STRATEGIES FOR FUTURE

EFFECTIVE FINANCIAL management contributes a lot to the speedier development and growth of a University Institution. It also creates in the university community a healthy atmosphere and feeling of security. The Government of India constituted various Committees/ Commissions for University Management from time to time. Based on the recommendations of such Committees/Commissions several important coordinating bodies like the University Grants Commission, the Indian Council of Agricultural Research, the Council of Scientific and Industrial Research, the Indian Council of Medical Research etc. have been established in the country for the promotion and coordination of university education. Accordingly Agricultural Universities, Engineering Universities and Health Universities have come up in the country apart from a large number of multi-faculty general universities. The number of University Institutions has increased from twenty-eight as it stood at the time of independence to one hundred and seventy-six by December, 1987. Enrolment of students has gone up from 11,90,713 to 35,70,897 over a period of twenty years from 1966-67 to 1985-86 at a compound rate of 2.4 per cent per year. The annual non-plan expenditure on education under the central and state budgets has increased by more than fifty times over the last thirty-five years, that is, from Rupees 114 crores in 1950-51 to more than Rupees 6,000 crores in 1984-85. The expenditure on education has increased from 1.2 per cent of the Gross National Product from the period 1950-51 to 4.0 per cent in 1984-85, yet this share is quite low when these figures are compared with those of other less developed countries. Though substantial increase has been made in many University Institutions and in terms of expenditure on university education yet the financial position of most of the existing University Institutions is far from satisfactory and many universities in the country are facing rough weather and are operating with heavy deficits. There is a general feeling that there is unplanned growth together with lack of efficient and effective management in most of the universities. As universities are autonomous they do not exercise effective control in the management of their finances due to budget deficit and paucity of funds. Thus, the management of university finances is presently undergoing several internal stresses and strains, resulting in low academic standard and performance. The problem of management of finances in University Institutions is attributed to lack of uniformity in the governance of all types of University Institutions as well as in various parameters of management such as the compositions, powers and functions of authorities/bodies, representation of all sections of the university community to such authorities/bodies, powers and functions of Finance Officers/Comptrollers, delegation of powers, functional and financial autonomy, pattern of funding and expenditure, grants-in-aid rules, criteria for fixation of grants, etc. Besides, there is no sound and uniform budgeting system and above all no serious thought seems to have been given to the planning process in different types of University Institutions. There is no proper and uniform system of maintenance of accounts and auditing in university Institutions. Most of the State Governments have not enacted Common Acts for governance of universities, where more than one university is established. The Central Universities, Deemed Universities and Institutions of National Importance, which are mainly financed by the Government of India/University Grants Commission are on a better financial footing as compared with the State General and Agricultural Universities. The findings so arrived at as a result of the present study as detailed in different chapters lead to the inference that there is great scope for the improvement of the existing financial management system of University Institutions in India. The effective and efficient financial management system can go a long way in bringing the University Institutions out of the present financial crisis and in helping them to achieve set objectives/goals.

The following measures are suggested for the improvement of the existing financial management system of University Institutions in India:

1. The Act of University Institutions and Model Act of Indian Council of Agricultural Research should be reviewed and revised in the light of recommendations of the Committee on the Model Act and the Gajendragadkar Committee.
2. The State which have more than one State General University

should enact a Common Act for the governance of universities to ensure uniformity.

3. All powers for laying down the financial policies and procedures should be vested with the Syndicate (Executive Council/Board of Management) which should be assisted by the Finance Committee.
4. All sections of the University Community be given representation on the Senate (Court/Council) and the Syndicate (Executive Council/Board of Management). The students should have no voting right on the agenda concerning appointment of examiners, financial matters and selection of employees. The students and non-teaching employees should not be represented on the Academic Council.
5. The Court (Senate/Council) should not be the supreme authority and should not exercise the powers to approve the budget, make, amend or repeal the statutes and to create posts. It should exercise general supervision over the affairs of the University Institutions. The financial powers should be vested with the Syndicate (Executive Council/Board of Management). All financial matters should be first considered by the Finance Committee.
6. There should be representation from the Central Government and from the University Grants Commission on the Finance Committee of Central Universities, Deemed Universities and Institutions of National Importance. The Finance Secretary to the Government and Secretary to the Government dealing with University affairs should be represented on the Finance Committee of the State General Universities and State Agricultural Universities. The representation to Deans/Directors and Professors and Heads of the Departments should also be provided on the Finance Committee of all types of University Institutions. The Finance Officer/Comptroller should be a Member Secretary and the Registrar should be a permanent invitee to the Finance Committee. The Vice-Chancellors/Directors should be the Chairmen of the Finance Committee.
7. The Model composition of the Finance Committee should be as suggested under the heading, "Composition of Finance Committee" in Chapter 3.
8. The post of Finance Officer/Comptroller should be designated

as Controller of Finances. The Finance Officer/Comptroller should be a statutory officer appointed by the university on the recommendation of the selection committee. He should work under the control of the Vice-Chancellor/Director and should be directly responsible to him. He should be the principal financial advisor and should be of the same rank and status as that of Registrar and should be a permanent invitee to all meetings of the authorities of the University Institution.

9. The system of decentralisation and delegation of powers as is being followed by the State Agricultural Universities should be adopted in all types of University Institutions. The Heads of the Departments and other functionaries should be delegated adequate financial powers with supporting ministerial staff. Only the compilation of accounts and issuance of cheques should be centralised with the Finance Department of the University Institution.
10. The Government should not exercise any power to approve the budget and to allow creation of posts in respect of University Institutions once the quantum of financial assistance is determined by the Government and the University Institution is in a position to bear additional liability from its existing resources. Financial control can be exercised by the Government through the system of audit and submission of audited accounts along with audit reports to the Government.
11. Functional and financial autonomy should be provided to all types of University Institutions, particularly the State General Universities. The University Institutions should enjoy functional and financial autonomy for raising funds, plan pattern of expenditure and management of funds. They should be provided funds additionally when a new programme or scheme is started and when there is an increase in students enrolment. Once the grant is earmarked for the University Institution the same should be released as per time schedule mutually decided by the University Institution and the funding agency.
12. The Professors and Heads of the departments should be associated in the preparation of agenda for the Senate (Court/Council) and Syndicate (Executive Council/Board of Management) which is all the more necessary so that they feel concerned regarding the running of affairs of the University

Institutions.

13. Adequate funds, flexibility in allocation, timely allotment and release of funds by the Government/funding agencies and an efficient system of auditing should be ensured for running the activities of various departments of a University Institution.
14. The University Grants Commission should provide liberal, if not adequate funds as are being provided to the Central Universities without asking for matching grants from the State General Universities to meet development requirements. The funds provided to the State General Universities and State Agricultural Universities should be earmarked by the Finance Commission and the Planning Commission of India at the time of determining the quantum of Non-Plan and Plan grants to the State Government.
15. The grants-in-aid to the University Institutions should be reflected as a minor head under a major head of the department concerned with the caption 'Grants-in-aid to the University Institution (Name)'. The grants-in-aid should be released by various departments without seeking sanction of the Finance Department of the Government once it has been provided in the budget.
16. In the beginning of the quarter/quarterly grants should be released to the University Institutions and the funding agency should issue a sanction letter in the beginning of the financial year, specifying the month and date on which the quarterly grant is to be paid to the University Institution. The funding agencies should remit the grant on their own every quarter as specified in the sanction letter through bank draft only.
17. The revenue grant should be lapsable after one year from the date of its sanction/payment. The capital grant should not lapse with the close of the financial year and should be allowed to be expended even beyond the plan period if the situations so warrants.
18. The block grants should be paid to the University Institution with freedom to utilise the same on various activities in the manner it deems fit. The University Institutions should also be provided with specific grants especially for the execution of development works and specific schemes/projects. Adequate grants should be provided to University Institutions and the quantum should be decided by the funding agencies after taking

into account the existing programmes and new schemes/projects which should coincide with the period of Finance Commission and Planning Commission of the Government of India.

19. Uniform grants-in-aid rules should be formulated for all types of University Institutions in the country so that there are no varying standards for their financing. Model grants-in-aid rules for funding of the University Institutions should be as suggested under heading, 'Model Grants-in-Aid Rules' under Chapter 4.
20. There should be a national body in the country which should have a say in financial matters especially with regard to giving uniform guidelines to the Central or State Governments for funding of University Institutions. The University Grants Commission should act as a co-ordinating agency for fixation of block/maintenance grants to the State General Universities and Institutions of National Importance. Similarly, the Indian Council of Agricultural Research should act as a co-ordinating agency for fixation of block/maintenance grants to the State Agricultural Universities.
21. The Model Criteria/Formulae for fixation of grants to the University Institutions should be as suggested under heading, 'Model Criteria for Fixation of Grants-in-Aid' in Chapter 4.
22. The normative pattern of expenditure, both recurring and non-recurring should be as suggested under the heading, 'Normative Pattern of Expenditure' under Chapter 5.
23. The existing format for preparation of the budget as suggested by the University Grants Commission should be critically examined and a model proforma for preparation of the budget be formulated after taking into account the modern techniques of budgeting. The budget should be prepared on the estimated income and expenditure. The Heads of the Departments should be actively associated in preparation of the budget and it should be prepared after getting their proposals and discussing the same with them before it is included or rejected.
24. The budget should be prepared well in advance of the time schedule so fixed by the Government/Funding Agency and should be submitted to the Government so that it could scrutinise the same in consultation with the University Institution.
25. New schemes which have been approved by the authorities of the University Institution should be included in the budget and

there is no need to get prior approval of the Government/Funding Agency because such a new schemes when incorporated in the budget should be discussed at the time of discussions for determining the grants to the University Institution.

26. The budget should be approved by the authorities of the University Institution and only then it should be sent to the Government.
27. The allocation of available funds to the departments should be invariably done after discussing the requirements with the Heads of the Departments so that their active participation is also ensured.
28. Performance budgeting (with planning programming and budgeting system in respect of commercial units) is suggested for University Institutions.
29. University Institutions should prepare long term, five-year and annual plans fully reflecting their requirements and submit the same to the Government so that their plan requirements could be assessed and funds provided.
30. Each University Institution should constitute a Planning Committee under the chairmanship of the Vice-Chancellor/Director consisting of fifteen members both internal and outside experts to be nominated by the Vice-Chancellor/Director for a period of three years. While nominating membership to the said committee it should be ensured that all sections of the University Institution are represented, may be by rotation and only those outside experts are nominated who are well conversant with an educational planning.
31. The Vice-Chancellor, Director should be a permanent invitee to the Planning Board, if not member, and their representatives should be associated by the Government while discussing the plan requirements with the Planning Commission, Government of India.
32. The sanction/allocation for the five-year and annual plans should be communicated to the University Institutions without any time lag so that they could plan their programmes and expenditure accordingly.
33. The accounts of the University Institutions should be prepared on single entry system and compiled as Receipt and Payment

Account with classified abstract. The balance sheet should be prepared only in respect of commercial units of the University Institutions which should be attached with the main account of the University Institution as annexure.

34. There should be one University Account in the name of the Comptroller/Finance Officer, to be centrally operated. The drawing and disbursing officers should only keep a separate bank account for imprest moneys sanctioned for them in case the imprest amount exceeds rupees two thousand.
35. There should be no multiplicity of bank accounts in the University Institutions and only one General/Main Account should be maintained for all types of grants and the accounts should be prepared in a consolidated manner incorporating therein the position of balances in respect of each type of grant.
36. A separate fund should be created for retiring benefits of employees and kept in a separate account outside the General Account.
37. The students fund should be kept outside the General Account.
38. All the funds should be initially deposited in the Current Bank Account and the barest minimum amount should be kept in the Current Account to meet day-to-day expenditure. The surplus amount should be kept in saving bank account so as to earn interest and thereby create additional resources to University Institution.
39. The accounts should be compiled centrally by the Finance Wing and the drawing and disbursing officers should maintain the books of income and expenditure for reconciliation of expenditure with the central office.
40. All the University Institutions should prepare their own Accounts Manuals and the State Governments/Government of India Rules should be followed only where the financial rules of the University Institutions are silent.
41. The pre-audit system with strong internal inspection should be followed in all the University Institutions and the test check audit should be done by the Comptroller and Auditor General of India in case the expenditure under government grant exceeds 75 per cent of the total expenditure.
42. The audited annual accounts should be sent to the Government only for information and not for laying on the table of State Assembly/Parliaments, keeping in view the autonomous

character of the University Institutions as also suggested by the Committee on Model Act.

The adoption of the above measures will doubtlessly help the University Institutions to improve their financial management systems for the ultimate fulfilment of the objectives/goals for which they have been established. The improved financial management practices will help the University Institutions to utilise the available resources more efficiently, generate additional funds, gain confidence of the Government/Funding Agencies and make them feel that University Institutions through autonomous in character are exercising effective control over their finances. These measures will also serve as guidelines to the Central and State Governments as well as co-ordinating agencies like the University Grants Commission and the Indian Council of Agricultural Research for better understanding of the problems of the University Institutions encountered by them in the field of finances. Thus the dreams of our planners to accelerate the process of raising the socio-economic standards for its masses by providing better facilities in the field of higher education, could be translated into reality.

INDEX